MIT 3.091

Introduction to Solid State Chemistry Course Supplement

Materials selected from:

Materials Science and Engineering: An Introduction, 4th Edition
by William D. Callister, Jr.

Introduction to Materials Science and Engineering
by Kenneth M. Ralls, Thomas H. Courtney, & John Wulff

X-Ray Structure Determination: A Practical Guide, 2nd Edition
by George H. Stout & Lyle H. Jensen

X-ray Diffraction Methods by E.W. Nuffield

for use by
Massachusetts Institute of Technology
Department of Materials Science

WILEY
Custom Services

Printed in the United States of America.

ISBN 0-471-32297-0

Contents

FOURTH EDITION

Materials Science and Engineering

An Introduction

William D. Callister, Jr.
Department of Metallurgical Engineering
The University of Utah

John Wiley & Sons, Inc.
New York Chichester Brisbane Toronto Singapore Weinheim

Front Cover: The aggregate of sphere-like objects on the front cover represents a unit cell of the high critical temperature superconducting material $YBa_2Cu_3O_7$. Red, green, orange, and purple spheres represent oxygen, copper, barium, and yttrium ions, respectively. This material has a superconducting critical temperature of about 92 K, and was the first of this new generation of superconductors to have been recently discovered.

Back Cover: Top view of the $YBa_2Cu_3O_7$ unit cell that is shown on the front cover.

Acquisitions Editor Cliff Robichaud
Marketing Manager Harper Mooy
Senior Production Manager Lucille Buonocore
Senior Production Editor Nancy Prinz
Text Designer Karin Gerdes Kincheloe
Cover Type Design Carol Grobe
Cover Design Director Karin Gerdes Kincheloe
Cover Illustration Roy Wiemann
Manufacturing Manager Mark Cirillo
Photo Editor Mary Ann Price
Illustration Editor Sigmund Malinowski

This book was set in Times Ten by Bi-Comp, Inc., and printed and bound by Donnelly/Willard. The cover was printed by Phoenix Color.

Recognizing the importance of preserving what has been written, it is a policy of John Wiley & Sons, Inc. to have books of enduring value published in the United States printed on acid-free paper, and we exert our best efforts to that end.

The paper in this book was manufactured by a mill whose forest management programs include sustained yield harvesting of its timberlands. Sustained yield harvesting principles ensure that the number of trees cut each year does not exceed the amount of new growth.

Library of Congress Cataloging-in-Publication Data

Callister, William D., 1940–
Materials science and engineering : an introduction / William D. Callister, Jr.—4th ed.
p. cm.
Includes bibliographical references and index.
ISBN 0-471-13459-7 (cloth : alk. paper)
1. Materials. I. Title.
TA403.C23 1996
620.1'1—dc20 96-1878
CIP

Printed in the United States of America

10 9 8 7 6 5 4 3

3

The Structure of Crystalline Solids

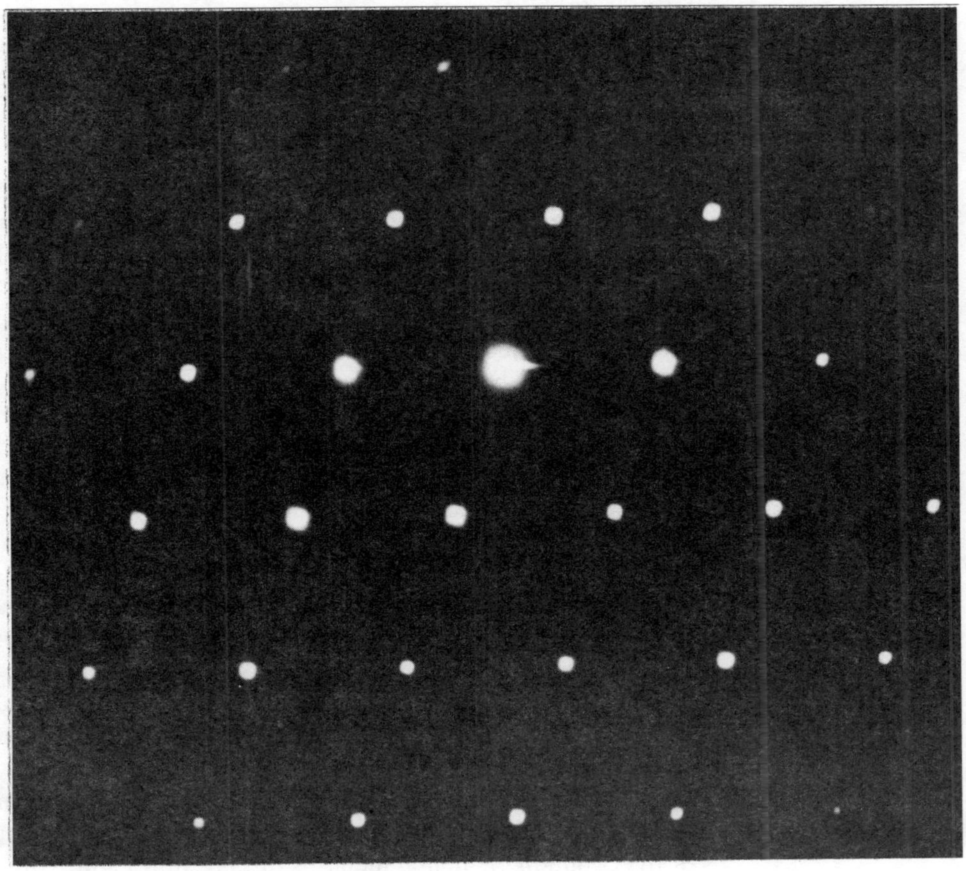

High velocity electron beams that are produced when electrons are accelerated across large voltages become wavelike in character. Their wavelengths are shorter than interatomic spacings, and, thus, these beams may be diffracted by atomic planes in crystalline materials, in the same manner as x-rays experience diffraction.

This photograph shows a diffraction pattern produced for a single crystal of gallium arsenide using a transmission electron microscope. The brightest spot near the center is produced by the incident electron beam which is parallel to a ⟨110⟩ crystallographic direction. Each of the other white spots results from an electron beam that is diffracted by a specific set of crystallographic planes. (Photograph courtesy of Dr. Raghaw S. Rai, Motorola, Inc., Austin, Texas.)

3.1 Introduction

Chapter 2 was concerned primarily with the various types of atomic bonding, which are determined by the electron structure of the individual atoms. The present discussion is devoted to the next level of the structure of materials, specifically, to some of the arrangements that may be assumed by atoms in the solid state. Within this framework, concepts of crystallinity and noncrystallinity are introduced. For crystalline solids the notion of crystal structure is presented, specified in terms of a unit cell. The three common crystal structures found in metals are then detailed, along with the scheme by which crystallographic directions and planes are expressed. Single crystals, polycrystalline, and noncrystalline materials are considered.

CRYSTAL STRUCTURES

3.2 Fundamental Concepts

Solid materials may be classified according to the regularity with which atoms or ions are arranged with respect to one another. A **crystalline** material is one in which the atoms are situated in a repeating or periodic array over large atomic distances; that is, long-range order exists, such that upon solidification, the atoms will position themselves in a repetitive three-dimensional pattern, in which each atom is bonded to its nearest-neighbor atoms. All metals, many ceramic materials, and certain polymers form crystalline structures under normal solidification conditions. For those that do not crystallize, this long-range atomic order is absent; these *noncrystalline* or *amorphous* materials are discussed briefly at the end of this chapter.

Some of the properties of crystalline solids depend on the **crystal structure** of the material, the manner in which atoms, ions, or molecules are spatially arranged. There is an extremely large number of different crystal structures all having long-range atomic order; these vary from relatively simple structures for metals, to exceedingly complex ones, as displayed by some of the ceramic and polymeric materials. The present discussion deals with several common metallic crystal structures. Chapters 13 and 15 are devoted to crystal structures for ceramics and polymers, respectively.

When describing crystalline structures, atoms (or ions) are thought of as being solid spheres having well-defined diameters. This is termed the *atomic hard sphere model* in which spheres representing nearest-neighbor atoms touch one another. An example of the hard sphere model for the atomic arrangement found in some of the common elemental metals is displayed in Figure 3.1*c*. In this particular case all the atoms are identical. Sometimes the term **lattice** is used in the context of crystal structures; in this sense "lattice" means a three-dimensional array of points coinciding with atom positions (or sphere centers).

3.3 Unit Cells

The atomic order in crystalline solids indicates that small groups of atoms form a repetitive pattern. Thus, in describing crystal structures, it is often convenient to subdivide the structure into small repeat entities called **unit cells.** Unit cells for most crystal structures are parallelepipeds or prisms having three sets of parallel faces; one is drawn within the aggregate of spheres (Figure 3.1*c*), which in this case happens to be a cube. A unit cell is chosen to represent the symmetry of the

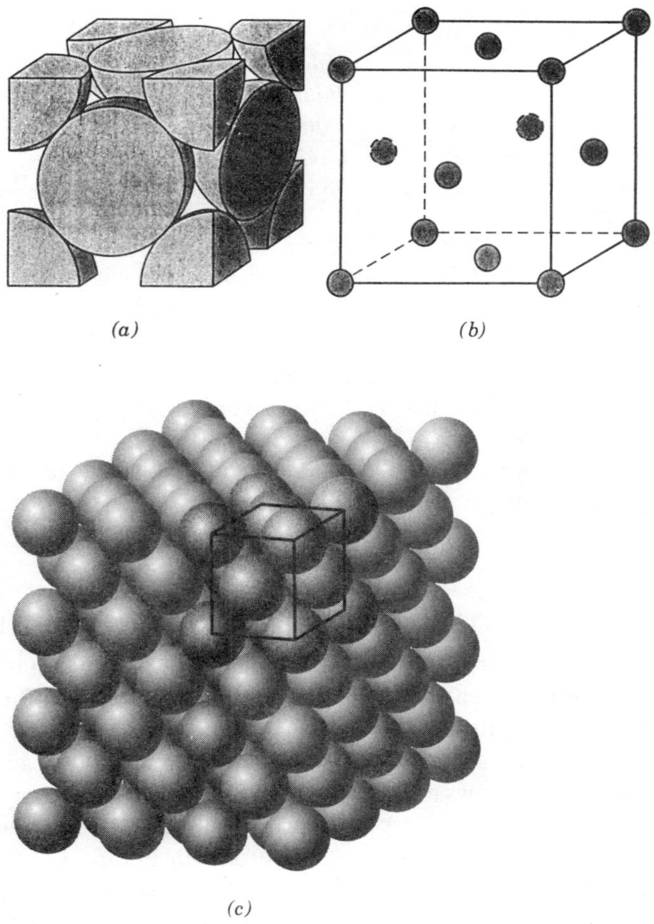

FIGURE 3.1 For the face-centered cubic crystal structure: (*a*) a hard sphere unit cell representation, (*b*) a reduced-sphere unit cell, and (*c*) an aggregate of many atoms. (Figure *c* adapted from W. G. Moffatt, G. W. Pearsall, and J. Wulff, *The Structure and Properties of Materials*, Vol. I, *Structure*, p. 51. Copyright © 1964 by John Wiley & Sons, New York. Reprinted by permission of John Wiley & Sons, Inc.)

crystal structure, wherein all the atom positions in the crystal may be generated by translations of the unit cell integral distances along each of its edges. Thus, the unit cell is the basic structural unit or building block of the crystal structure and defines the crystal structure by virtue of its geometry and the atom positions within. Convenience usually dictates that parallelepiped corners coincide with centers of the hard sphere atoms. Furthermore, more than a single unit cell may be chosen for a particular crystal structure; however, we generally use the unit cell having the highest level of geometrical symmetry.

3.4 Metallic Crystal Structures

The atomic bonding in this group of materials is metallic, and thus nondirectional in nature. Consequently, there are no restrictions as to the number and position of nearest-neighbor atoms; this leads to relatively large numbers of nearest neighbors and dense atomic packings for most metallic crystal structures. Also, for metals, using the hard sphere model for the crystal structure, each sphere represents an ion core. Table 3.1 presents the atomic radii for a number of metals. Three relatively simple crystal structures are found for most of the common metals: face-centered cubic, body-centered cubic, and hexagonal close-packed.

Table 3.1 Atomic Radii and Crystal Structures for 16 Metals

Metal	*Crystal Structure*[a]	*Atomic Radius*[b] *(nm)*	*Metal*	*Crystal Structure*	*Atomic Radius (nm)*
Aluminum	FCC	0.1431	Molybdenum	BCC	0.1363
Cadmium	HCP	0.1490	Nickel	FCC	0.1246
Chromium	BCC	0.1249	Platinum	FCC	0.1387
Cobalt	HCP	0.1253	Silver	FCC	0.1445
Copper	FCC	0.1278	Tantalum	BCC	0.1430
Gold	FCC	0.1442	Titanium (α)	HCP	0.1445
Iron (α)	BCC	0.1241	Tungsten	BCC	0.1371
Lead	FCC	0.1750	Zinc	HCP	0.1332

[a] FCC = face-centered cubic; HCP = hexagonal close-packed; BCC = body-centered cubic.

[b] A nanometer (nm) equals 10^{-9} m; to convert from nanometers to angstrom units (Å), multiply the nanometer value by 10.

THE FACE-CENTERED CUBIC CRYSTAL STRUCTURE

The crystal structure found for many metals has a unit cell of cubic geometry, with atoms located at each of the corners and the centers of all the cube faces. It is aptly called the **face-centered cubic (FCC)** crystal structure. Some of the familiar metals having this crystal structure are copper, aluminum, silver, and gold (see also Table 3.1). Figure 3.1*a* shows a hard sphere model for the FCC unit cell, whereas in Figure 3.1*b* the atom centers are represented by small circles to provide a better perspective of atom positions. The aggregate of atoms in Figure 3.1*c* represents a section of crystal consisting of many FCC unit cells. These spheres or ion cores touch one another across a face diagonal; the cube edge length a and the atomic radius R are related through

$$a = 2R\sqrt{2} \tag{3.1}$$

This result is obtained as an example problem.

For the FCC crystal structure, each corner atom is shared among eight unit cells, whereas a face-centered atom belongs to only two. Therefore, one eighth of each of the eight corner atoms and one half of each of the six face atoms, or a total of four whole atoms, may be assigned to a given unit cell. This is depicted in Figure 3.1*a*, where only sphere portions are represented within the confines of the cube. The cell comprises the volume of the cube, which is generated from the centers of the corner atoms as shown in the figure.

Corner and face positions are really equivalent; that is, translation of the cube corner from an original corner atom to the center of a face atom will not alter the cell structure.

Two other important characteristics of a crystal structure are the **coordination number** and the **atomic packing factor (APF).** For metals, each atom has the same number of nearest-neighbor or touching atoms, which is the coordination number. For face-centered cubics, the coordination number is 12. This may be confirmed by examination of Figure 3.1*a*; the front face atom has four corner nearest-neighbor atoms surrounding it, four face atoms that are in contact from behind, and four other equivalent face atoms residing in the next unit cell to the front, which is not shown.

The APF is the fraction of solid sphere volume in a unit cell, assuming the atomic hard sphere model, or

$$\text{APF} = \frac{\text{volume of atoms in a unit cell}}{\text{total unit cell volume}} \tag{3.2}$$

For the FCC structure, the atomic packing factor is 0.74, which is the maximum packing possible for spheres all having the same diameter. Computation of this APF is also included as an example problem. Metals typically have relatively large atomic packing factors to maximize the shielding provided by the free electron cloud.

THE BODY-CENTERED CUBIC CRYSTAL STRUCTURE

Another common metallic crystal structure also has a cubic unit cell with atoms located at all eight corners and a single atom at the cube center. This is called a **body-centered cubic (BCC)** crystal structure. A collection of spheres depicting this crystal structure is shown in Figure 3.2*c*, whereas Figures 3.2*a* and 3.2*b* are diagrams of BCC unit cells with the atoms represented by hard sphere and reduced-sphere models, respectively. Center and corner atoms touch one another along cube diagonals, and unit cell length a and atomic radius R are related through

$$a = \frac{4R}{\sqrt{3}} \tag{3.3}$$

Chromium, iron, tungsten, as well as several other metals listed in Table 3.1 exhibit a BCC structure.

Two atoms are associated with each BCC unit cell: the equivalence of one atom from the eight corners, each of which is shared among eight unit cells, and the single center atom, which is wholly contained within its cell. In addition, corner and center atom positions are equivalent. The coordination number for the BCC crystal structure is 8; each center atom has as nearest neighbors its eight corner atoms. Since the coordination number is less for BCC than FCC, so also is the atomic packing factor for BCC lower—0.68 versus 0.74.

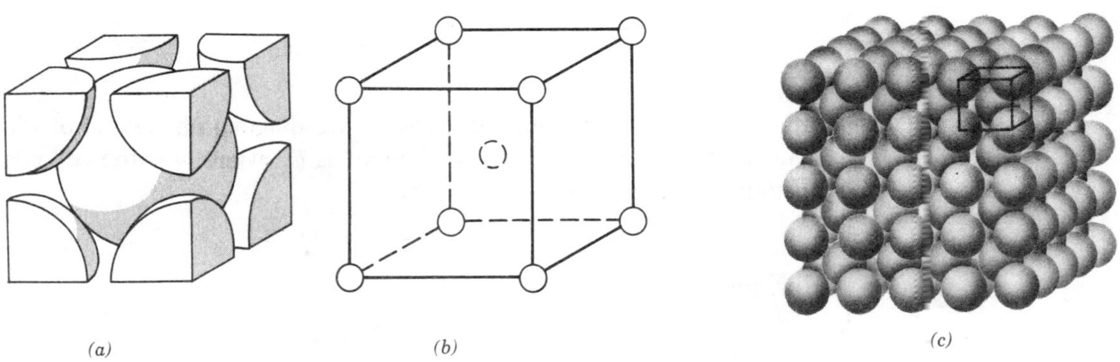

FIGURE 3.2 For the body-centered cubic crystal structure, (*a*) a hard sphere unit cell representation, (*b*) a reduced-sphere unit cell, and (*c*) an aggregate of many atoms. (Figure (*c*) from W. G. Moffatt, G. W. Pearsall, and J. Wulff, *The Structure and Properties of Materials*, Vol. I, *Structure*, p. 51. Copyright © 1964 by John Wiley & Sons, New York. Reprinted by permission of John Wiley & Sons, Inc.)

THE HEXAGONAL CLOSE-PACKED CRYSTAL STRUCTURE

Not all metals have unit cells with cubic symmetry; the final common metallic crystal structure to be discussed has a unit cell that is hexagonal. Figure 3.3*a* shows a reduced-sphere unit cell for this structure, which is termed **hexagonal close-packed (HCP);** an assemblage of several HCP unit cells is presented in Figure 3.3*b*. The top and bottom faces of the unit cell consist of six atoms that form regular hexagons and surround a single atom in the center. Another plane that provides three additional atoms to the unit cell is situated between the top and bottom planes. The atoms in this midplane have as nearest neighbors atoms in both of the adjacent two planes. The equivalence of six atoms is contained in each unit cell; one-sixth of each of the 12 top and bottom face corner atoms, one-half of each of the 2 center face atoms, and all the 3 midplane interior atoms. If a and c represent, respectively, the short and long unit cell dimensions of Figure 3.3*a*, the c/a ratio should be 1.633; however, for some HCP metals this ratio deviates from the ideal value.

The coordination number and the atomic packing factor for the HCP crystal structure are the same as for FCC: 12 and 0.74, respectively. The HCP metals include cadmium, magnesium, titanium, and zinc; some of these are listed in Table 3.1.

EXAMPLE PROBLEM 3.1

Calculate the volume of an FCC unit cell in terms of the atomic radius R.

SOLUTION

In the FCC unit cell illustrated,

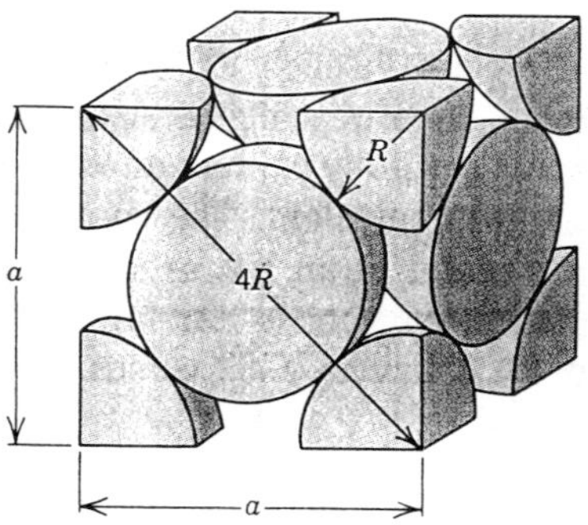

the atoms touch one another across a face-diagonal the length of which is $4R$. Since the unit cell is a cube, its volume is a^3, where a is the cell edge length. From the right triangle on the face,

$$a^2 + a^2 = (4R)^2$$

or, solving for a,

$$a = 2R\sqrt{2} \tag{3.1}$$

The FCC unit cell volume V_C may be computed from

$$V_C = a^3 = (2R\sqrt{2})^3 = 16R^3\sqrt{2} \tag{3.4}$$

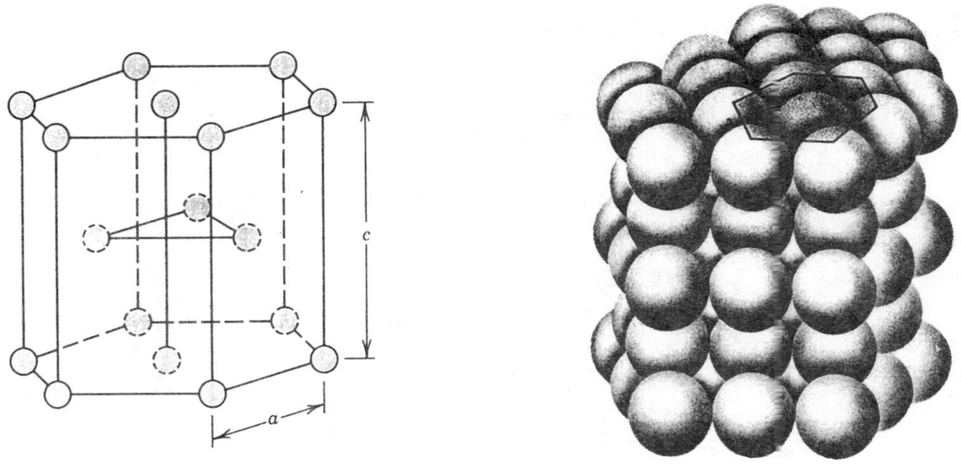

(a) (b)

FIGURE 3.3 For the hexagonal close-packed crystal structure, (*a*) a reduced-sphere unit cell (*a* and *c* represent the short and long edge lengths, respectively), and (*b*) an aggregate of many atoms. (Figure (*b*) from W. G. Moffatt, G. W. Pearsall, and J. Wulff, *The Structure and Properties of Materials,* Vol. I, *Structure,* p. 51. Copyright © 1964 by John Wiley & Sons, New York. Reprinted by permission of John Wiley & Sons, Inc.)

EXAMPLE PROBLEM 3.2

Show that the atomic packing factor for the FCC crystal structure is 0.74.

SOLUTION

The APF is defined as the fraction of solid sphere volume in a unit cell, or

$$\text{APF} = \frac{\text{total sphere volume}}{\text{total unit cell volume}} = \frac{V_S}{V_C}$$

Both the total sphere and unit cell volumes may be calculated in terms of the atomic radius R. The volume for a sphere is $\frac{4}{3}\pi R^3$, and since there are four atoms per FCC unit cell, the total FCC sphere volume is

$$V_S = (4)\frac{4}{3}\pi R^3 = \frac{16}{3}\pi R^3$$

From Example Problem 3.1, the total unit cell volume is

$$V_C = 16R^3\sqrt{2}$$

Therefore, the atomic packing factor is

$$\text{APF} = \frac{V_S}{V_C} = \frac{(\frac{16}{3})\pi R^3}{16R^3\sqrt{2}} = 0.74$$

3.5 Density Computations

A knowledge of the crystal structure of a metallic solid permits computation of its true density ρ through the relationship

$$\rho = \frac{nA}{V_C N_A} \tag{3.5}$$

where

n = number of atoms associated with each unit cell

A = atomic weight

V_C = volume of the unit cell

N_A = Avogadro's number (6.023×10^{23} atoms/mol)

Example Problem 3.3

Copper has an atomic radius of 0.128 nm (1.28 Å), an FCC crystal structure, and an atomic weight of 63.5 g/mol. Compute its density and compare the answer with its measured density.

Solution

Equation 3.5 is employed in the solution of this problem. Since the crystal structure is FCC, n, the number of atoms per unit cell, is 4. Furthermore, the atomic weight A_{Cu} is given as 63.5 g/mol. The unit cell volume V_C for FCC was determined in Example Problem 3.1 as $16R^3\sqrt{2}$, where R, the atomic radius, is 0.128 nm.

Substitution for the various parameters into Equation 3.5 yields

$$\rho = \frac{nA_{Cu}}{V_C N_A} = \frac{nA_{Cu}}{(16R^3\sqrt{2})N_A}$$

$$= \frac{(4 \text{ atoms/unit cell})(63.5 \text{ g/mol})}{[16\sqrt{2}(1.28 \times 10^{-8} \text{ cm})^3/\text{unit cell}](6.023 \times 10^{23} \text{ atoms/mol})}$$

$$= 8.89 \text{ g/cm}^3$$

The literature value for the density of copper is 8.94 g/cm^3, which is in very close agreement with the foregoing result.

3.6 Polymorphism and Allotropy

Some metals, as well as nonmetals, may have more than one crystal structure, a phenomenon known as **polymorphism.** When found in elemental solids, the condition is often termed **allotropy.** The prevailing crystal structure depends on both the temperature and the external pressure. One familiar example is found in carbon: graphite is the stable polymorph at ambient conditions, whereas diamond is formed at extremely high pressures. Also, pure iron has a BCC crystal structure at room temperature, which changes to FCC iron at 912°C (1674°F). Most often a modifica-

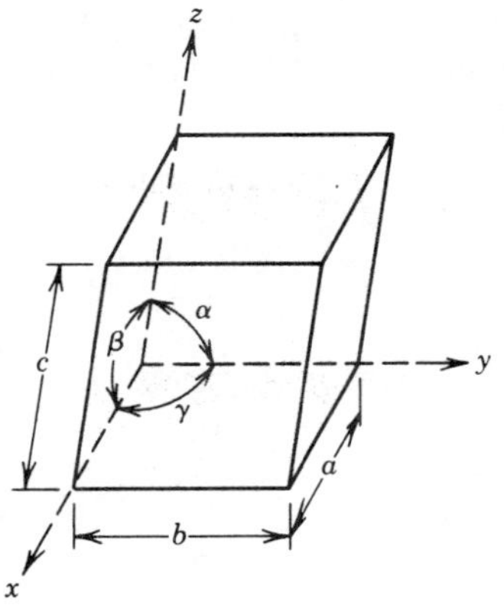

FIGURE 3.4 A unit cell with *x*, *y*, and *z* coordinate axes, showing axial lengths (*a*, *b*, and *c*) and interaxial angles (α, β, and γ).

tion of the density and other physical properties accompanies a polymorphic transformation.

3.7 Crystal Systems

Since there are many different possible crystal structures, it is sometimes convenient to divide them into groups according to unit cell configurations and/or atomic arrangements. One such scheme is based on the unit cell geometry, that is, the shape of the appropriate unit cell parallelepiped without regard to the atomic positions in the cell. Within this framework, an *x*, *y*, *z* coordinate system is established with its origin at one of the unit cell corners; each of the *x*, *y*, and *z* axes coincides with one of the three parallelepiped edges that extend from this corner, as illustrated in Figure 3.4. The unit cell geometry is completely defined in terms of six parameters: the three edge lengths *a*, *b*, and *c*, and the three interaxial angles α, β, and γ. These are indicated in Figure 3.4, and are sometimes termed the **lattice parameters** of a crystal structure.

On this basis there are found crystals having seven different possible combinations of *a*, *b*, and *c*, and α, β, and γ, each of which represents a distinct **crystal system.** These seven crystal systems are cubic, tetragonal, hexagonal, orthorhombic, rhombohedral, monoclinic, and triclinic. The lattice parameter relationships and unit cell sketches for each are represented in Table 3.2. The cubic system, for which $a = b = c$ and $\alpha = \beta = \gamma = 90°$, has the greatest degree of symmetry. Least symmetry is displayed by the triclinic system, since $a \neq b \neq c$ and $\alpha \neq \beta \neq \gamma$.

From the discussion of metallic crystal structures, it should be apparent that both FCC and BCC structures belong to the cubic crystal system, whereas HCP falls within hexagonal. The conventional hexagonal unit cell really consists of three parallelepipeds situated as shown in Table 3.2.

CRYSTALLOGRAPHIC DIRECTIONS AND PLANES

When dealing with crystalline materials, it often becomes necessary to specify some particular crystallographic plane of atoms or a crystallographic direction. Labeling conventions have been established in which three integers or indices are used to designate directions and planes. The basis for determining index values is the unit

Table 3.2 Lattice Parameter Relationships and Figures Showing Unit Cell Geometries for the Seven Crystal Systems

Crystal System	*Axial Relationships*	*Interaxial Angles*	*Unit Cell Geometry*
Cubic	$a = b = c$	$\alpha = \beta = \gamma = 90°$	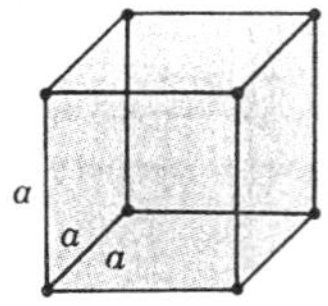
Hexagonal	$a = b \neq c$	$\alpha = \beta = 90°, \gamma = 120°$	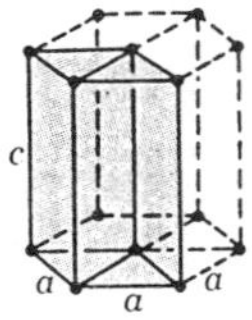
Tetragonal	$a = b \neq c$	$\alpha = \beta = \gamma = 90°$	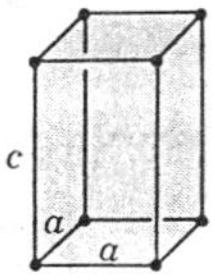
Rhombohedral	$a = b = c$	$\alpha = \beta = \gamma \neq 90°$	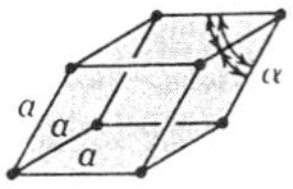
Orthorhombic	$a \neq b \neq c$	$\alpha = \beta = \gamma = 90°$	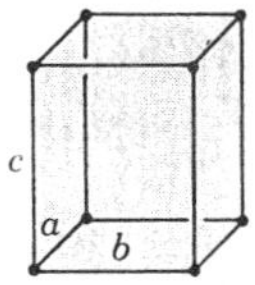
Monoclinic	$a \neq b \neq c$	$\alpha = \gamma = 90° \neq \beta$	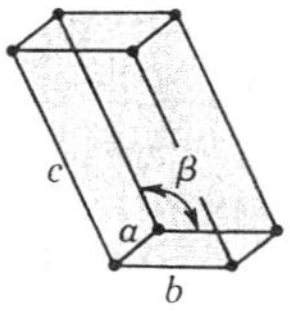
Triclinic	$a \neq b \neq c$	$\alpha \neq \beta \neq \gamma \neq 90°$	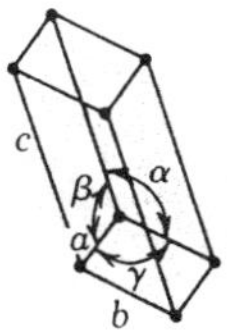

cell, with a coordinate system consisting of three (x, y, and z) axes situated at one of the corners and coinciding with the unit cell edges, as shown in Figure 3.4. For some crystal systems—namely, hexagonal, rhombohedral, monoclinic, and triclinic—the three axes are *not* mutually perpendicular, as in the familiar Cartesian coordinate scheme.

3.8 Crystallographic Directions

A crystallographic direction is defined as a line between two points, or a vector. The following steps are utilized in the determination of the three directional indices:

1. A vector of convenient length is positioned such that it passes through the origin of the coordinate system. Any vector may be translated throughout the crystal lattice without alteration, if parallelism is maintained.
2. The length of the vector projection on each of the three axes is determined; *these are measured in terms of the unit cell dimensions a, b, and c.*
3. These three numbers are multiplied or divided by a common factor to reduce them to the smallest integer values.
4. The three indices, not separated by commas, are enclosed in square brackets, thus: [uvw]. The u, v, and w integers correspond to the reduced projections along the x, y, and z axes, respectively.

For each of the three axes, there will exist both positive and negative coordinates. Thus negative indices are also possible, which are represented by a bar over the appropriate index. For example, the [$1\bar{1}1$] direction would have a component in the $-y$ direction. Also, changing the signs of all indices produces an antiparallel direction; that is, [$\bar{1}1\bar{1}$] is directly opposite to [$1\bar{1}1$]. If more than one direction or plane is to be specified for a particular crystal structure, it is imperative for the maintaining of consistency that a positive–negative convention, once established, not be changed.

The [100], [110], and [111] directions are common ones; they are drawn in the unit cell shown in Figure 3.5.

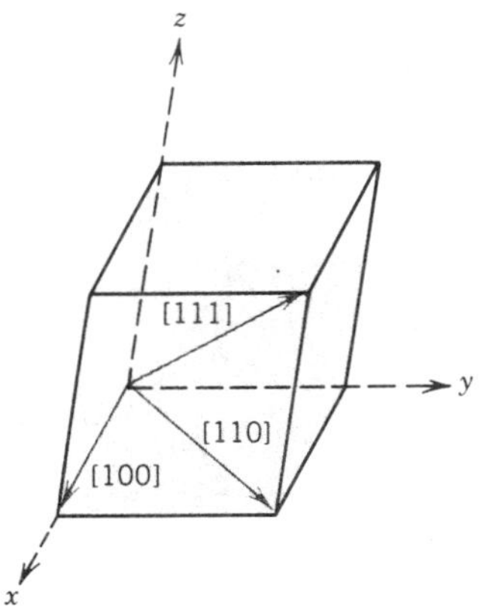

Figure 3.5 The [100], [110], and [111] directions within a unit cell.

Example Problem 3.4

Determine the indices for the direction shown in the accompanying figure.

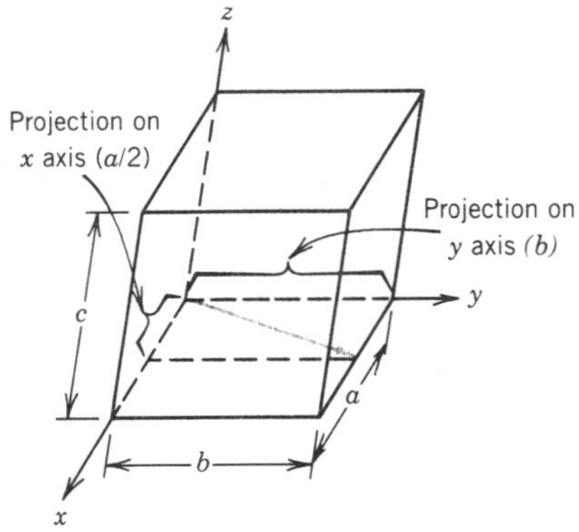

Solution

The vector, as drawn, passes through the origin of the coordinate system, and therefore no translation is necessary. Projections of this vector onto the x, y, and z axes are, respectively, $a/2$, b, and $0c$, which become $\frac{1}{2}$, 1, and 0 in terms of the unit cell parameters (i.e., when the a, b, and c are dropped). Reduction of these numbers to the lowest set of integers is accompanied by multiplication of each by the factor 2. This yields the integers 1, 2, and 0, which are then enclosed in brackets as [120].

This procedure may be summarized as follows:

	x	y	z
Projections	$a/2$	b	$0c$
Projections (in terms of a, b, and c)	$\frac{1}{2}$	1	0
Reduction	1	2	0
Enclosure		[120]	

Example Problem 3.5

Draw a $[1\bar{1}0]$ direction within a cubic unit cell.

Solution

First construct an appropriate unit cell and coordinate axes system. In the accompanying figure the unit cell is cubic, and the origin of the coordinate system, point O, is located at one of the cube corners.

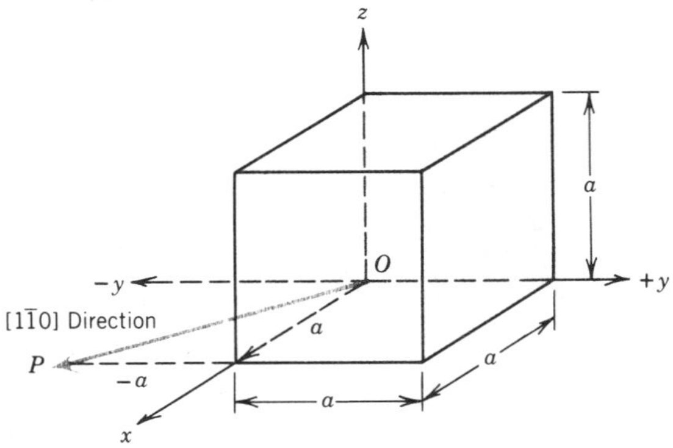

This problem is solved by reversing the procedure of the preceding example. For this $[1\bar{1}0]$ direction, the projections along x, y, z axes are a, $-a$, and $0a$, respectively. This direction is defined by a vector passing from the origin to point P, which is located by first moving along the x axis a units, and from this position, parallel to the y axis $-a$ units, as indicated in the figure. There is no z component to the vector, since the z projection is zero.

For some crystal structures, several nonparallel directions with different indices are actually equivalent; this means that the spacing of atoms along each direction is the same. For example, in cubic crystals, all the directions represented by the following indices are equivalent: [100], $[\bar{1}00]$, [010], $[0\bar{1}0]$, [001], and $[00\bar{1}]$. As a convenience, equivalent directions are grouped together into a *family*, which are enclosed in angle brackets, thus: ⟨100⟩. Furthermore, directions in cubic crystals having the same indices without regard to order or sign, for example, [123] and $[\bar{2}1\bar{3}]$, are equivalent. This is, in general, not true for other crystal systems. For example, for crystals of tetragonal symmetry, [100] and [010] directions are equivalent, whereas [100] and [001] are not.

HEXAGONAL CRYSTALS

A problem arises for crystals having hexagonal symmetry in that some crystallographic equivalent directions will not have the same set of indices. This is circumvented by utilizing a four-axis, or *Miller-Bravais*, coordinate system as shown in Figure 3.6. The three a_1, a_2, and a_3 axes are all contained within a single plane (called the basal plane), and at 120° angles to one another. The z axis is perpendicular to this basal plane. Directional indices, which are obtained as described above, will be denoted by four indices, as $[uvtw]$; by convention, the first three indices pertain to projections along the respective a_1, a_2, and a_3 axes in the basal plane.

Conversion from the three-index system to the four-index system,

$$[u'v'w'] \longrightarrow [uvtw]$$

is accomplished by the following formulas:

$$u = \frac{n}{3}(2u' - v') \tag{3.6a}$$

$$v = \frac{n}{3}(2v' - u') \tag{3.6b}$$

$$t = -(u + v) \tag{3.6c}$$

$$w = nw' \tag{3.6d}$$

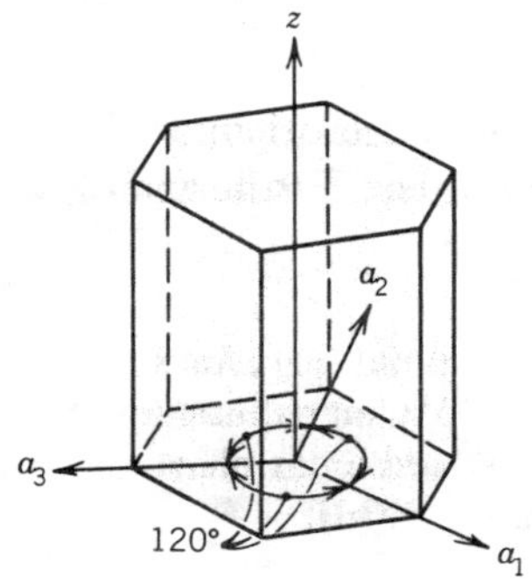

FIGURE 3.6 Coordinate axis system for a hexagonal unit cell (Miller–Bravais scheme).

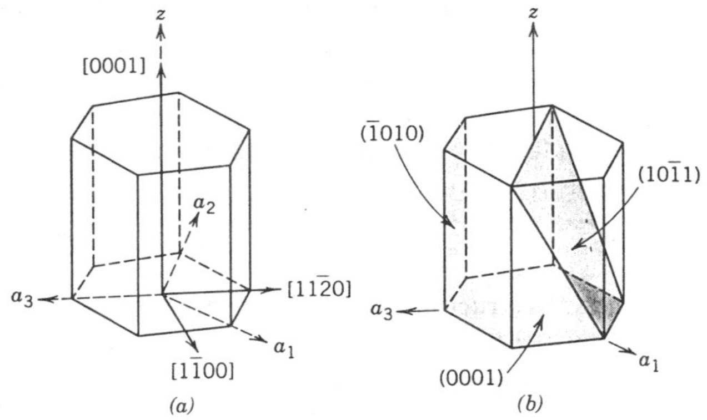

FIGURE 3.7 For the hexagonal crystal system, (*a*) [0001], $[1\bar{1}00]$, and $[11\bar{2}0]$ directions, and (*b*) the (0001), $(10\bar{1}1)$, and $(\bar{1}010)$ planes.

where primed indices are associated with the three-index scheme and unprimed, with the new Miller–Bravais four-index system; n is a factor that may be required to reduce u, v, t, and w to the smallest integers. For example, using this conversion the [010] direction becomes $[\bar{1}2\bar{1}0]$. Several different directions are indicated in the hexagonal unit cell (Figure 3.7*a*).

3.9 Crystallographic Planes

The orientations of planes for a crystal structure are represented in a similar manner. Again, the unit cell is the basis, with the three-axis coordinate system as represented in Figure 3.4. In all but the hexagonal crystal system, crystallographic planes are specified by three **Miller indices** as (hkl). Any two planes parallel to each other are equivalent and have identical indices. The procedure employed in determination of the h, k, and l index numbers is as follows:

1. If the plane passes through the selected origin, either another parallel plane must be constructed within the unit cell by an appropriate translation, or a new origin must be established at the corner of another unit cell.
2. At this point the crystallographic plane either intersects or parallels each of the three axes; the length of the planar intercept for each axis is determined in terms of the lattice parameters a, b, and c.
3. The reciprocals of these numbers are taken. A plane that parallels an axis may be considered to have an infinite intercept, and, therefore, a zero index.
4. If necessary, these three numbers are changed to the set of smallest integers by multiplication or division by a common factor.[1]
5. Finally, the integer indices, not separated by commas, are enclosed within parentheses, thus: (hkl).

An intercept on the negative side of the origin is indicated by a bar or minus sign positioned over the appropriate index. Furthermore, reversing the directions

[1] On occasion, index reduction is not carried out (e.g., for x-ray diffraction studies that are described in Section 3.15); for example, (002) is not reduced to (001). In addition, for ceramic materials, the ionic arrangement for a reduced-index plane may be different than that for a nonreduced one [see Problems 13.25(a) and (b)].

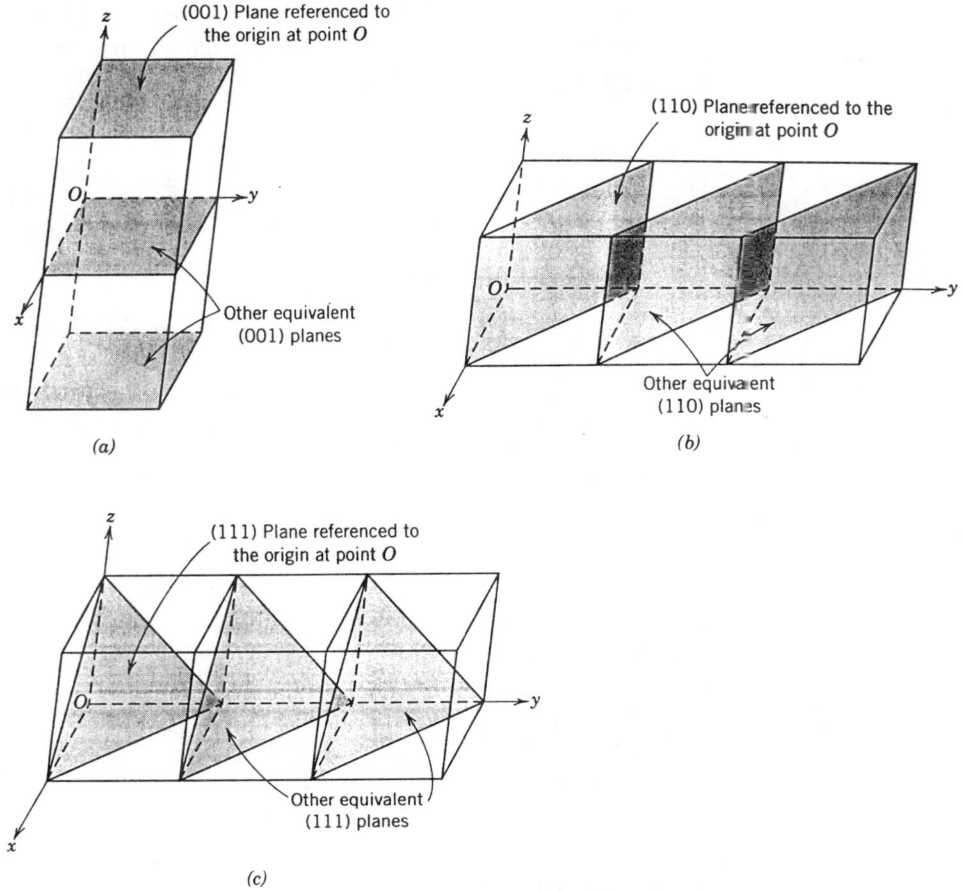

FIGURE 3.8 Representations of a series each of (*a*) (001), (*b*) (110), and (*c*) (111) crystallographic planes.

of all indices specifies another plane parallel to, on the opposite side of and equidistant from, the origin. Several low-index planes are represented in Figure 3.8.

One interesting and unique characteristic of cubic crystals is that planes and directions having the same indices are perpendicular to one another; however, for other crystal systems there are no simple geometrical relationships between planes and directions having the same indices.

EXAMPLE PROBLEM 3.6

Determine the Miller indices for the plane shown in the accompanying sketch (*a*).

SOLUTION

Since the plane passes through the selected origin O, a new origin must be chosen at the corner of an adjacent unit cell, taken as O', and shown in sketch (*b*). This plane is parallel to the x axis, and the intercept may be taken as ∞a. The y and z axes intersections, referenced to the new origin O', are $-b$, and $c/2$, respectively. Thus, in terms of the lattice parameters a, b, and c, these intersections are ∞, -1, and $\frac{1}{2}$. The reciprocals of these numbers are 0, -1, and 2; and since all are integers, no further reduction is necessary. Finally, enclosure in parentheses yields $(0\bar{1}2)$.

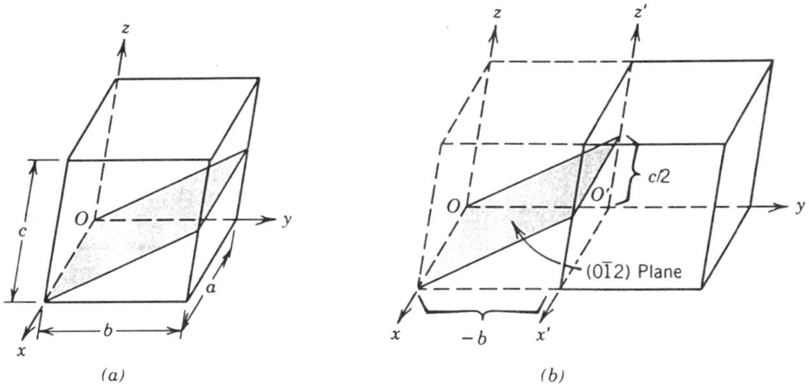

These steps are briefly summarized below:

	x	y	z
Intercepts	∞a	$-b$	$c/2$
Intercepts (in terms of lattice parameters)	∞	-1	$\frac{1}{2}$
Reciprocals	0	-1	2
Reductions (unnecessary)			
Enclosure		$(0\bar{1}2)$	

Example Problem 3.7

Construct a $(0\bar{1}1)$ plane within a cubic unit cell.

Solution

To solve this problem, carry out the procedure used in the preceding example in reverse order. To begin, the indices are removed from the parentheses, and reciprocals are taken, which yields ∞, -1, and 1. This means that the particular plane parallels the x axis while intersecting the y and z axes at $-b$ and c, respectively, as indicated in the accompanying sketch (a). This plane has been drawn in sketch (b). A plane is indicated by lines representing its intersections

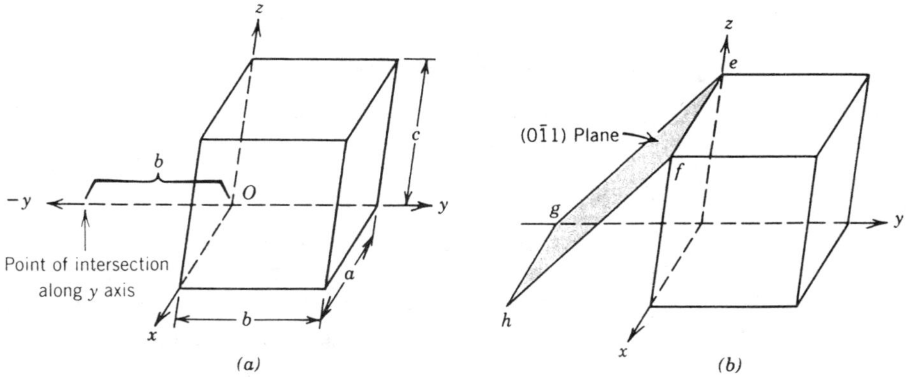

with the planes that constitute the faces of the unit cell or their extensions. For example, in this figure, line *ef* is the intersection between the $(0\bar{1}1)$ plane and the top face of the unit cell; also, line *gh* represents the intersection between this same $(0\bar{1}1)$ plane and the plane of the bottom unit cell face extended. Similarly, lines *eg* and *fh* are the intersections between $(0\bar{1}1)$ and back and front cell faces, respectively.

ATOMIC ARRANGEMENTS

The atomic arrangement for a crystallographic plane, which is often of interest, depends on the crystal structure. The (110) atomic planes for FCC and BCC crystal structures are represented in Figures 3.9 and 3.10; reduced-sphere unit cells are also included. Note that the atomic packing is different for each case. The circles represent atoms lying in the crystallographic planes as would be obtained from a slice taken through the centers of the full-sized hard spheres.

A "family" of planes contains all those planes that are crystallographically equivalent—that is, having the same atomic packing; and a family is designated by indices that are enclosed in braces—e.g., {100}. For example, in cubic crystals the (111), $(\bar{1}\bar{1}\bar{1})$, $(\bar{1}11)$, $(1\bar{1}\bar{1})$, $(11\bar{1})$, $(\bar{1}1\bar{1})$, $(\bar{1}\bar{1}1)$, and $(1\bar{1}1)$ planes all belong to the {111} family. On the other hand, for tetragonal crystal structures, the {100} family would contain only the (100), $(\bar{1}00)$, (010), and $(0\bar{1}0)$ since the (001) and $(00\bar{1})$ planes are not crystallographically equivalent. Also, in the cubic system only, planes having the same indices, irrespective of order and sign, are equivalent. For example, both $(1\bar{2}3)$ and $(3\bar{1}2)$ belong to the {123} family.

HEXAGONAL CRYSTALS

For crystals having hexagonal symmetry, it is desirable that equivalent planes have the same indices; as with directions, this is accomplished by the Miller-Bravais

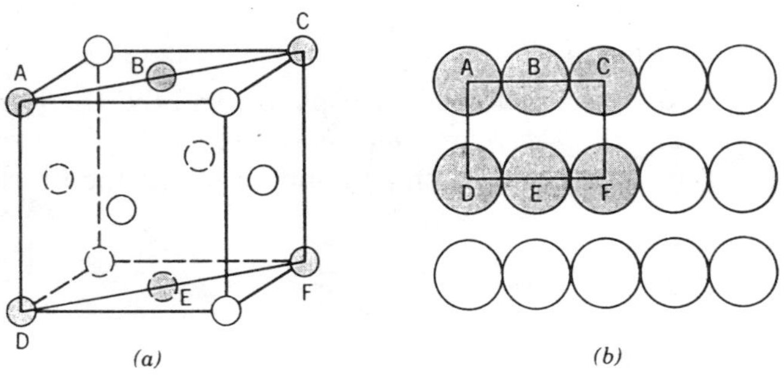

FIGURE 3.9 (*a*) Reduced-sphere FCC unit cell with (110) plane. (*b*) Atomic packing of an FCC (110) plane. Corresponding atom positions from (*a*) are indicated.

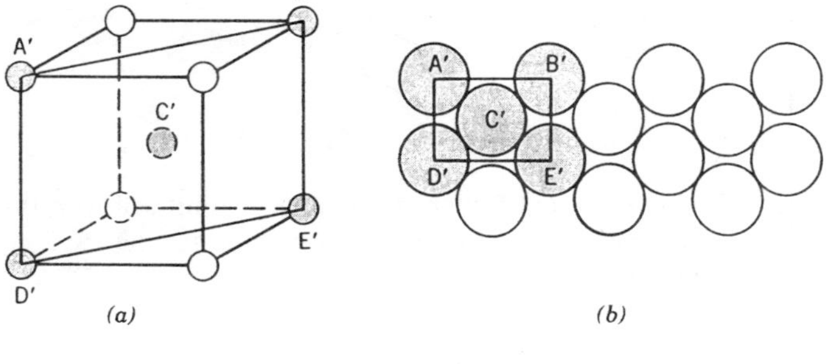

FIGURE 3.10 (*a*) Reduced-sphere BCC unit cell with (110) plane. (*b*) Atomic packing of a BCC (110) plane. Corresponding atom positions from (*a*) are indicated.

system shown in Figure 3.6. This convention leads to the four-index (*hkil*) scheme, which is favored in most instances, since it more clearly identifies the orientation of a plane in a hexagonal crystal. There is some redundancy in that *i* is determined by the sum of *h* and *k* through

$$i = -(h + k) \tag{3.7}$$

Otherwise the three *h*, *k*, and *l* indices are identical for both indexing systems. Figure 3.7*b* presents several of the common planes that are found for crystals having hexagonal symmetry.

3.10 Linear and Planar Atomic Densities

The two previous sections discussed the equivalency of nonparallel directions and planes, where equivalency is related to the degree of atomic spacing or atomic packing. It is felt appropriate at this time to introduce the concepts of atomic linear and planar densities. *Linear density* corresponds to the fraction of line length in a particular crystallographic direction that passes through atom centers. Similarly, *planar density* is simply the fraction of total crystallographic plane area that is occupied by atoms (represented as circles); the plane must pass through an atom's center for the particular atom to be included. These concepts, the one- and two-dimensional analogs of the atomic packing factor, are illustrated in the following example problems.

Example Problem 3.8

Calculate the linear density of the [100] direction for BCC.

Solution

A BCC unit cell (reduced sphere) and the [100] direction therein are shown in Figure 3.11*a*; represented in Figure 3.11*b* is the linear packing in this direction. As a basis for our computation let us use the line length within the unit cell,

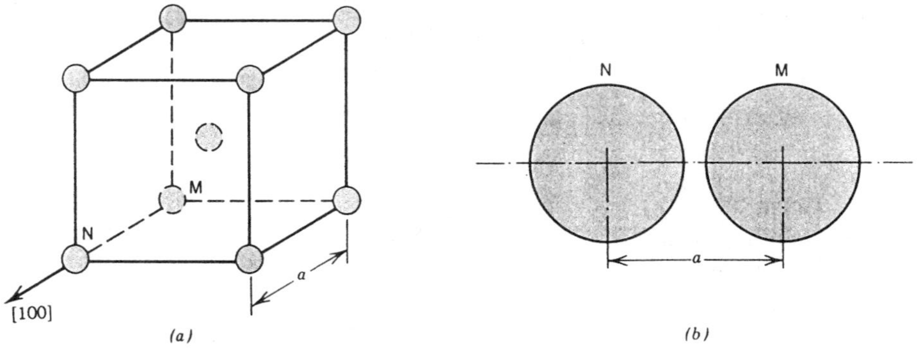

Figure 3.11 (*a*) Reduced-sphere BCC unit cell with the [100] direction indicated. (*b*) Atomic spacing in the [100] direction for the BCC crystal structure—between atoms M and N in (*a*).

L_l, which in this case is the lattice parameter a—the distance between the centers of atoms M and N. In terms of the atomic radius R,

$$L_l = a = \frac{4R}{\sqrt{3}} \qquad \text{(see Equation 3.3)}$$

Now, the total line length intersecting circles (atoms M and N), L_c, is equal to $2R$. And, the linear density LD is just the following ratio:

$$\text{LD} = \frac{L_c}{L_l} = \frac{2R}{4R/\sqrt{3}} = 0.866$$

EXAMPLE PROBLEM 3.9

Calculate the planar density of the (110) plane for FCC.

SOLUTION

The atomic packing of this plane is represented in Figure 3.9*b*. Consider that portion of the plane that intersects a unit cell (Figure 3.9*b*), and then compute both this planar area and total circle area in terms of the atomic radius R. Planar density, then, is just the ratio of these two areas.

The unit cell plane area, A_p, is simply that of the rectangle circumscribed by the centers of the atoms A, C, D, and F (Figure 3.9*b*). The rectangle length ($\overline{\text{AC}}$) and width ($\overline{\text{AD}}$) are, respectively,

$$\overline{\text{AC}} = 4R$$
$$\overline{\text{AD}} = 2R\sqrt{2} \qquad \text{(see Equation 3.1)}$$

Therefore,

$$A_p = (\overline{\text{AC}})(\overline{\text{AD}})$$
$$= (4R)(2R\sqrt{2}) = 8R^2\sqrt{2}$$

Now, for the total circle area, one fourth of each of atoms A, C, D, and F and one half of atoms B and E reside within this rectangle, which gives a total of 2 equivalent circles. Thus the total circle area A_c is just

$$A_c = (2)\pi R^2$$

Finally, the planar density PD is just

$$\text{PD} = \frac{A_c}{A_p} = \frac{2\pi R^2}{8R^2\sqrt{2}} = 0.555$$

Linear and planar densities are important considerations relative to the process of slip—that is, the mechanism by which metals plastically deform (Section 7.4). Slip occurs on the most densely packed crystallographic planes and, in those planes, along directions having the greatest atomic packing.

3.11 Close-Packed Crystal Structures

It may be remembered from the discussion on metallic crystal structures that both face-centered cubic and hexagonal close-packed crystal structures have atomic packing factors of 0.74, which is the most efficient packing of equal-sized spheres or atoms. In addition to unit cell representations, these two crystal structures may be described in terms of close-packed planes of atoms (i.e., planes having a maximum atom or sphere-packing density); a portion of one such plane is illustrated in Figure 3.12*a*. Both crystal structures may be generated by the stacking of these close-packed planes on top of one another; the difference between the two structures lies in the stacking sequence.

Let the centers of all the atoms in one close-packed plane be labeled *A*. Associated with this plane are two sets of equivalent triangular depressions formed by three adjacent atoms, into which the next close-packed plane of atoms may rest. Those having the triangle vertex pointing up are arbitrarily designated as *B* positions, while the remaining depressions are those with the down vertices, which are marked *C* in Figure 3.12*a*.

A second close-packed plane may be positioned with the centers of its atoms over either *B* or *C* sites; at this point both are equivalent. Suppose that the *B* positions are arbitrarily chosen; the stacking sequence is termed *AB*, which is illustrated in Figure 3.12*b*. The real distinction between FCC and HCP lies in where the third close-packed layer is positioned. For HCP, the centers of this layer are aligned directly above the original *A* positions. This stacking sequence, *ABABAB* . . . , is repeated over and over. Of course, the *ACACAC* . . . arrangement would be equivalent. These close-packed planes for HCP are (0001)-type planes, and the correspondence between this and the unit cell representation is shown in Figure 3.13.

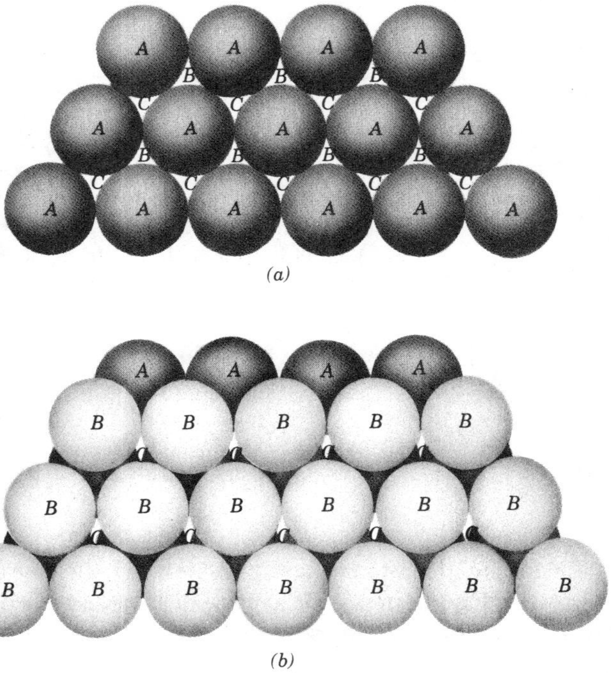

Figure 3.12 (*a*) A portion of a close-packed plane of atoms; *A*, *B*, and *C* positions are indicated. (*b*) The *AB* stacking sequence for close-packed atomic planes. (Adapted from W. G. Moffatt, G. W. Pearsall, and J. Wulff, *The Structure and Properties of Materials*, Vol. I, *Structure*, p. 50. Copyright © 1964 by John Wiley & Sons, New York. Reprinted by permission of John Wiley & Sons, Inc.)

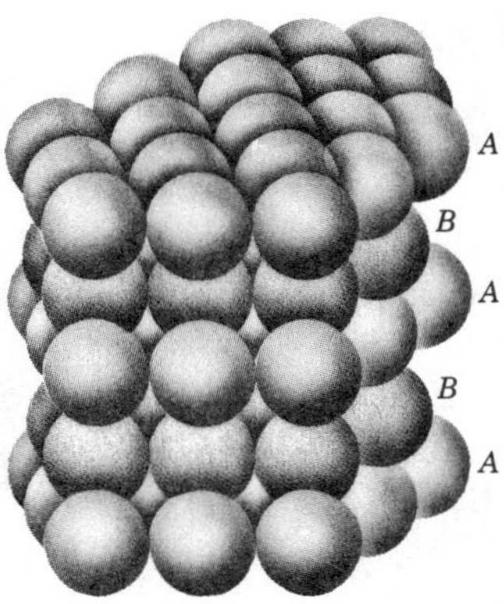

FIGURE 3.13 Close-packed plane stacking sequence for hexagonal close-packed. (Adapted from W. G. Moffatt, G. W. Pearsall, and J. Wulff, *The Structure and Properties of Materials,* Vol. I, *Structure,* p. 51. Copyright © 1964 by John Wiley & Sons, New York. Reprinted by permission of John Wiley & Sons, Inc.)

For the face-centered crystal structure, the centers of the third plane are situated over the C sites of the first plane (Figure 3.14a). This yields an $ABCABCABC$ . . . stacking sequence; that is, the atomic alignment repeats every third plane. It is more difficult to correlate the stacking of close-packed planes to the FCC unit cell. However, this relationship is demonstrated in Figure 3.14b; these planes are of the (111) type. The significance of these FCC and HCP close-packed planes will become apparent in Chapter 7.

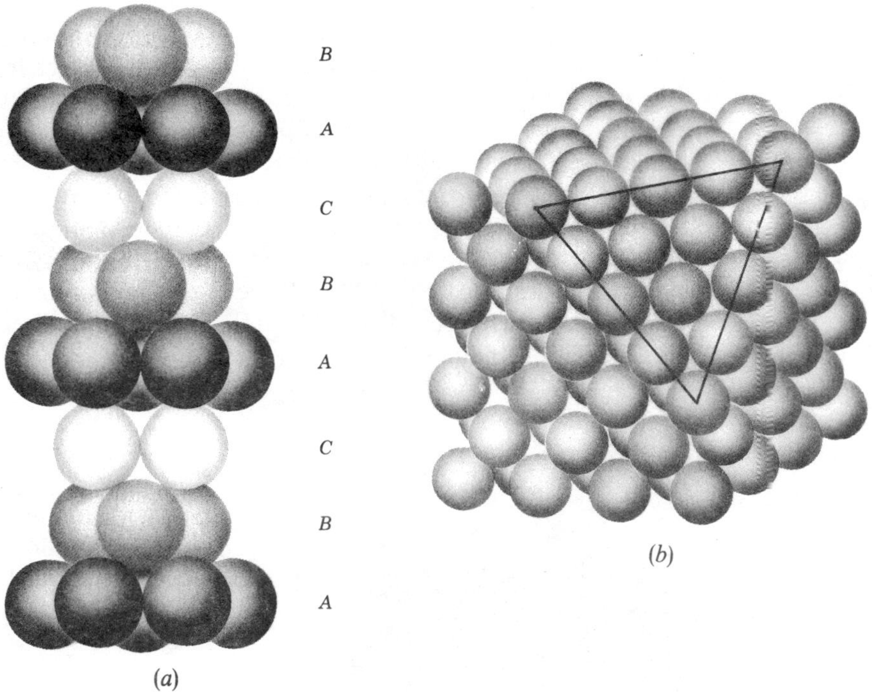

FIGURE 3.14 (a) Close-packed stacking sequence for face-centered cubic. (b) A corner has been removed to show the relation between the stacking of close-packed planes of atoms and the FCC crystal structure; the heavy triangle outlines a (111) plane. (Figure (b) from W. G. Moffatt, G. W. Pearsall, and J. Wulff, *The Structure and Properties of Materials,* Vol. I, *Structure,* p. 51. Copyright © 1964 by John Wiley & Sons, New York. Reprinted by permission of John Wiley & Sons, Inc.)

CRYSTALLINE AND NONCRYSTALLINE MATERIALS

3.12 Single Crystals

For a crystalline solid, when the periodic and repeated arrangement of atoms is perfect or extends throughout the entirety of the specimen without interruption, the result is a **single crystal.** All unit cells interlock in the same way and have the same orientation. Single crystals exist in nature, but they may also be produced artificially. They are ordinarily difficult to grow, because the environment must be carefully controlled.

If the extremities of a single crystal are permitted to grow without any external constraint, the crystal will assume a regular geometric shape having flat faces, as with some of the gem stones; the shape is indicative of the crystal structure. A photograph of several single crystals is shown in Figure 3.15. Within the past few years, single crystals have become extremely important in many of our modern technologies, in particular electronic microcircuits, which employ single crystals of silicon and other semiconductors.

3.13 Polycrystalline Materials

Most crystalline solids are composed of a collection of many small crystals or **grains;** such materials are termed **polycrystalline.** Various stages in the solidification of a polycrystalline specimen are represented schematically in Figure 3.16. Initially, small crystals or nuclei form at various positions. These have random crystallographic orientations, as indicated by the square grids. The small grains grow by the successive addition from the surrounding liquid of atoms to the structure of each. The extremities of adjacent grains impinge on one another as the solidification process approaches completion. As indicated in Figure 3.16, the crystallographic orientation varies from grain to grain. Also, there exists some atomic mismatch within the region where two grains meet; this area, called a **grain boundary,** is discussed in more detail in Section 4.5.

FIGURE 3.15 Photograph showing several single crystals of fluorite, CaF_2. (Smithsonian Institution photograph number 38181P.)

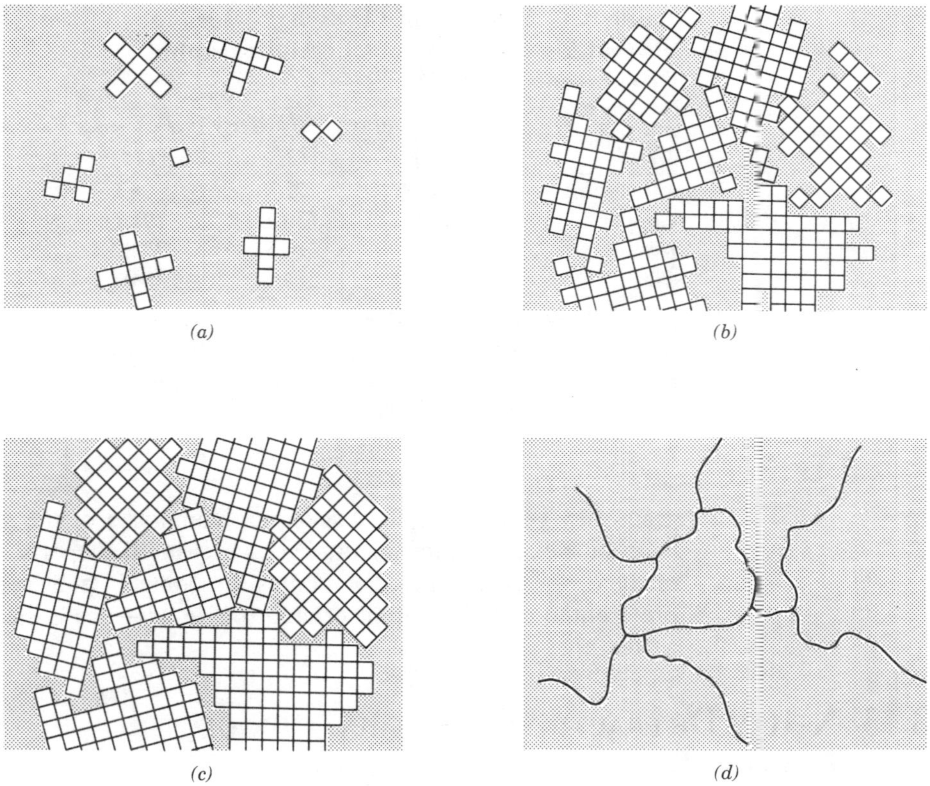

FIGURE 3.16 Schematic diagrams of the various stages in the solidification of a polycrystalline material; the square grids depict unit cells. (*a*) Small crystallite nuclei. (*b*) Growth of the crystallites; the obstruction of some grains that are adjacent to one another is also shown. (*c*) Upon completion of solidification, grains having irregular shapes have formed. (*d*) The grain structure as it would appear under the microscope; dark lines are the grain boundaries. (Adapted from W. Rosenhain, *An Introduction to the Study of Physical Metallurgy*, 2nd edition, Constable & Company Ltd., London, 1915.)

3.14 ANISOTROPY

The physical properties of single crystals of some substances depend on the crystallographic direction in which measurements are taken. For example, the elastic modulus, the electrical conductivity, and the index of refraction may have different values in the [100] and [111] directions. This directionality of properties is termed **anisotropy,** and it is associated with the variance of atomic or ionic spacing with crystallographic direction. Substances in which measured properties are independent of the direction of measurement are **isotropic.** The extent and magnitude of anisotropic effects in crystalline materials are functions of the symmetry of the crystal structure; the degree of anisotropy increases with decreasing structural symmetry—triclinic structures normally are highly anisotropic. The modulus of elasticity values at [100], [110], and [111] orientations for several materials are presented in Table 3.3.

For many polycrystalline materials, the crystallographic orientations of the individual grains are totally random. Under these circumstances, even though each

Table 3.3 **Modulus of Elasticity Values for Several Metals at Various Crystallographic Orientations**

	Modulus of Elasticity (GPa)		
Metal	*[100]*	*[110]*	*[111]*
Aluminum	63.7	72.6	76.1
Copper	66.7	130.3	191.1
Iron	125.0	210.5	272.7
Tungsten	384.6	384.6	384.6

Source: R. W. Hertzberg, *Deformation and Fracture Mechanics of Engineering Materials,* 3rd edition. Copyright © 1989 by John Wiley & Sons, New York. Reprinted by permission of John Wiley & Sons, Inc.

grain may be anisotropic, a specimen composed of the grain aggregate behaves isotropically. Also, the magnitude of a measured property represents some average of the directional values. Sometimes the grains in polycrystalline materials have a preferential crystallographic orientation, in which case the material is said to have a "texture."

3.15 X-Ray Diffraction: Determination of Crystal Structures

Historically much of our understanding regarding the atomic and molecular arrangements in solids has resulted from x-ray diffraction investigations; furthermore, x-rays are still very important in developing new materials. A brief overview of the diffraction phenomenon and how, using x-rays, atomic interplanar distances and crystal structures are deduced will now be given.

THE DIFFRACTION PHENOMENON

Diffraction occurs when a wave encounters a series of regularly spaced obstacles, that (1) are capable of scattering the wave, and (2) have spacings that are comparable in magnitude to the wavelength. Furthermore, diffraction is a consequence of specific phase relationships that are established between two or more waves that have been scattered by the obstacles.

Consider waves 1 and 2 in Figure 3.17*a*, which have the same wavelength (λ) and are in phase at point O–O'. Now let us suppose that both waves are scattered in such a way that they traverse different paths. The phase relationship between the scattered waves, which will depend upon the difference in path length, is important. One possibility results when this path length difference is an integral number of wavelengths. As noted in Figure 3.17*a*, these scattered waves (now labeled $1'$ and $2'$) are still in phase. They are said to mutually reinforce (or constructively interfere with) one another; and, when amplitudes are added, the wave shown on the right side of the figure results. This is a manifestation of **diffraction,** and we refer to a diffracted beam as one composed of a large number of scattered waves that mutually reinforce one another.

Other phase relationships are possible between scattered waves that will not lead to this mutual reinforcement. The other extreme is that demonstrated in Figure

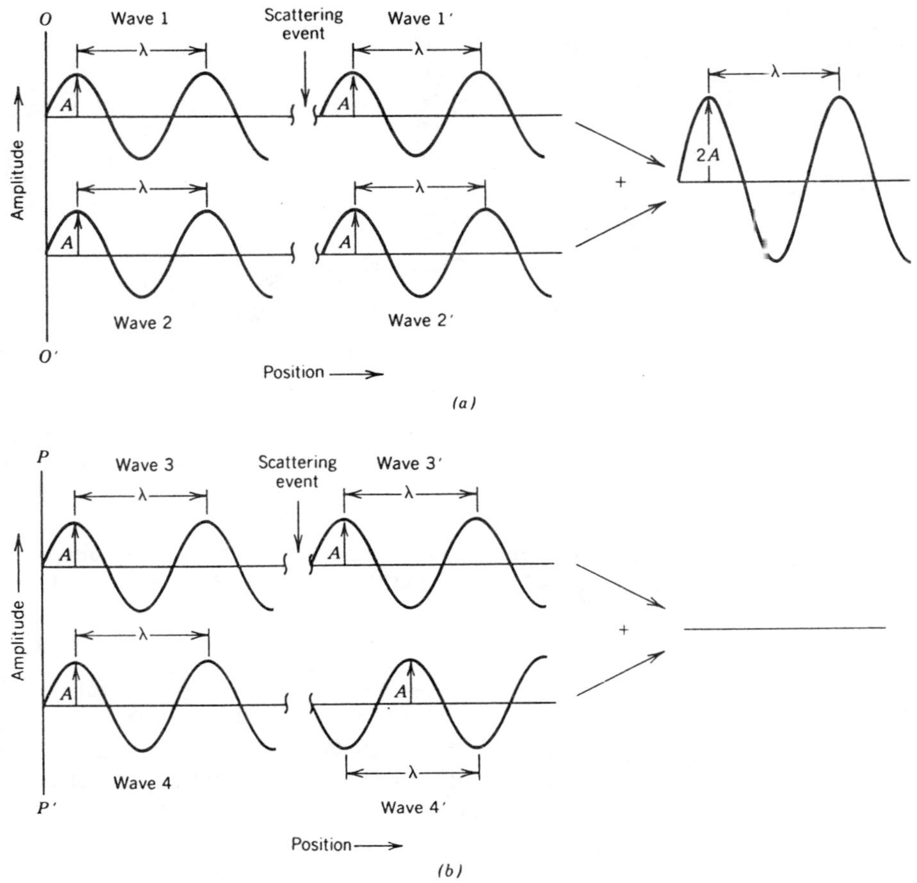

FIGURE 3.17 (*a*) Demonstration of how two waves (labeled 1 and 2) that have the same wavelength λ and remain in phase after a scattering event (waves 1′ and 2′) constructively interfere with one another. The amplitudes of the scattered waves add together in the resultant wave. (*b*) Demonstration of how two waves (labeled 3 and 4) that have the same wavelength and become out of phase after a scattering event (waves 3′ and 4′) destructively interfere with one another. The amplitudes of the two scattered waves cancel one another.

3.17*b*, wherein the path length difference after scattering is some integral number of *half* wavelengths. The scattered waves are out of phase—that is, corresponding amplitudes cancel or annul one another, or destructively interfere (i.e., the resultant wave has zero amplitude), as indicated on the extreme right side of the figure. Of course, phase relationships intermediate between these two extremes exist, resulting in only partial reinforcement.

X-RAY DIFFRACTION AND BRAGG'S LAW

X-Rays are a form of electromagnetic radiation that have high energies and short wavelengths—wavelengths on the order of the atomic spacings for solids. When a beam of x-rays impinges on a solid material, a portion of this beam will be scattered in all directions by the electrons associated with each atom or ion that lies within the beam's path. Let us now examine the necessary conditions for diffraction of x-rays by a periodic arrangement of atoms.

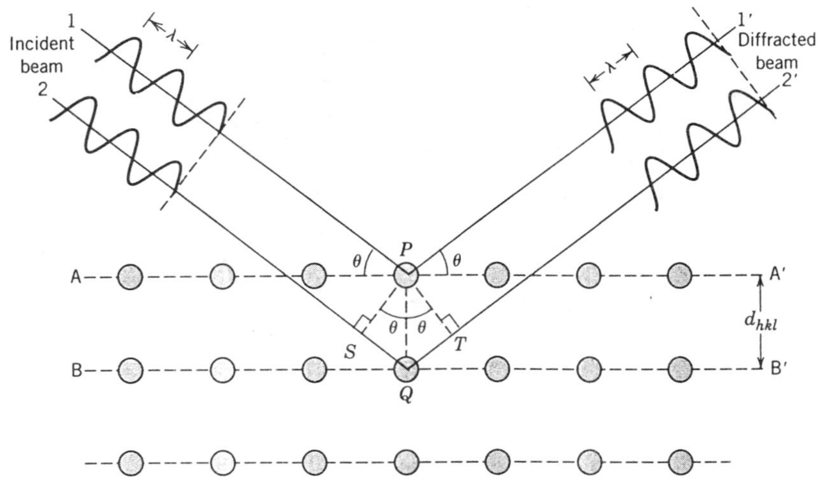

FIGURE 3.18 Diffraction of x-rays by planes of atoms (A–A′ and B–B′).

Consider the two parallel planes of atoms A–A′ and B–B′ in Figure 3.18, which have the same h, k, and l Miller indices and are separated by the interplanar spacing d_{hkl}. Now assume that a parallel, monochromatic, and coherent (in-phase) beam of x-rays of wavelength λ is incident on these two planes at an angle θ. Two rays in this beam, labeled 1 and 2, are scattered by atoms P and Q. Constructive interference of the scattered rays 1′ and 2′ occurs also at an angle θ to the planes, if the path length difference between 1–P–1′ and 2–Q–2′ (i.e., $\overline{SQ} + \overline{QT}$) is equal to a whole number, n, of wavelengths. That is, the condition for diffraction is

$$n\lambda = \overline{SQ} + \overline{QT} \tag{3.8}$$

or

$$n\lambda = d_{hkl} \sin\theta + d_{hkl} \sin\theta = 2d_{hkl} \sin\theta \tag{3.9}$$

Equation 3.9 is known as **Bragg's law;** also, n is the order of reflection, which may be any integer (1, 2, 3, . . .) consistent with sin θ not exceeding unity. Thus, we have a simple expression relating the x-ray wavelength and interatomic spacing to the angle of the diffracted beam. If Bragg's law is not satisfied, then the interference will be nonconstructive in nature so as to yield a very low-intensity diffracted beam.

The magnitude of the distance between two adjacent and parallel planes of atoms (i.e., the interplanar spacing d_{hkl}) is a function of the Miller indices (h, k, and l) as well as the lattice parameter(s). For example, for crystal structures having cubic symmetry,

$$d_{hkl} = \frac{a}{\sqrt{h^2 + k^2 + l^2}} \tag{3.10}$$

in which a is the lattice parameter (unit cell edge length). Relationships similar to Equation 3.10, but which are more complex, exist for the other six crystal systems noted in Table 3.2.

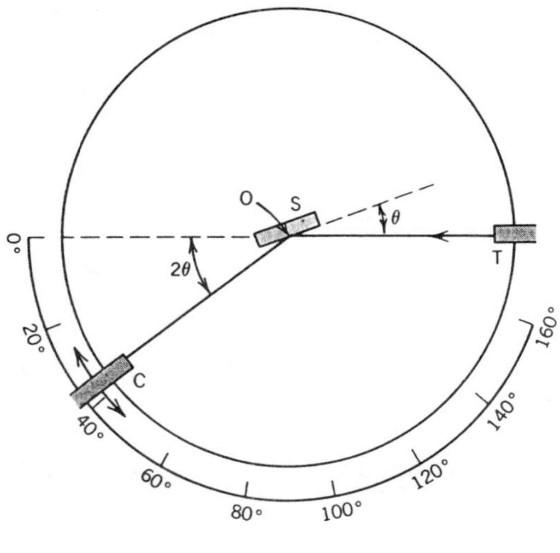

FIGURE 3.19 Schematic diagram of an x-ray diffractometer; T = x-ray source, S = specimen, C = detector, and O = the axis around which the specimen and detector rotate.

Bragg's law, Equation 3.9, is a necessary but not sufficient condition for diffraction by real crystals. It specifies when diffraction will occur for unit cells having atoms positioned only at cell corners. However, atoms situated at other sites (e.g., face and interior unit cell positions as with FCC and BCC) act as extra scattering centers, which can produce out-of-phase scattering at certain Bragg angles. The net result is the absence of some diffracted beams which, according to Equation 3.9, should be present. For example, for the BCC crystal structure, $h + k + l$ must be even if diffraction is to occur, whereas for FCC, h, k, and l must all be either odd or even.

DIFFRACTION TECHNIQUES

One common diffraction technique employs a powdered or polycrystalline specimen consisting of many fine and randomly oriented particles that are exposed to monochromatic x-radiation. Each powder particle (or grain) is a crystal, and having a large number of them with random orientations ensures that some particles are properly oriented such that every possible set of crystallographic planes will be available for diffraction.

The *diffractometer* is an apparatus used to determine the angles at which diffraction occurs for powdered specimens; its features are represented schematically in Figure 3.19. A specimen S in the form of a flat plate is supported so that rotations about the axis labeled O are possible; this axis is perpendicular to the plane of the page. The monochromatic x-ray beam is generated at point T, and the intensities of diffracted beams are detected with a counter labeled C in the figure. The specimen, x-ray source, and counter are all coplanar.

The counter is mounted on a movable carriage which may also be rotated about the O axis; its angular position in terms of 2θ is marked on a graduated scale.[2] Carriage and specimen are mechanically coupled such that a rotation of the specimen

[2] It should be pointed out that the symbol θ has been used in two different contexts for this discussion. Here, θ represents the angular locations of both x-ray source and counter relative to the specimen surface. Previously (e.g., Equation 3.9), it denoted the angle at which the Bragg criterion for diffraction is satisfied.

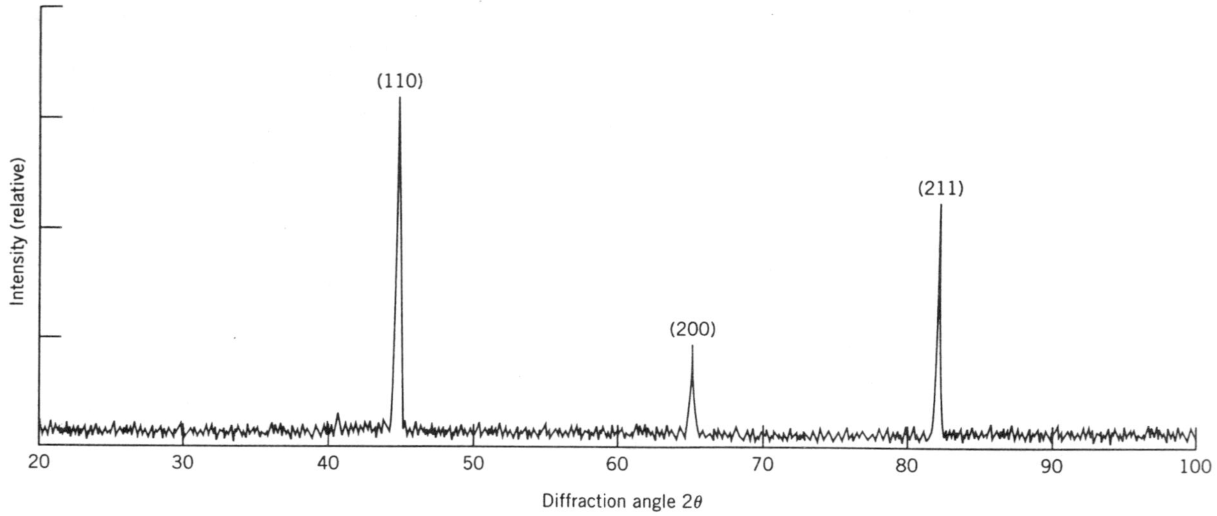

FIGURE 3.20 Diffraction pattern for polycrystalline α-iron.

through θ is accompanied by a 2θ rotation of the counter; this assures that the incident and reflection angles are maintained equal to one another (Figure 3.19). Collimators are incorporated within the beam path to produce a well-defined and focused beam. Utilization of a filter provides a near-monochromatic beam.

As the counter moves at constant angular velocity, a recorder automatically plots the diffracted beam intensity (monitored by the counter) as a function of 2θ; 2θ is termed the *diffraction angle,* which is measured experimentally. Figure 3.20 shows a diffraction pattern for a polycrystalline specimen of iron. The high-intensity peaks result when the Bragg diffraction condition is satisfied by some set of crystallographic planes. These peaks are plane-indexed in the figure.

Other powder techniques have been devised wherein diffracted beam intensity and position are recorded on a photographic film instead of being measured by a counter.

One of the primary uses of x-ray diffractometry is for the determination of crystal structure. The unit cell size and geometry may be resolved from the angular positions of the diffraction peaks, whereas arrangement of atoms within the unit cell is associated with the relative intensities of these peaks.

X-Rays, as well as electron and neutron beams, are also used in other types of material investigations. For example, crystallographic orientations of single crystals are possible using x-ray diffraction (or Laue) photographs. On page 29 is shown a photograph that was generated using an incident electron beam that was directed on a gallium arsenide crystal; each spot (with the exception of the brightest one near the center) resulted from an electron beam that was diffracted by a specific set of crystallographic planes. Other uses of x-rays include qualitative and quantitative chemical identifications, and the determination of residual stresses and crystal size.

EXAMPLE PROBLEM 3.10

For BCC iron, compute (a) the interplanar spacing, and (b) the diffraction angle for the (220) set of planes. The lattice parameter for Fe is 0.2866 nm

(2.886 Å). Also, assume that monochromatic radiation having a wavelength of 0.1790 nm (1.790 Å) is used, and the order of reflection is 1.

SOLUTION

(a) The value of the interplanar spacing d_{hkl} is determined using Equation 3.10, with $a = 0.2866$ nm, and $h = 2$, $k = 2$, and $l = 0$, since we are considering the (220) planes. Therefore,

$$d_{hkl} = \frac{a}{\sqrt{h^2 + k^2 + l^2}}$$

$$= \frac{0.2866 \text{ nm}}{\sqrt{(2)^2 + (2)^2 + (0)^2}} = 0.1013 \text{ nm } (1.013 \text{ Å})$$

(b) The value of θ may now be computed using Equation 3.9, with $n = 1$, since this is a first-order reflection:

$$\sin\theta = \frac{n\lambda}{2d_{hkl}} = \frac{(1)(0.1790 \text{ nm})}{(2)(0.1013 \text{ nm})} = 0.884$$

$$\theta = \sin^{-1}(0.884) = 62.13°$$

The diffraction angle is 2θ, or

$$2\theta = (2)(62.13°) = 124.26°$$

3.16 Noncrystalline Solids

It has been mentioned that **noncrystalline** solids lack a systematic and regular arrangement of atoms over relatively large atomic distances. Sometimes such materials are also called **amorphous** (meaning literally without form), or supercooled liquids inasmuch as their atomic structure resembles that of a liquid.

An amorphous condition may be illustrated by comparison of the crystalline and noncrystalline structures of the ceramic compound silicon dioxide (SiO_2), which may exist in both states. Figures 3.21*a* and 3.21*b* present two-dimensional schematic

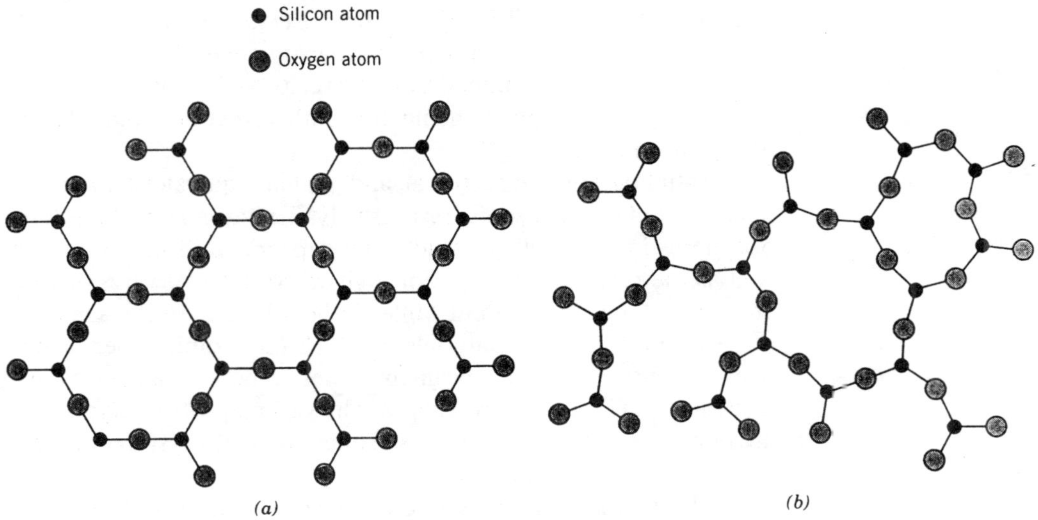

FIGURE 3.21 Two-dimensional schemes of the structure of (*a*) crystalline silicon dioxide and (*b*) noncrystalline silicon dioxide.

diagrams for both structures of SiO_2. Even though each silicon ion bonds to three oxygen ions for both states, beyond this, the structure is much more disordered and irregular for the noncrystalline structure.

Whether a crystalline or amorphous solid forms depends on the ease with which a random atomic structure in the liquid can transform to an ordered state during solidification. Amorphous materials, therefore, are characterized by atomic or molecular structures that are relatively complex and become ordered only with some difficulty. Furthermore, rapidly cooling through the freezing temperature favors the formation of a noncrystalline solid, since little time is allowed for the ordering process.

Metals normally form crystalline solids; but some ceramic materials are crystalline, whereas others, the inorganic glasses, are amorphous. Polymers may be completely crystalline, entirely noncrystalline, or a mixture of the two. More about the structure and properties of amorphous ceramics and polymers is contained in Chapters 13 and 15.

SUMMARY

Atoms in crystalline solids are positioned in an orderly and repeated pattern, which is in contrast to the random and disordered atomic distribution found in noncrystalline or amorphous materials. Atoms may be represented as solid spheres, and, for crystalline solids, crystal structure is just the spatial arrangement of these spheres. The various crystal structures are specified in terms of parallelepiped unit cells, which are characterized by geometry and atom positions within.

Most common metals exist in at least one of three relatively simple crystal structures: face-centered cubic (FCC), body-centered cubic (BCC), and hexagonal close-packed (HCP). Two features of a crystal structure are coordination number (or number of nearest-neighbor atoms) and atomic packing factor (the fraction of solid sphere volume in the unit cell). Coordination number and atomic packing factor are the same for both FCC and HCP crystal structures, each of which may be generated by the stacking of close-packed planes of atoms.

Crystallographic planes and directions are specified in terms of an indexing scheme. The basis for the determination of each index is a coordinate axis system defined by the unit cell for the particular crystal structure. Directional indices are computed in terms of vector projections on each of the coordinate axes, whereas planar indices are determined from the reciprocals of axial intercepts. For hexagonal unit cells, a four-index scheme for both directions and planes is found to be more convenient.

Crystallographic directional and planar equivalencies are related to atomic linear and planar densities, respectively. The atomic packing (i.e., planar density) of spheres in a crystallographic plane depends on both the indices of the plane as well as the crystal structure. For a given crystal structure, planes having identical atomic packing yet different Miller indices belong to the same family.

Single crystals are materials in which the atomic order extends uninterrupted over the entirety of the specimen; under some circumstances, they may have flat faces and regular geometric shapes. The vast majority of crystalline solids, however, are polycrystalline, being composed of many small crystals or grains having different crystallographic orientations.

X-Ray diffractometry is used for crystal structure and interplanar spacing determinations. A beam of x-rays directed on a crystalline material may experience diffraction (constructive interference) as a result of its interaction with a series of parallel atomic planes according to Bragg's law. Interplanar spacing is a function of the Miller indices and lattice parameter(s) as well as the crystal structure.

IMPLICATIONS

A knowledge and understanding of the concepts discussed in this chapter are important for a number of reasons; some of these are as follows:

1. Some of the properties of materials (e.g., ductility [Section 6.6]) may be dependent on their crystal structure.

2. Being able to specify crystallographic planes and directions allows us to understand and explain the mechanism of plastic deformation for most crystalline metals and ceramics (Section 7.4).

3. Anisotropic properties in single crystals must necessarily be specified in terms of crystallographic directions.

4. Anisotropic effects often need to be considered in the applications and processing of materials.

5. Thermodynamic principles relating to solid materials involve understanding allotropic and polymorphic transformations.

6. The properties and the applications of materials may depend on whether they are single crystals or polycrystalline.

7. X-ray analytical techniques are often used to characterize materials.

8. The crystal structures of materials and other important crystallographic information may be deduced through x-ray diffraction analyses.

IMPORTANT TERMS AND CONCEPTS

Allotropy	Crystal system	Lattice
Amorphous	Crystalline	Lattice parameters
Anisotropy	Diffraction	Miller indices
Atomic packing factor (APF)	Face-centered cubic (FCC)	Noncrystalline
Body-centered cubic (BCC)	Grain	Polycrystalline
Bragg's law	Grain boundary	Polymorphism
Coordination number	Hexagonal close-packed (HCP)	Single crystal
Crystal structure	Isotropic	Unit cell

REFERENCES

Azaroff, L. F., *Elements of X-Ray Crystallography,* McGraw-Hill Book Company, New York, 1968. Reprinted by TechBooks, Fairfax, VA.

Barrett, C. S. and T. B. Massalski, *Structure of Metals,* 3rd edition, Pergamon Press, Oxford, 1980.

Buerger, M. J., *Elementary Crystallography,* John Wiley & Sons, New York, 1956.

Cohen, J. B., *Diffraction Methods in Materials Science,* The Macmillan Co., New York, 1966.

Cullity, B. D., *Elements of X-Ray Diffraction,* 2nd edition, Addison-Wesley Publishing Co., Reading, MA, 1978.

Schwartz, L. H. and J. B. Cohen, *Diffraction from Materials,* 2nd edition, Springer-Verlag, New York, 1987.

Wyckoff, R. W. G., *Crystal Structures,* 2nd edition, Interscience Publishers, 1963. Reprinted by Krieger Publishing Company, Melbourne, FL, 1986.

QUESTIONS AND PROBLEMS

3.1 What is the difference between atomic structure and crystal structure?

3.2 What is the difference between a crystal structure and a crystal system?

3.3 If the atomic radius of lead is 0.175 nm, calculate the volume of its unit cell in cubic meters.

3.4 Show for the body-centered cubic crystal structure that the unit cell edge length a and the atomic radius R are related through $a = 4R/\sqrt{3}$.

3.5 For the HCP crystal structure, show that the ideal c/a ratio is 1.633.

3.6 Show that the atomic packing factor for BCC is 0.68.

3.7 Show that the atomic packing factor for HCP is 0.74.

3.8 Molybdenum has a BCC crystal structure, an atomic radius of 0.1363 nm, and an atomic weight of 95.94 g/mol. Compute and compare its density with the experimental value found in Table C.1, Appendix C.

3.9 Calculate the radius of a palladium atom, given that Pd has an FCC crystal structure, a density of 12.0 g/cm^3, and an atomic weight of 106.4 g/mol.

3.10 Calculate the radius of a tantalum atom, given that Ta has a BCC crystal structure, a density of 16.6 g/cm^3, and an atomic weight of 180.9 g/mol.

3.11 Some hypothetical metal has the simple cubic crystal structure shown in Figure 3.22. If its atomic weight is 70.4 g/mol and the atomic radius is 0.126 nm, compute its density.

3.12 Zirconium has an HCP crystal structure and a density of 6.51 g/cm^3.

(a) What is the volume of its unit cell in cubic meters?

(b) If the c/a ratio is 1.593, compute the values of c and a.

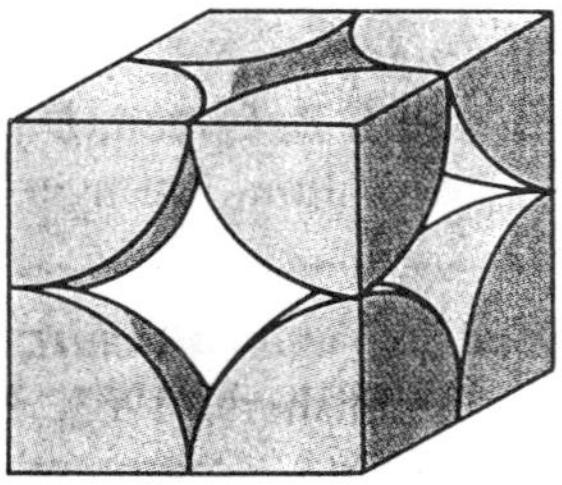

FIGURE 3.22 Hard-sphere unit cell representation of the simple cubic crystal structure.

3.13 Using atomic weight, crystal structure, and atomic radius data tabulated inside the front cover, compute the theoretical densities of lead, chromium, copper, and cobalt, and then compare these values with the measured densities listed in this same table. The c/a ratio for cobalt is 1.623.

3.14 Rhodium has an atomic radius of 0.1345 nm (1.345 Å) and a density of 12.41 g/cm^3. Determine whether it has an FCC or BCC crystal structure.

3.15 Below are listed the atomic weight, density, and atomic radius for three hypothetical alloys. For each determine whether its crystal structure is FCC, BCC, or simple cubic and then justify your determination. A simple cubic unit cell is shown in Figure 3.22.

Alloy	*Atomic Weight (g/mol)*	*Density (g/cm³)*	*Atomic Radius (nm)*
A	77.4	8.22	0.125
B	107.6	13.42	0.133
C	127.3	9.23	0.142

3.16 The unit cell for tin has tetragonal symmetry, with a and b lattice parameters of 0.583 and 0.318 nm, respectively. If its density, atomic weight, and atomic radius are 7.30 g/cm^3, 118.69 g/mol, and 0.151 nm, respectively, compute the atomic packing factor.

3.17 Iodine has an orthorhombic unit cell for which the a, b, and c lattice parameters are 0.479, 0.725, and 0.978 nm, respectively.

(a) If the atomic packing factor and atomic radius are 0.547 and 0.177 nm, respectively, determine the number of atoms in each unit cell.

(b) The atomic weight of iodine is 126.91 g/mol; compute its density.

3.18 Titanium has an HCP unit cell for which the ratio of the lattice parameters c/a is 1.58. If the radius of the Ti atom is 0.1445 nm, **(a)** determine the unit cell volume, and **(b)** calculate the density of Ti and compare it with the literature value.

3.19 Zinc has an HCP crystal structure, a c/a ratio of 1.856, and a density of 7.13 g/cm^3. Calculate the atomic radius for Zn.

3.20 Rhenium has an HCP crystal structure, an atomic radius of 0.137 nm, and a c/a ratio of 1.615. Compute the volume of the unit cell for Re.

3.21 This is a unit cell for a hypothetical metal:

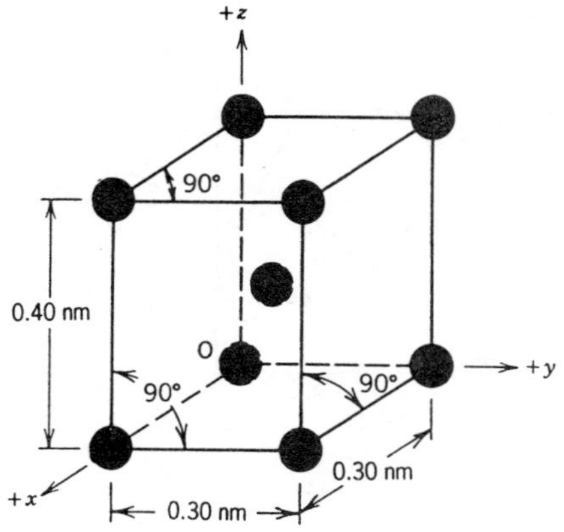

(a) To which crystal system does this unit cell belong?

(b) What would this crystal structure be called?

(c) Calculate the density of the material, given that its atomic weight is 114 g/mol.

3.22 Sketch a unit cell for the body-centered orthorhombic crystal structure.

3.23 Draw an orthorhombic unit cell, and within that cell a $[2\bar{1}1]$ direction and a $(02\bar{1})$ plane.

3.24 Sketch a monoclinic unit cell, and within that cell a $[\bar{1}01]$ direction and a (200) plane.

3.25 Here are unit cells for two hypothetical metals:

(a) What are the indices for the directions indicated by the two vectors in sketch (a)?

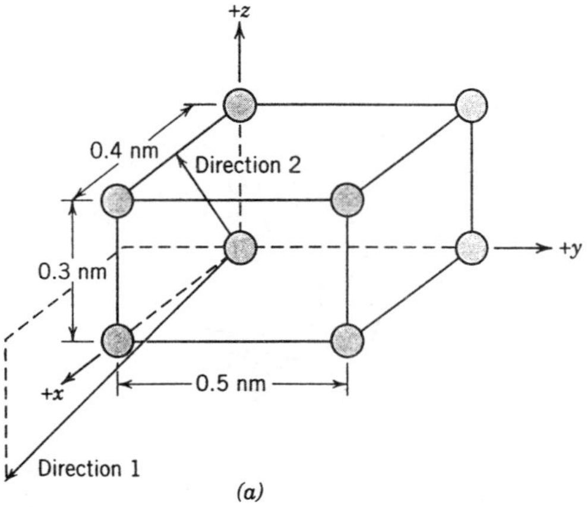

(a)

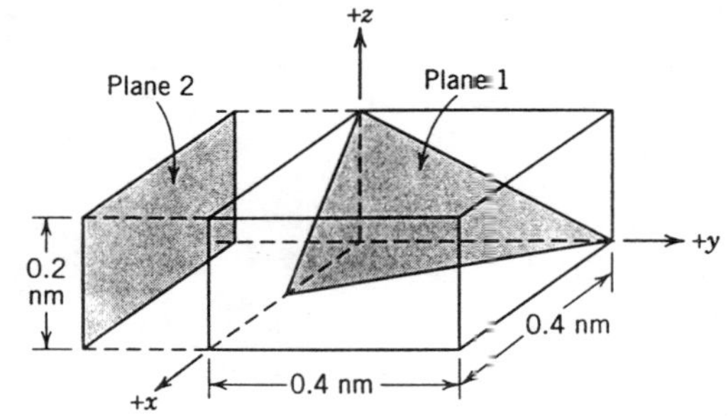

(b)

(b) What are the indices for the two planes drawn in sketch (b)?

3.26 Within a cubic unit cell, sketch the following directions:

(a) $[\bar{1}10]$; **(d)** $[1\bar{3}3]$; **(g)** $[\bar{1}2\bar{3}]$;
(b) $[\bar{1}\bar{2}1]$; **(e)** $[\bar{1}11]$; **(h)** $[\bar{1}03]$.
(c) $[0\bar{1}2]$; **(f)** $[\bar{1}22]$;

3.27 Determine the indices for the directions shown in the following cubic unit cell:

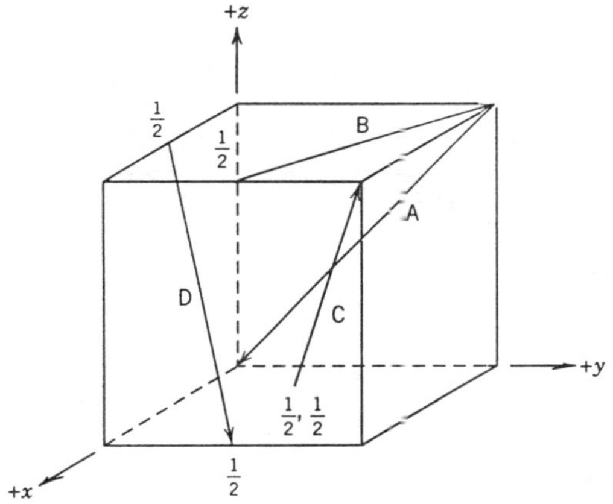

3.28 Determine the indices for the directions shown in the following cubic unit cell:

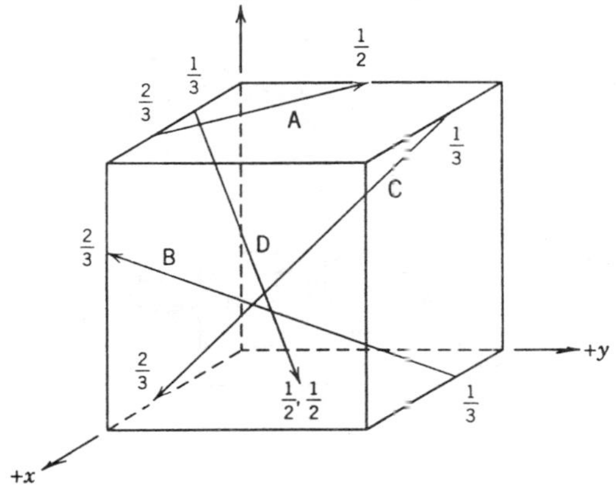

3.29 For tetragonal crystals, cite the indices of directions that are equivalent to each of the following directions:

(a) [101];

(b) [110];

(c) [010].

3.30 (a) Convert the [110] and [00$\bar{1}$] directions into the four-index Miller–Bravais scheme for hexagonal unit cells.

(b) Make the same conversion for the (111) and (0$\bar{1}$2) planes.

3.31 Determine the Miller indices for the planes shown in the following unit cell:

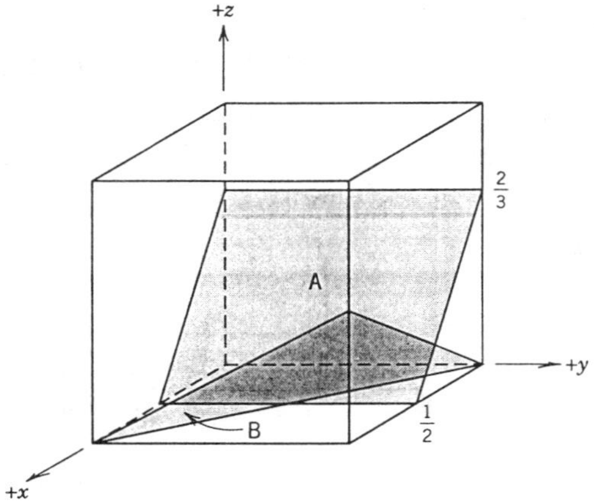

3.32 Determine the Miller indices for the planes shown in the following unit cell:

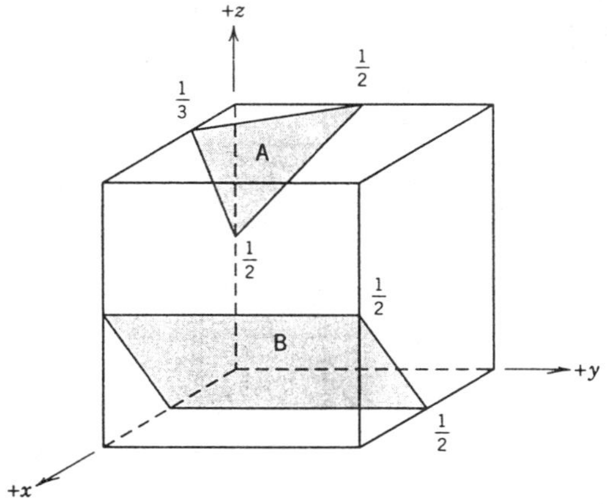

3.33 Determine the Miller indices for the planes shown in the following unit cell:

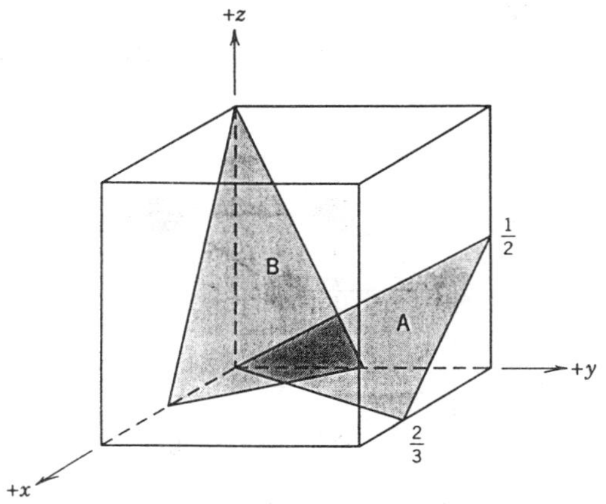

3.34 Sketch the (1$\bar{1}$01) and (11$\bar{2}$0) planes in a hexagonal unit cell.

3.35 Determine the indices for the planes shown in the hexagonal unit cells shown below.

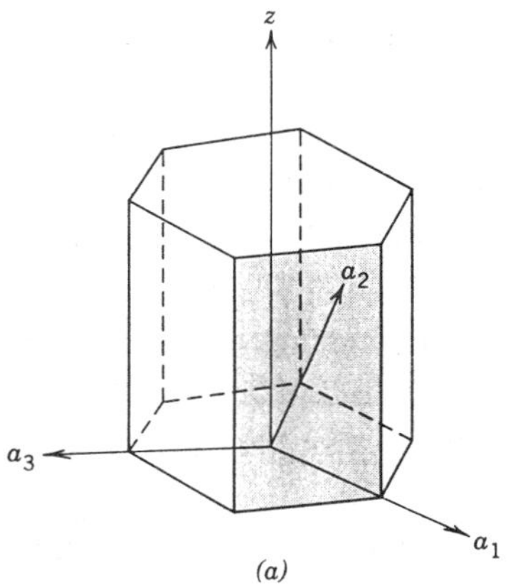

(a)

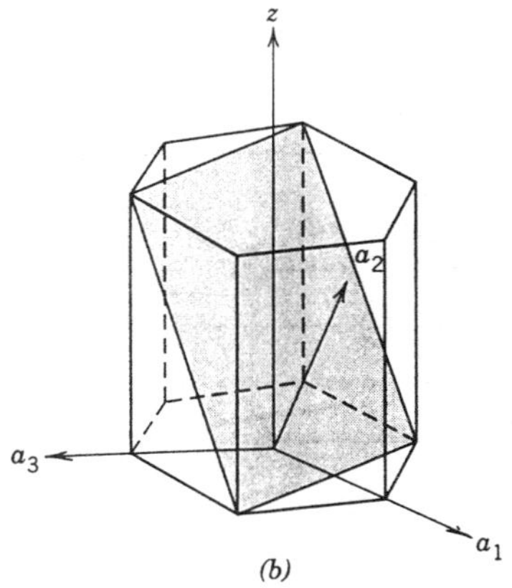

(b)

3.36 Sketch within a cubic unit cell the following planes:

(a) $(0\bar{1}\bar{1})$;

(b) $(11\bar{2})$;

(c) $(10\bar{2})$;

(d) $(1\bar{3}1)$;

(e) $(\bar{1}1\bar{1})$;

(f) $(1\bar{2}\bar{2})$;

(g) $(\bar{1}2\bar{3})$;

(h) $(0\bar{1}\bar{3})$.

3.37 Sketch the atomic packing of **(a)** the (100) plane for the FCC crystal structure, and **(b)** the (111) plane for the BCC crystal structure (similar to Figures 3.9*b* and 3.10*b*).

3.38 Consider the reduced-sphere unit cell shown in Problem 3.21, having an origin of the coordinate system positioned at the atom labeled with an O. For the following sets of planes, determine which are equivalent:

(a) (100), $(0\bar{1}0)$, and (001).

(b) (110), (101), (011), and $(\bar{1}10)$.

(c) (111), $(1\bar{1}1)$, $(11\bar{1})$, and $(\bar{1}1\bar{1})$.

3.39 Cite the indices of the direction that results from the intersection of each of the following pair of planes within a cubic crystal: **(a)** (110) and (111) planes; **(b)** (110) and $(1\bar{1}0)$ planes; and **(c)** $(10\bar{1})$ and (001) planes.

3.40 Compute and compare the linear densities of the [100], [110], and [111] directions for FCC.

3.41 Compute and compare the linear densities of the [110] and [111] directions for BCC.

3.42 Calculate and compare the planar densities of the (100) and (111) planes for FCC.

3.43 Calculate and compare the planar densities of the (100) and (110) planes for BCC.

3.44 Calculate the planar density of the (0001) plane for HCP.

3.45 Here are shown the atomic packing schemes for several different crystallographic directions for some hypothetical metal. For each direction the circles represent only those atoms contained within a unit cell, which circles are reduced from their actual size.

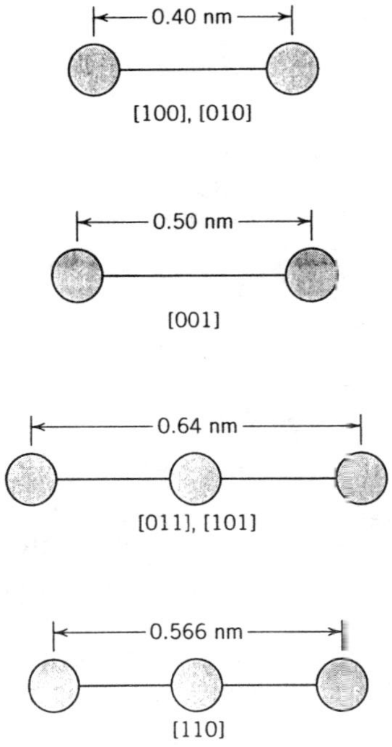

(a) To what crystal system does the unit cell belong?

(b) What would this crystal structure be called?

3.46 Below are shown three different crystallographic planes for a unit cell of some hypothetical metal; the circles represent atoms:

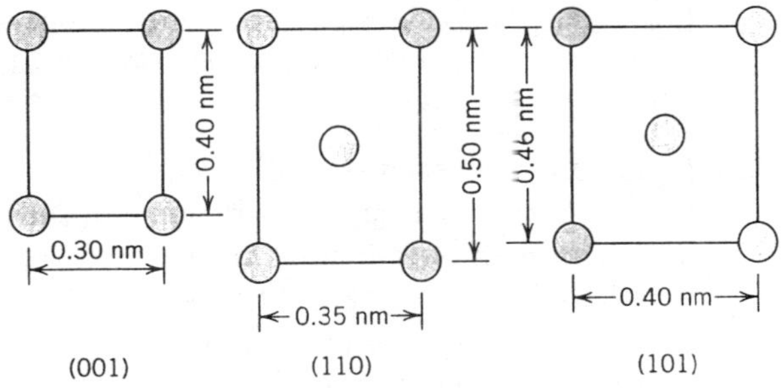

(a) To what crystal system does the unit cell belong?

(b) What would this crystal structure be called?

(c) If the density of this metal is 8.95 g/cm^3, determine its atomic weight.

3.47 Explain why the properties of polycrystalline materials are most often isotropic.

3.48 Using the data for molybdenum in Table 3.1, compute the interplanar spacing for the (111) set of planes.

3.49 Determine the expected diffraction angle for the first-order reflection from the (113) set of planes for FCC platinum when monochromatic radiation of wavelength 0.1542 nm is used.

3.50 Using the data for aluminum in Table 3.1, compute the interplanar spacings for the (110) and (221) sets of planes.

3.51 The metal iridium has an FCC crystal structure. If the angle of diffraction for the (220) set of planes occurs at 69.22° (first-order reflection) when monochromatic x-radiation having a wavelength of 0.1542 nm is used, compute **(a)** the interplanar spacing for this set of planes, and **(b)** the atomic radius for an iridium atom.

3.52 The metal rubidium has a BCC crystal structure. If the angle of diffraction for the (321) set of planes occurs at 27.00° (first-order reflection) when monochromatic x-radiation having a wavelength of 0.0711 nm is used, compute **(a)** the interplanar spacing for this set of planes, and **(b)** the atomic radius for the rubidium atom.

3.53 For which set of crystallographic planes will a first-order diffraction peak occur at a diffraction angle of 46.21° for BCC iron when monochromatic radiation having a wavelength of 0.0711 nm is used?

3.54 Figure 3.20 shows an x-ray diffraction pattern for α-iron taken using a diffractometer and monochromatic x-radiation having a wavelength of 0.1542 nm; each diffraction peak on the pattern has been indexed. Compute the interplanar spacing for each set of planes indexed; also determine the lattice parameter of Fe for each of the peaks.

3.55 The diffraction peaks shown in Figure 3.20 are indexed according to the reflection rules for BCC (i.e., the sum $h + k + l$ must be even). Cite the h, k, and l indices for the first four diffraction peaks for FCC crystals consistent with h, k, and l all being either odd or even.

3.56 Figure 3.23 shows the first four peaks of the x-ray diffraction pattern for copper which has an FCC crystal structure; monochromatic x-radiation having a wavelength of 0.1542 nm was used.

(a) Index (i.e., give h, k, and l indices) for each of these peaks.

(b) Determine the interplanar spacing for each of the peaks.

(c) For each peak, determine the atomic radius for Cu and compare these with the value presented in Table 3.1.

3.57 Would you expect a material in which the atomic bonding is predominantly ionic in nature to be more or less likely to form a noncrystalline solid upon solidification than a covalent material? Why? (See Section 2.6.)

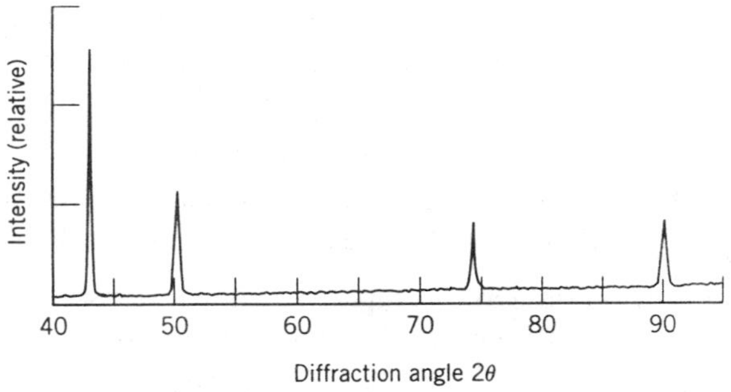

FIGURE 3.23 Diffraction pattern for polycrystalline copper.

4

Imperfections in Solids

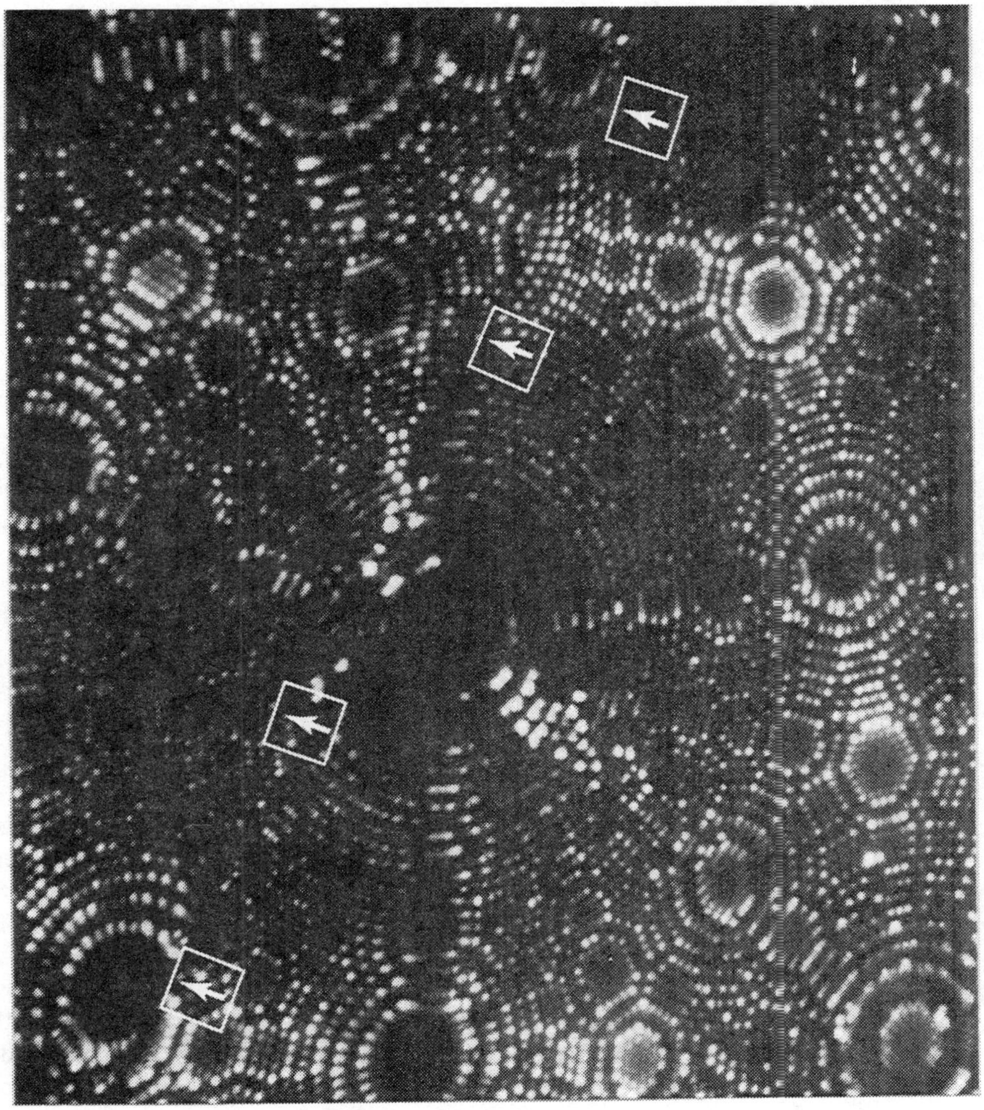

A field ion micrograph taken at the tip of a pointed tungsten specimen. Field ion microscopy is a sophisticated and fascinating technique that permits observation of individual atoms in a solid, which are represented by white spots. The symmetry and regularity of the atom arrangements are evident from the positions of the spots in this micrograph. A disruption of this symmetry occurs along a grain boundary which is traced by the arrows. Approximately 3,460,000×. (Photomicrograph courtesy of J. J. Hren and R. W. Newman.)

4.1 Introduction

Thus far it has been tacitly assumed that perfect order exists throughout crystalline materials on an atomic scale. However, such an idealized solid does not exist; all contain large numbers of various defects or imperfections. As a matter of fact, many of the properties of materials are profoundly sensitive to deviations from crystalline perfection; the influence is not always adverse, and often specific characteristics are deliberately fashioned by the introduction of controlled amounts or numbers of particular defects, as detailed in succeeding chapters.

By "crystalline defect" is meant a lattice irregularity having one or more of its dimensions on the order of an atomic diameter. Classification of crystalline imperfections is frequently made according to geometry or dimensionality of the defect. Several different imperfections are discussed in this chapter, including point defects (those associated with one or two atomic positions), linear (or one-dimensional) defects, as well as interfacial defects, or boundaries, which are two-dimensional. Impurities in solids are also discussed, since impurity atoms may exist as point defects. Finally, techniques for the microscopic examination of defects and the structure of materials are briefly described.

POINT DEFECTS

4.2 Vacancies and Self-Interstitials

The simplest of the point defects is a **vacancy,** or vacant lattice site, one normally occupied from which an atom is missing (Figure 4.1). Vacancies are formed during solidification, and also as a result of atomic vibrations, which can cause the displacement of atoms from their normal lattice sites.

The equilibrium number of vacancies N_v for a given quantity of material depends on and increases with temperature according to

$$N_v = N \exp\left(-\frac{Q_v}{kT}\right) \tag{4.1}$$

In this expression, N is the total number of atomic sites, Q_v is the energy required for the formation of a vacancy, T is the absolute temperature,[1] in kelvins, and k is the gas or **Boltzmann's constant.** The value of k is 1.38×10^{-23} J/atom-K, or 8.62×10^{-5} eV/atom-K, depending on the units of Q_v.[2] Thus, the number of vacancies increases exponentially with temperature; that is, as T in Equation 4.1 increases, so does also the expression $\exp -(Q_v/kT)$. For most metals, the fraction of vacancies N_v/N just below the melting temperature is on the order of 10^{-4}; that is, one lattice site out of 10,000 will be empty. As ensuing discussions indicate, a number of other material parameters have an exponential dependence on temperature similar to that of Equation 4.1.

A **self-interstitial** is an atom from the crystal that is crowded into an interstitial site, a small void space that under ordinary circumstances is not occupied. This kind of defect is also represented in Figure 4.1. In metals, a self-interstitial introduces

[1] Absolute temperature in kelvins (K) is equal to °C + 273.

[2] Boltzmann's constant per mole of atoms becomes the gas constant R; in such a case R = 8.31 J/mol-K, or 1.987 cal/mol-K.

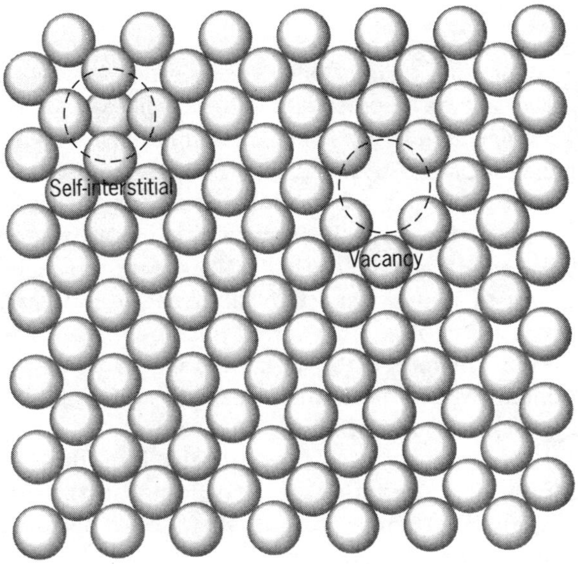

FIGURE 4.1 Two-dimensional representations of a vacancy and a self-interstitial. (Adapted from W. G. Moffatt, G. W. Pearsall and J. Wulff, *The Structure and Properties of Materials,* Vol. I, *Structure,* p. 77. Copyright © 1964 by John Wiley & Sons, New York. Reprinted by permission of John Wiley & Sons, Inc.)

relatively large distortions in the surrounding lattice because the atom is substantially larger than the interstitial position in which it is situated. Consequently, the formation of this defect is not highly probable, and it exists in very small concentrations, which are significantly lower than for vacancies.

EXAMPLE PROBLEM 4.1

Calculate the equilibrium number of vacancies per cubic meter for copper at 1000°C. The energy for vacancy formation is 0.9 eV/atom; the atomic weight and density (at 1000°C) for copper are 63.5 g/mol and 8.4 g/cm³, respectively.

SOLUTION

This problem may be solved by using Equation 4.1; it is first necessary, however, to determine the value of N, the number of atomic sites per cubic meter for copper from its atomic weight A_{Cu}, its density ρ, and Avogadro's number N_A, according to

$$N = \frac{N_A \rho}{A_{Cu}} \tag{4.2}$$

$$= \frac{(6.023 \times 10^{23} \text{ atoms/mol})(8.4 \text{ g/cm}^3)(10^6 \text{ cm}^3/\text{m}^3)}{63.5 \text{ g/mol}}$$

$$= 8.0 \times 10^{28} \text{ atoms/m}^3$$

Thus, the number of vacancies at 1000°C (1273 K) is equal to

$$N_v = N \exp\left(-\frac{Q_v}{kT}\right)$$

$$= (8.0 \times 10^{28} \text{ atoms/m}^3) \exp\left[-\frac{(0.9 \text{ eV})}{(8.62 \times 10^{-5} \text{ eV/K})(1273 \text{ K})}\right]$$

$$= 2.2 \times 10^{25} \text{ vacancies/m}^3$$

4.3 Impurities in Solids

A pure metal consisting of only one type of atom just isn't possible; impurity or foreign atoms will always be present, and some will exist as crystalline point defects. In fact, even with relatively sophisticated techniques, it is difficult to refine metals to a purity in excess of 99.9999%. At this level, on the order of 10^{22} to 10^{23} impurity atoms will be present in one cubic meter of material. Most familiar metals are not highly pure; rather, they are **alloys,** in which impurity atoms have been added intentionally to impart specific characteristics to the material. Ordinarily alloying is used in metals to improve mechanical strength and corrosion resistance. For example, sterling silver is a 92.5% silver–7.5% copper alloy. In normal ambient environments, pure silver is highly corrosion resistant, but also very soft. Alloying with copper enhances the mechanical strength significantly, without depreciating the corrosion resistance appreciably.

The addition of impurity atoms to a metal will result in the formation of a **solid solution** and/or a new *second phase,* depending on the kinds of impurity, their concentrations, and the temperature of the alloy. The present discussion is concerned with the notion of a solid solution; treatment of the formation of a new phase is deferred to Chapter 9.

Several terms relating to impurities and solid solutions deserve mention. With regard to alloys, **solute** and **solvent** are terms that are commonly employed. "Solvent" represents the element or compound that is present in the greatest amount; on occasion, solvent atoms are also called *host atoms.* "Solute" is used to denote an element or compound present in a minor concentration.

Solid Solutions

A solid solution forms when, as the solute atoms are added to the host material, the crystal structure is maintained, and no new structures are formed. Perhaps it is useful to draw an analogy with a liquid solution. If two liquids, soluble in each other (such as water and alcohol) are combined, a liquid solution is produced as the molecules intermix, and its composition is homogeneous throughout. A solid solution is also compositionally homogeneous; the impurity atoms are randomly and uniformly dispersed within the solid.

Impurity point defects are found in solid solutions, of which there are two types: **substitutional** and **interstitial.** For substitutional, solute or impurity atoms replace or substitute for the host atoms (Figure 4.2). There are several features of the solute and solvent atoms that determine the degree to which the former dissolves in the latter; these are as follows:

1. *Atomic size factor.* Appreciable quantities of a solute may be accommodated in this type of solid solution only when the difference in atomic radii between the two atom types is less than about ±15%. Otherwise the solute atoms will create substantial lattice distortions and a new phase will form.
2. *Crystal structure.* For appreciable solid solubility the crystal structures for metals of both atom types must be the same.
3. *Electronegativity.* The more electropositive one element and the more electronegative the other, the greater is the likelihood that they will form an intermetallic compound instead of a substitutional solid solution.
4. *Valences.* Other factors being equal, a metal will have more of a tendency to dissolve another metal of higher valency than one of a lower valency.

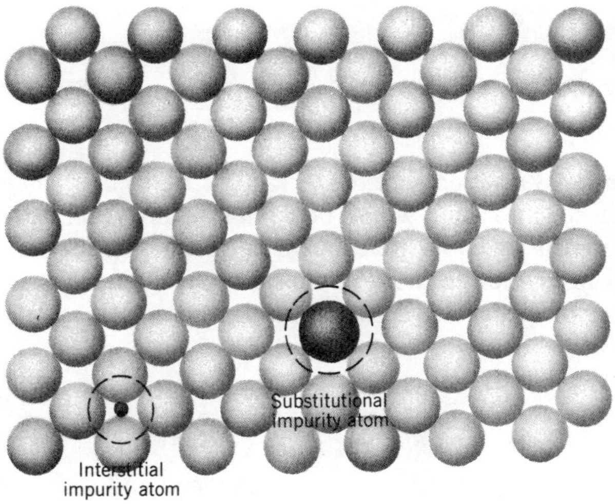

FIGURE 4.2 Two-dimensional schematic representations of substitutional and interstitial impurity atoms. (Adapted from W. G. Moffatt, G. W. Pearsall, and J. Wulff, *The Structure and Properties of Materials,* Vol. I, *Structure,* p. 77. Copyright © 1964 by John Wiley & Sons, New York. Reprinted by permission of John Wiley & Sons, Inc.)

An example of a substitutional solid solution is found for copper and nickel. These two elements are completely soluble in one another at all proportions. With regard to the aforementioned rules that govern degree of solubility, the atomic radii for copper and nickel are 0.128 and 0.125 nm (1.28 and 1.25 Å), respectively, both have the FCC crystal structure, and their electronegativities are 1.9 and 1.8 (Figure 2.7); finally, the most common valences are +1 for copper (although it sometimes can be +2) and +2 for nickel.

For interstitial solid solutions, impurity atoms fill the voids or interstices among the host atoms (see Figure 4.2). For metallic materials that have relatively high atomic packing factors, these interstitial positions are relatively small. Consequently, the atomic diameter of an interstitial impurity must be substantially smaller than that of the host atoms. Normally, the maximum allowable concentration of interstitial impurity atoms is low (less than 10%). Even very small impurity atoms are ordinarily larger than the interstitial sites, and as a consequence they introduce some lattice strains on the adjacent host atoms. Problem 4.5 calls for determination of the radii of impurity atoms (in terms of R, the host atom radius) that will just fit into interstitial positions without introducing any lattice strains for both FCC and BCC crystal structures.

Carbon forms an interstitial solid solution when added to iron; the maximum concentration of carbon is about 2%. The atomic radius of the carbon atom is much less than that for iron: 0.071 nm (0.71 Å) versus 0.124 nm (1.24 Å). Solid solutions are also possible for ceramic materials, as discussed in Section 13.5.

SPECIFICATION OF COMPOSITION

It is often necessary to express the **composition** (or *concentration*)[3] of an alloy in terms of its constituent elements. The two most common ways to specify composition are weight (or mass) percent and atom percent. The basis for **weight percent** (wt%) is the weight of a particular element relative to the total alloy weight. For an alloy that contains two hypothetical atoms denoted by 1 and 2, the concentration of 1

[3] The terms *composition* and *concentration* will be assumed to have the same meaning in this book (i.e., the relative content of a specific element or constituent in an alloy) and will be used interchangeably.

in wt%, C_1, is defined as

$$C_1 = \frac{m_1}{m_1 + m_2} \times 100 \tag{4.3}$$

where m_1 and m_2 represent the weight (or mass) of elements 1 and 2, respectively. The concentration of 2 would be computed in an analogous manner.

The basis for **atom percent** (at%) calculations is the number of moles of an element in relation to the total moles of the elements in the alloy. The number of moles in some specified mass of a hypothetical element 1, n_{m1}, may be computed as follows:

$$n_{m1} = \frac{m_1'}{A_1} \tag{4.4}$$

Here, m_1' and A_1 denote the mass (in grams) and atomic weight, respectively, for element 1.

Concentration in terms of atom percent of element 1 in an alloy containing 1 and 2 atoms, C_1', is defined by[4]

$$C_1' = \frac{n_{m1}}{n_{m1} + n_{m2}} \times 100 \tag{4.5}$$

In like manner, the atom percent of 2 may be determined.

Atom percent computations also can be carried out on the basis of the number of atoms instead of moles, since one mole of all substances contains the same number of atoms.

COMPOSITION CONVERSIONS

Sometimes it is necessary to convert from one composition scheme to another—e.g., from weight percent to atom percent. We will now present equations for making these conversions in terms of the two hypothetical elements 1 and 2. Using the convention of the previous section (i.e., weight percents denoted by C_1 and C_2, atom percents by C_1' and C_2', and atomic weights as A_1 and A_2), these conversion expressions are as follows:

$$C_1' = \frac{C_1 A_2}{C_1 A_2 + C_2 A_1} \times 100 \tag{4.6a}$$

$$C_2' = \frac{C_2 A_1}{C_1 A_2 + C_2 A_1} \times 100 \tag{4.6b}$$

$$C_1 = \frac{C_1' A_1}{C_1' A_1 + C_2' A_2} \times 100 \tag{4.7a}$$

$$C_2 = \frac{C_2' A_2}{C_1' A_1 + C_2' A_2} \times 100 \tag{4.7b}$$

---

[4] In order to avoid confusion in notations and symbols that are being used in this section, it should be pointed out that the prime (as in C_1' and m_1') is used to designate both composition, in atom percent, as well as mass of material in units of grams.

Since we are considering only two elements, computations involving the preceding equations are simplified when it is realized that

$$C_1 + C_2 = 100 \tag{4.8a}$$

$$C_1' + C_2' = 100 \tag{4.8b}$$

In addition, it sometimes becomes necessary to convert concentration from weight percent to mass of one component per unit volume of material (i.e., from units of wt% to kg/m^3); this latter composition scheme is often used in diffusion computations (Section 5.3). Concentrations in terms of this basis will be denoted using a double prime (i.e., C_1'' and C_2''), and the relevant equations are as follows:

$$C_1'' = \left(\frac{C_1}{\dfrac{C_1}{\rho_1} + \dfrac{C_2}{\rho_2}} \right) \times 10^3 \tag{4.9a}$$

$$C_2'' = \left(\frac{C_2}{\dfrac{C_1}{\rho_1} + \dfrac{C_2}{\rho_2}} \right) \times 10^3 \tag{4.9b}$$

For density ρ in units of g/cm^3, these expressions yield C_1'' and C_2'' in kg/m^3.

Furthermore, on occasion we desire to determine the density and atomic weight of a binary alloy given the composition in terms of either weight percent or atom percent. If we represent alloy density and atomic weight by ρ_{ave} and A_{ave}, respectively, then

$$\rho_{\text{ave}} = \frac{100}{\dfrac{C_1}{\rho_1} + \dfrac{C_2}{\rho_2}} \tag{4.10a}$$

$$\rho_{\text{ave}} = \frac{C_1'A_1 + C_2'A_2}{\dfrac{C_1'A_1}{\rho_1} + \dfrac{C_2'A_2}{\rho_2}} \tag{4.10b}$$

$$A_{\text{ave}} = \frac{100}{\dfrac{C_1}{A_1} + \dfrac{C_2}{A_2}} \tag{4.11a}$$

$$A_{\text{ave}} = \frac{C_1'A_1 + C_2'A_2}{100} \tag{4.11b}$$

It should be noted that Equations 4.9 and 4.11 are not always exact. In their derivations, it is assumed that total alloy volume is exactly equal to the sum of the volumes of the individual elements. This normally is not the case for most alloys; however, it is a reasonably valid assumption and does not lead to significant errors for dilute solutions and over composition ranges where solid solutions exist.

Example Problem 4.2

Derive Equation 4.6a.

Solution

To simplify this derivation, it will be assumed that masses are expressed in units of grams, and denoted with a prime (e.g., m_1'). Furthermore, the total alloy mass (in grams) M' is

$$M' = m_1' + m_2' \tag{4.12}$$

Using the definition of C_1' (Equation 4.5) and incorporation of the expression for n_{m1}, Equation 4.4, and the analogous expression for n_{m2} yields

$$C_1' = \frac{n_{m1}}{n_{m1} + n_{m2}} \times 100$$

$$= \frac{\dfrac{m_1'}{A_1}}{\dfrac{m_1'}{A_1} + \dfrac{m_2'}{A_2}} \times 100 \tag{4.13}$$

Rearrangement of the mass-in-grams equivalent of Equation 4.3 leads to

$$m_1' = \frac{C_1 M'}{100} \tag{4.14}$$

Substitution of this expression and its m_2' equivalent into Equation 4.13 gives

$$C_1' = \frac{\dfrac{C_1 M'}{100 A_1}}{\dfrac{C_1 M'}{100 A_1} + \dfrac{C_2 M'}{100 A_2}} \times 100 \tag{4.15}$$

And upon simplification we have

$$C_1' = \frac{C_1 A_2}{C_1 A_2 + C_2 A_1} \times 100$$

which is identical to Equation 4.6a.

Example Problem 4.3

Determine the composition, in atom percent, of an alloy that consists of 97 wt% aluminum and 3 wt% copper.

Solution

If we denote the respective weight percent compositions as $C_{Al} = 97$ and $C_{Cu} = 3$, substitution into Equations 4.6a and 4.6b yields

$$C_{Al}' = \frac{C_{Al} A_{Cu}}{C_{Al} A_{Cu} + C_{Cu} A_{Al}} \times 100$$

$$= \frac{(97)(63.55\ \text{g/mol})}{(97)(63.55\ \text{g/mol}) + (3)(26.98\ \text{g/mol})} \times 100$$

$$= 98.7\ \text{at\%}$$

And

$$C'_{Cu} = \frac{C_{Cu}A_{Al}}{C_{Cu}A_{Al} + C_{Al}A_{Cu}} \times 100$$

$$= \frac{(3)(26.98\ \text{g/mol})}{(3)(26.98\ \text{g/mol}) + (97)(63.55\ \text{g/mol})} \times 100$$

$$= 1.30\ \text{at\%}$$

MISCELLANEOUS IMPERFECTIONS

4.4 Dislocations — Linear Defects

A *dislocation* is a linear or one-dimensional defect around which some of the atoms are misaligned. One type of dislocation is represented in Figure 4.3: an extra portion of a plane of atoms, or half-plane, the edge of which terminates within the crystal. This is termed an **edge dislocation;** it is a linear defect that centers around the line that is defined along the end of the extra half-plane of atoms. This is sometimes termed the **dislocation line,** which, for the edge dislocation in Figure 4.3, is perpendicular to the plane of the page. Within the region around the dislocation line there is some localized lattice distortion. The atoms above the dislocation line in Figure 4.3 are squeezed together, and those below are pulled apart; this is reflected in the slight curvature for the vertical planes of atoms as they bend around this extra half-plane. The magnitude of this distortion decreases with distance away from the dislocation line; at positions far removed, the crystal lattice is virtually perfect. Sometimes the edge dislocation in Figure 4.3 is represented by the symbol ⊥, which also indicates the position of the dislocation line. An edge dislocation may also be formed by an extra half-plane of atoms that is included in the bottom portion of the crystal; its designation is a ⊤.

Another type of dislocation, called a **screw dislocation,** exists, which may be thought of as being formed by a shear stress that is applied to produce the distortion

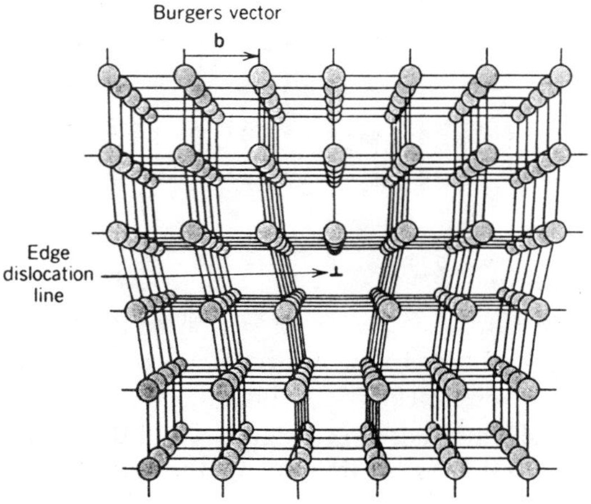

FIGURE 4.3 The atom positions around an edge dislocation; extra half-plane of atoms shown in perspective. (Adapted from A. G. Guy, *Essentials of Materials Science,* McGraw-Hill Book Company, New York, 1976, p. 153.)

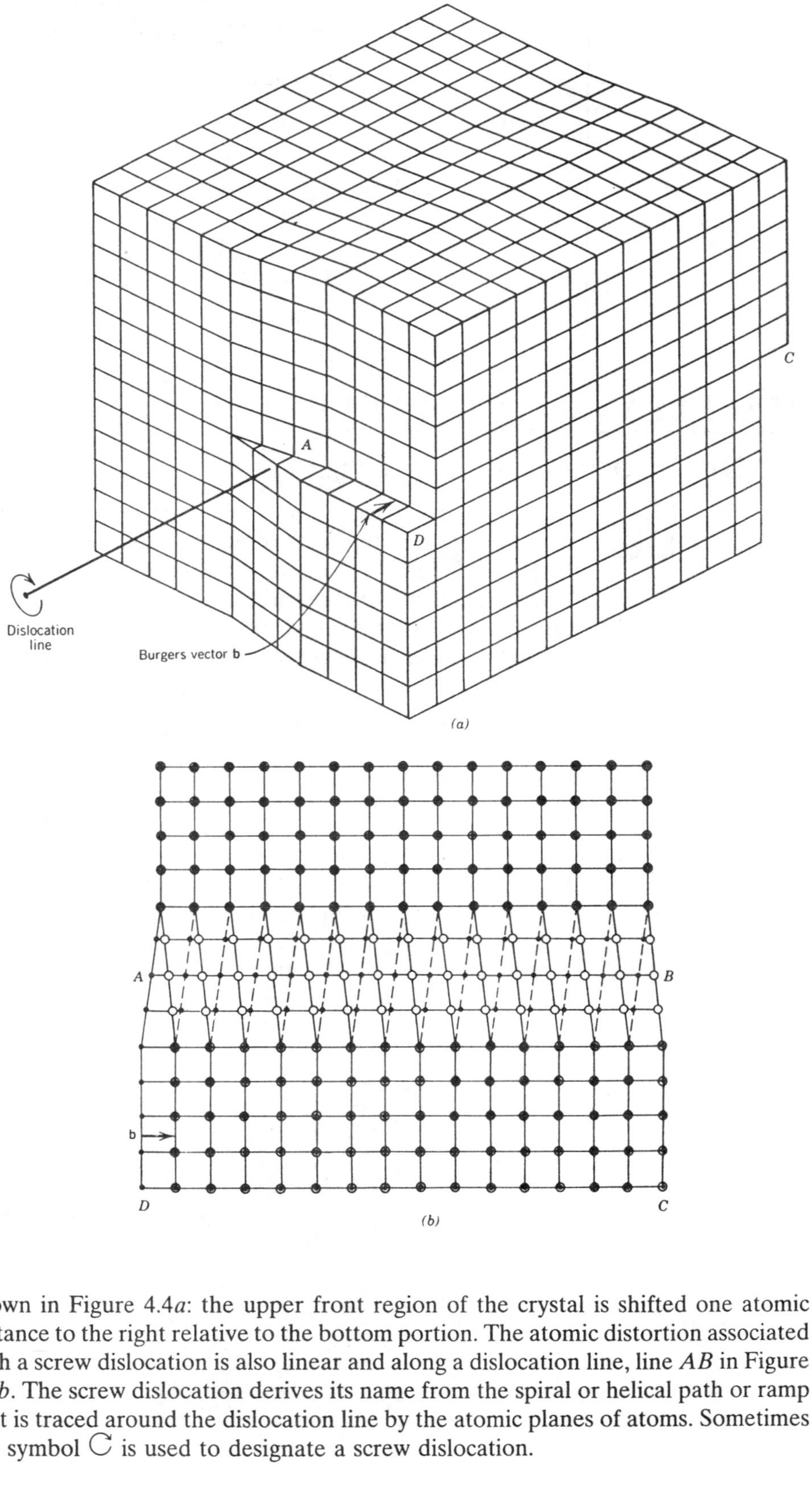

FIGURE 4.4 (*a*) A screw dislocation within a crystal. (*b*) The screw dislocation in (*a*) as viewed from above. The dislocation line extends along line *AB*. Atom positions above the slip plane are designated by open circles, those below by solid circles. (Figure (*b*) from W. T. Read, Jr., *Dislocations in Crystals,* McGraw-Hill Book Company, New York, 1953.)

shown in Figure 4.4*a*: the upper front region of the crystal is shifted one atomic distance to the right relative to the bottom portion. The atomic distortion associated with a screw dislocation is also linear and along a dislocation line, line *AB* in Figure 4.4*b*. The screw dislocation derives its name from the spiral or helical path or ramp that is traced around the dislocation line by the atomic planes of atoms. Sometimes the symbol ↻ is used to designate a screw dislocation.

Most dislocations found in crystalline materials are probably neither pure edge nor pure screw, but exhibit components of both types; these are termed **mixed dislocations.** All three dislocation types are represented schematically in Figure 4.5; the lattice distortion that is produced away from the two faces is mixed, having varying degrees of screw and edge character.

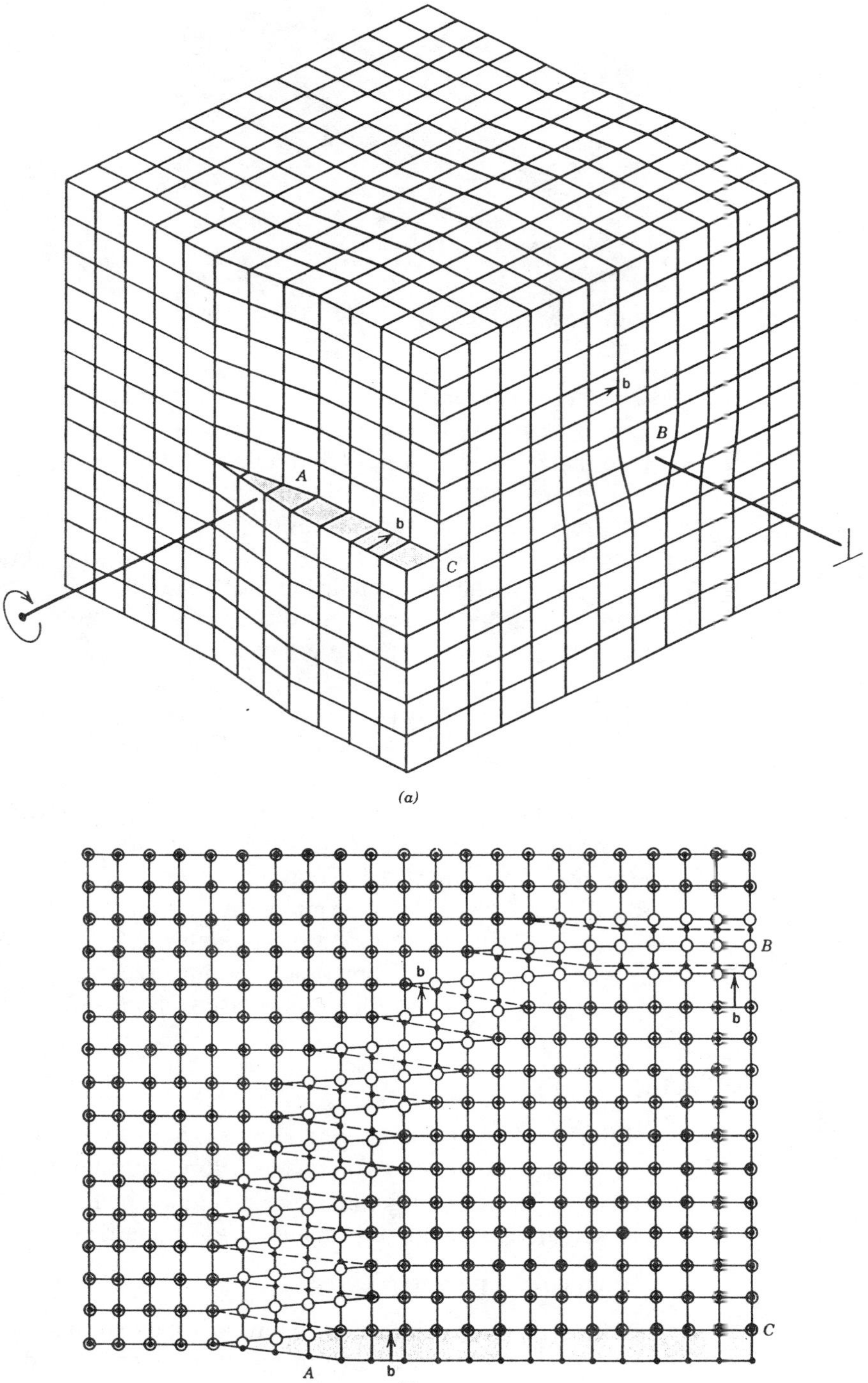

FIGURE 4.5 (*a*) Schematic representation of a dislocation that has edge, screw, and mixed character. (*b*) Top view, where open circles denote atom positions above the slip plane. Solid circles, atom positions below. At point *A*, the dislocation is pure screw, while at point *B*, it is pure edge. For regions in between where there is curvature in the dislocation line, the character is mixed edge and screw. (Figure (*b*) from W. T. Read, Jr., *Dislocations in Crystals,* McGraw-Hill Book Company, New York, 1953.)

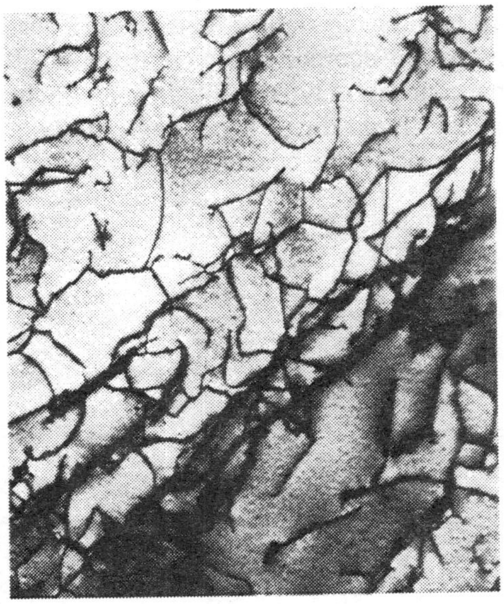

FIGURE 4.6 A transmission electron micrograph of a titanium alloy in which the dark lines are dislocations. 51,450×. (Courtesy of M. R. Plichta, Michigan Technological University.)

The magnitude and direction of the lattice distortion associated with a dislocation is expressed in terms of a **Burgers vector,** denoted by a **b**. Burgers vectors are indicated in Figures 4.3 and 4.4 for edge and screw dislocations, respectively. Furthermore, the nature of a dislocation (i.e., edge, screw, or mixed) is defined by the relative orientations of dislocation line and Burgers vector. For an edge, they are perpendicular (Figure 4.3), whereas for a screw, both are parallel (Figure 4.4); they are neither perpendicular nor parallel for a mixed dislocation. Also, even though a dislocation changes direction and nature within a crystal (e.g., from edge to mixed to screw), the Burgers vector will be the same at all points along its line. For example, all positions of the curved dislocation in Figure 4.5 will have the Burgers vector shown. For metallic materials, the Burgers vector for a dislocation will point in a close-packed crystallographic direction and will be of magnitude equal to the interatomic spacing.

Dislocations can be observed in crystalline materials using electron-microscopic techniques. In Figure 4.6, a high-magnification transmission electron micrograph, the dark lines are the dislocations.

Virtually all crystalline materials contain some dislocations that were introduced during solidification, during plastic deformation, and as a consequence of thermal stresses that result from rapid cooling. Dislocations are involved in the plastic deformation of crystalline materials, as discussed in Chapter 7.

4.5 Interfacial Defects

Interfacial defects are boundaries that have two dimensions and normally separate regions of the materials that have different crystal structures and/or crystallographic orientations. These imperfections include external surfaces, grain boundaries, twin boundaries, stacking faults, and phase boundaries.

External Surfaces

One of the most obvious boundaries is the external surface, along which the crystal structure terminates. Surface atoms are not bonded to the maximum number of nearest neighbors, and are therefore in a higher energy state than the atoms at interior positions. The bonds of these surface atoms that are not satisfied give rise to a surface energy, expressed in units of energy per unit area (J/m^2 or erg/cm^2). To reduce this energy, materials tend to minimize, if at all possible, the total surface area. For example, liquids assume a shape having a minimum area—the droplets become spherical. Of course, this is not possible with solids, which are mechanically rigid.

GRAIN BOUNDARIES

Another interfacial defect, the grain boundary, was introduced in Section 3.13 as the boundary separating two small grains or crystals having different crystallographic orientations in polycrystalline materials. A grain boundary is represented schematically from an atomic perspective in Figure 4.7. Within the boundary region, which is probably just several atom distances wide, there is some atomic mismatch in a transition from the crystalline orientation of one grain to that of an adjacent one.

Various degrees of crystallographic misalignment between adjacent grains are possible (Figure 4.7). When this orientation mismatch is slight, on the order of a few degrees, then the term *small-angle grain boundary* is used. These boundaries can be described in terms of dislocation arrays. One simple small-angle grain boundary is formed when edge dislocations are aligned in the manner of Figure 4.8. This type is called a *tilt boundary;* the angle of misorientation, θ, is also indicated in the figure. When the angle of misorientation is parallel to the boundary, a *twist boundary* results, which can be described by an array of screw dislocations.

The atoms are bonded less regularly along a grain boundary (e.g., bond angles are longer), and consequently, there is an interfacial or grain boundary energy similar to the surface energy described above. The magnitude of this energy is a function of the degree of misorientation, being larger for high-angle boundaries. Grain boundaries are more chemically reactive than the grains themselves as a consequence of this boundary energy. Furthermore, impurity atoms often preferentially segregate along these boundaries because of their higher energy state. The total interfacial energy is lower in large or coarse-grained materials than in fine-grained ones, since there is less total boundary area in the former. Grains grow at

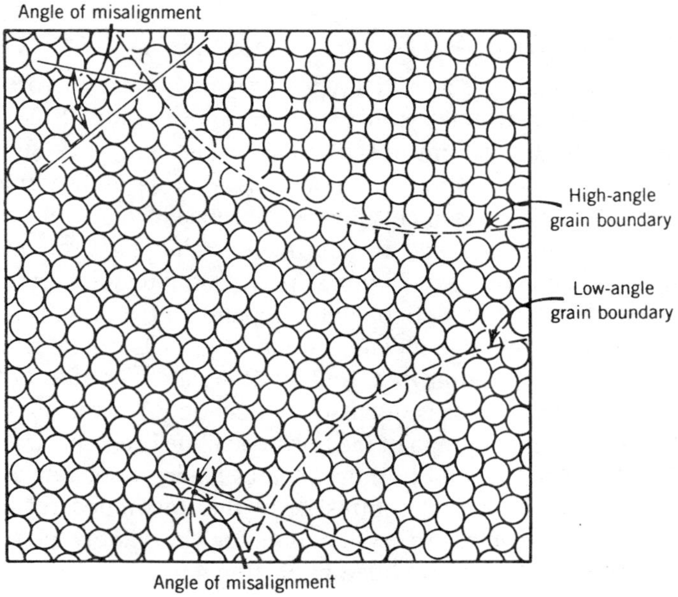

FIGURE 4.7 Schematic diagram showing low- and high-angle grain boundaries and the adjacent atom positions.

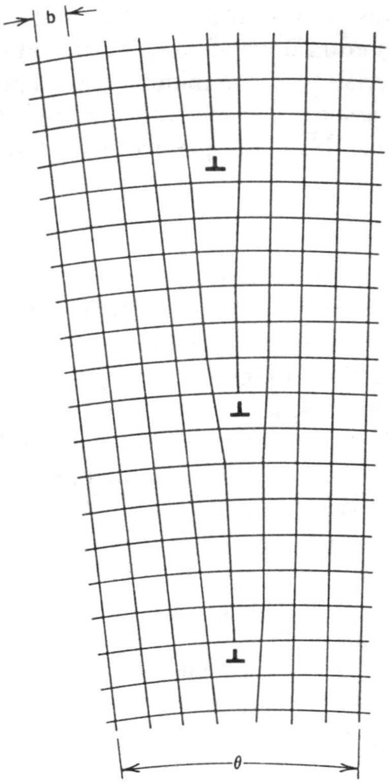

FIGURE 4.8 Demonstration of how a tilt boundary having an angle of misorientation θ results from an alignment of edge dislocations.

elevated temperatures to reduce the total boundary energy, a phenomenon explained in Section 7.13.

In spite of this disordered arrangement of atoms and lack of regular bonding along grain boundaries, a polycrystalline material is still very strong; cohesive forces within and across the boundary are present. Furthermore, the density of a polycrystalline specimen is virtually identical to that of a single crystal of the same material.

TWIN BOUNDARIES

A *twin boundary* is a special type of grain boundary across which there is a specific mirror lattice symmetry; that is, atoms on one side of the boundary are located in mirror image positions of the atoms on the other side (Figure 4.9). The region of material between these boundaries is appropriately termed a *twin.* Twins result from atomic displacements that are produced from applied mechanical shear forces (mechanical twins), and also during annealing heat treatments following deformation (annealing twins). Twinning occurs on a definite crystallographic plane and in a specific direction, both of which depend on the crystal structure. Annealing twins are typically found in metals that have the FCC crystal structure, while mechanical twins are observed in BCC and HCP metals. The role of mechanical twins in the deformation process is discussed in Section 7.7. Annealing twins may be observed in the photomicrograph of the polycrystalline brass specimen shown in Figure 4.11*c*. The twins correspond to those regions having relatively straight and parallel sides and a different visual contrast than the untwinned regions of the grains within which they reside. An explanation for the variety of textural contrasts in this photomicrograph is provided in Section 4.9.

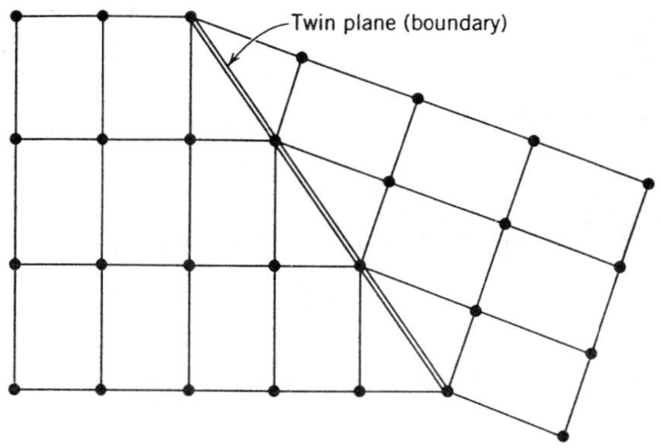

FIGURE 4.9 Schematic diagram showing a twin plane or boundary and the adjacent atom positions (dark circles).

MISCELLANEOUS INTERFACIAL DEFECTS

Other possible interfacial defects include stacking faults, phase boundaries, and ferromagnetic domain walls. Stacking faults are found in FCC metals when there is an interruption in the *ABCABCABC* . . . stacking sequence of close-packed planes (Section 3.11). Phase boundaries exist in multiphase materials (Section 9.3) across which there is a sudden change in physical and/or chemical characteristics. For ferromagnetic and ferrimagnetic materials, the boundary that separates regions having different directions of magnetization is termed a domain wall, which is discussed in Section 21.7.

Associated with each of the defects discussed in this section is an interfacial energy, the magnitude of which depends on boundary type, and which will vary from material to material. Normally, the interfacial energy will be greatest for external surfaces and least for domain walls.

4.6 Bulk or Volume Defects

Other defects exist in all solid materials that are much larger than those heretofore discussed. These include pores, cracks, foreign inclusions, and other phases. They are normally introduced during processing and fabrication steps. Some of these defects and their effects on the properties of materials are discussed in subsequent chapters.

4.7 Atomic Vibrations

Every atom in a solid material is vibrating very rapidly about its lattice position within the crystal. In a sense, these vibrations may be thought of as imperfections or defects. At any instant of time not all atoms vibrate at the same frequency and amplitude, nor with the same energy. At a given temperature there will exist a distribution of energies for the constituent atoms about an average energy. Over time the vibrational energy of any specific atom will also vary in a random manner. With rising temperature, this average energy increases, and, in fact, the temperature of a solid is really just a measure of the average vibrational activity of atoms and molecules. At room temperature, a typical vibrational frequency is on the order of 10^{13} vibrations per second, whereas the amplitude is a few thousandths of a nanometer.

Many properties and processes in solids are manifestations of this vibrational atomic motion. For example, melting occurs when the vibrations are vigorous enough to rupture large numbers of atomic bonds. A more detailed discussion of atomic vibrations and their influence on the properties of materials is presented in Chapter 20.

MICROSCOPIC EXAMINATION

4.8 General

On occasion it is necessary or desirable to examine the structural elements and defects that influence the properties of materials. The capacity to perform such examinations is important, first to ensure that the associations between the properties and structure (and defects) are properly understood, and second to predict the properties of materials once these relationships have been established. Several of the techniques that are commonly used in such investigations are discussed next.

Some structural elements are of *macroscopic* dimensions, that is, are large enough to be observed with the unaided eye. For example, the shape and average size or diameter of the grains for a polycrystalline specimen are important structural elements. Macroscopic grains are often evident on aluminum street light posts and also on garbage cans. Relatively large grains having different textures are clearly visible on the surface of the sectioned lead ingot shown in Figure 4.10. However, in most materials the constituent grains are of *microscopic* dimensions, having diameters that may be on the order of microns,[5] and their details must be investigated using some type of microscope. Grain size and shape are only two features of what is termed the **microstructure;** these and other microstructural characteristics are discussed in subsequent chapters.

4.9 Microscopy

Both optical and electron microscopes are commonly used in **microscopy.** These instruments aid in investigations of the microstructural features of all material types.

Figure 4.10 High-purity polycrystalline lead ingot in which the individual grains may be discerned. 0.7×. (Reproduced with permission from *Metals Handbook,* Vol. 9, 9th edition, *Metallography and Microstructures,* American Society for Metals, Metals Park, OH, 1985.)

[5] A micron (μm), sometimes called a micrometer, is 10^{-6} m.

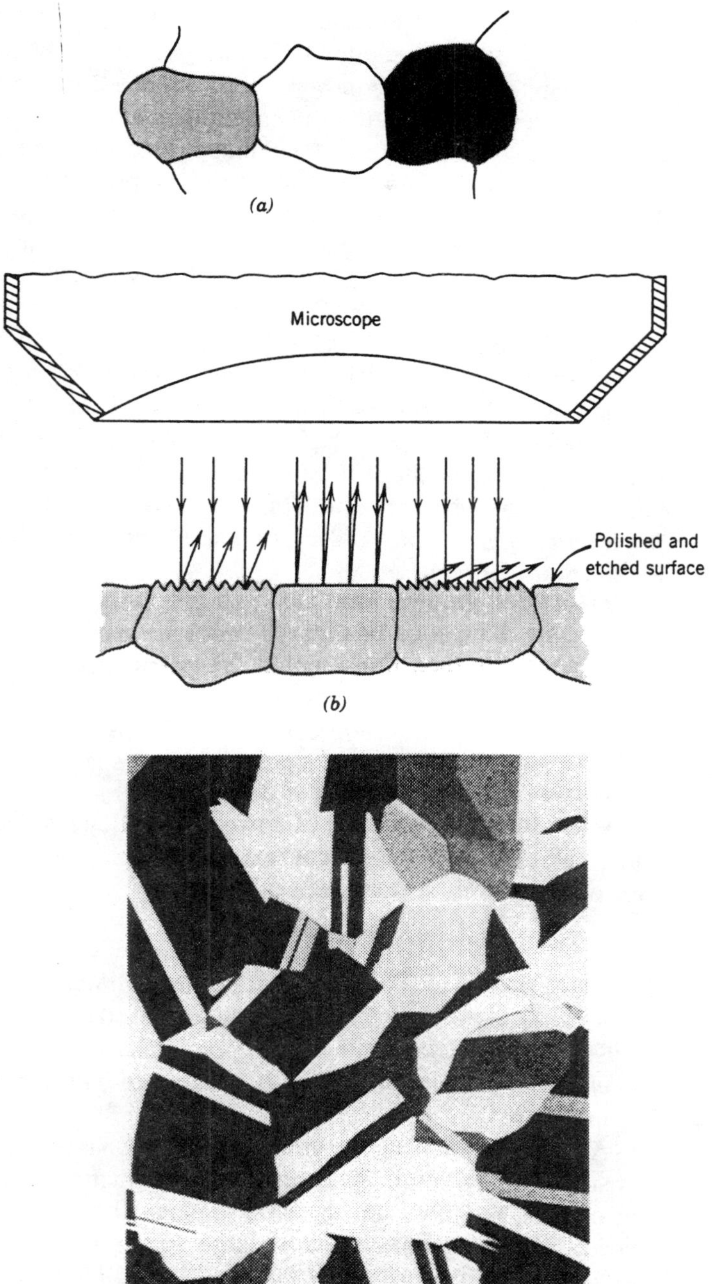

FIGURE 4.11 (*a*) Polished and etched grains as they might appear when viewed with an optical microscope. (*b*) Section taken through these grains showing how the etching characteristics and resulting surface texture vary from grain to grain because of differences in crystallographic orientation. (*c*) Photomicrograph of a polycrystalline brass specimen. 60×. (Photomicrograph courtesy of J. E. Burke, General Electric Co.)

Most of these techniques employ photographic equipment in conjunction with the microscope; the photograph on which the image is recorded is called a **photomicrograph.**

OPTICAL MICROSCOPY

With optical microscopy, the light microscope is used to study the microstructure; optical and illumination systems are its basic elements. For materials that are opaque to visible light (all metals and many ceramics and polymers), only the surface is subject to observation, and the light microscope must be used in a reflecting mode. Contrasts in the image produced result from differences in reflectivity of the various regions of the microstructure. Investigations of this type are often termed *metallographic,* since metals were first examined using this technique.

Normally, careful and meticulous surface preparations are necessary to reveal the important details of the microstructure. The specimen surface must first be ground and polished to a smooth and mirrorlike finish. This is accomplished by using successively finer abrasive papers and powders. The microstructure is revealed by a surface treatment using an appropriate chemical reagent in a procedure termed *etching.* The chemical reactivity of the grains of some single-phase materials depends on crystallographic orientation. Consequently, in a polycrystalline specimen, etching characteristics vary from grain to grain. Figure 4.11*b* shows how normally incident light is reflected by three etched surface grains, each having a different orientation. Figure 4.11*a* depicts the surface structure as it might appear when viewed with the microscope; the luster or texture of each grain depends on its reflectance properties. A photomicrograph of a polycrystalline specimen exhibiting these characteristics is shown in Figure 4.11*c*.

Also, small grooves form along grain boundaries as a consequence of etching. Since atoms along grain boundary regions are more chemically active, they dissolve at a greater rate than those within the grains. These grooves become discernible when viewed under a microscope because they reflect light at an angle different from that of the grains themselves; this effect is displayed in Figure 4.12*a*. Figure 4.12*b* is a photomicrograph of a polycrystalline specimen in which the grain boundary grooves are clearly visible as dark lines.

When the microstructure of a two-phase alloy is to be examined, an etchant is chosen that produces a different texture for each phase so that the different phases may be distinguished from each other.

ELECTRON MICROSCOPY

The upper limit to the magnification possible with an optical microscope is approximately 2000 diameters. Consequently, some structural elements are too fine or small to permit observation using optical microscopy. Under such circumstances the electron microscope, which is capable of much higher magnifications, may be employed.

An image of the structure under investigation is formed using beams of electrons instead of light radiation. According to quantum mechanics, a high-velocity electron will become wavelike, having a wavelength that is inversely proportional to its velocity. When accelerated across large voltages, electrons can be made to have wavelengths on the order of 0.003 nm (3 pm). High magnifications and resolving powers of these microscopes are consequences of the short wavelengths of electron beams. The electron beam is focused and the image formed with magnetic lenses; otherwise the geometry of the microscope components is essentially the same as with optical systems. Both transmission and reflection beam modes of operation are possible for electron microscopes.

Transmission Electron Microscopy

The image seen with a **transmission electron microscope (TEM)** is formed by an electron beam that passes through the specimen. Details of internal microstructural features are accessible to observation; contrasts in the image are produced by differences in beam scattering or diffraction produced between various elements of

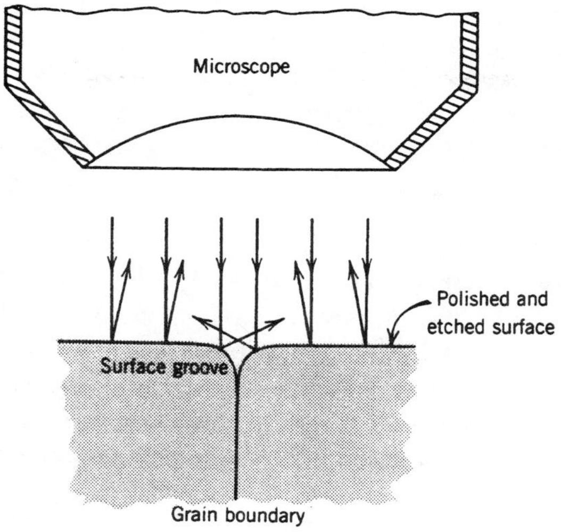

(a)

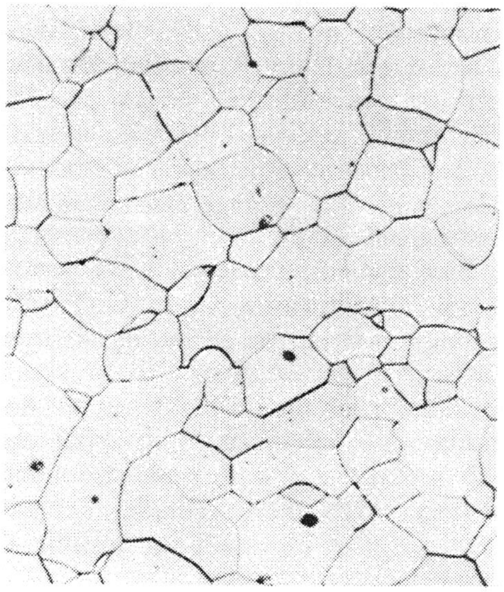

(b)

FIGURE 4.12 (a) Section of a grain boundary and its surface groove produced by etching; the light reflection characteristics in the vicinity of the groove are also shown. (b) Photomicrograph of the surface of a polished and etched polycrystalline specimen of an iron-chromium alloy in which the grain boundaries appear dark. 100×. (Photomicrograph courtesy of L. C. Smith and C. Brady, the National Bureau of Standards, Washington, DC.)

the microstructure or defect. Since solid materials are highly absorptive to electron beams, a specimen to be examined must be prepared in the form of a very thin foil; this ensures transmission through the specimen of an appreciable fraction of the incident beam. The transmitted beam is projected onto a fluorescent screen or a photographic film so that the image may be viewed. Magnifications approaching 1,000,000× are possible with transmission electron microscopy, which is frequently utilized in the study of dislocations.

Scanning Electron Microscopy

A more recent and extremely useful investigative tool, is the **scanning electron microscope (SEM).** The surface of a specimen to be examined is scanned with an electron beam, and the reflected (or back-scattered) beam of electrons is collected, then displayed at the same scanning rate on a cathode ray tube (similar to a TV screen). The image on the screen, which may be photographed, represents the surface features of the specimen. The surface may or may not be polished and etched, but it must be electrically conductive; a very thin metallic surface coating must be applied to nonconductive materials. Magnifications ranging from 10 to in excess of 50,000 diameters are possible, as are also very great depths-of-field. Accessory equipment permits qualitative and semiquantitative analysis of the elemental composition of very localized surface areas.

Microscopic examination is an extremely useful tool in the study and characterization of materials. This will become apparent in subsequent chapters that correlate the microstructure with various characteristics and properties. Examination of microstructure is also used to determine the mode of mechanical fracture, to predict the mechanical properties of alloys, to show whether an alloy has been correctly heat treated, and also to design alloys with new property combinations.

4.10 Grain Size Determination

The **grain size** is often determined when the properties of a polycrystalline material are under consideration. In this regard, there exist a number of techniques by which size is specified in terms of average grain volume, diameter, or area. Grain size may be estimated by using an intercept method, described as follows. Straight lines all the same length are drawn through several photomicrographs that show the grain structure. The grains intersected by each line segment are counted; the line length is then divided by an average of the number of grains intersected, taken over all the line segments. The average grain diameter is found by dividing this result by the linear magnification of the photomicrographs.

Probably the most common method utilized, however, is that devised by the American Society for Testing and Materials (ASTM).[6] The ASTM has prepared several standard comparison charts, all having different average grain sizes. To each is assigned a number ranging from 1 to 10, which is termed the *grain size number;* the larger this number, the smaller the grains. A specimen must be properly prepared to reveal the grain structure, which is photographed at a magnification of 100×. Grain size is expressed as the grain size number of the chart that most nearly matches the grains in the micrograph. Thus, a relatively simple and convenient visual determination of grain size number is possible. Grain size number is used extensively in the specification of steels.

The rationale behind the assignment of the grain size number to these various charts is as follows. Let n represent the grain size number, and N the average number of grains per square inch at a magnification of 100×. These two parameters are related to each other through the expression

$$N = 2^{n-1} \tag{4.16}$$

Summary

All solid materials contain large numbers of imperfections or deviations from crystalline perfection. The several types of imperfection are categorized on the basis of their geometry and size. Point defects are those associated with one or two atomic

[6] ASTM Standard E 112, "Standard Methods for Estimating the Average Grain Size for Metals."

positions, including vacancies (or vacant lattice sites), self-interstitials (host atoms that occupy interstitial sites), and impurity atoms.

A solid solution may form when impurity atoms are added to a solid, in which case the original crystal structure is retained and no new phases are formed. For substitutional solid solutions, impurity atoms substitute for host atoms, and appreciable solubility is possible only when atomic diameters and electronegativities for both atom types are similar, and when both elements have the same crystal structure and same valence. Interstitial solid solutions form for relatively small impurity atoms that occupy interstitial sites among the host atoms.

Composition of an alloy may be specified in weight percent or atom percent. The basis for weight percent computations is the weight (or mass) of each alloy constituent relative to the total alloy weight. Atom percents are calculated in terms of the number of moles for each constituent relative to the total moles of all the elements in the alloy.

Dislocations are one-dimensional crystalline defects of which there are two pure types: edge and screw. An edge may be thought of in terms of the lattice distortion along the end of an extra half-plane of atoms; a screw, by a helical planar ramp. For mixed dislocations, components of both pure edge and screw are found. The magnitude and direction of lattice distortion associated with a dislocation is specified by its Burgers vector. The relative orientations of Burgers vector and dislocation line are (1) perpendicular for edge, (2) parallel for screw, and (3) neither perpendicular nor parallel for mixed.

Other imperfections include interfacial defects [external surfaces, grain boundaries (both low- and high-angle), twin boundaries, etc.], volume defects (cracks, pores, etc.), and atomic vibrations. Each type of imperfection has some influence on the properties of a material.

Many of the important defects and structural elements of materials are of microscopic dimensions, and observation is possible only with the aid of a microscope. Both optical and electron microscopes are employed, usually in conjunction with photographic equipment. Transmissive and reflective modes are possible for each microscope type; preference is dictated by the nature of the specimen as well as the structural element or defect to be examined.

Grain size of polycrystalline materials is frequently determined using photomicrographic techniques. Two methods are commonly employed: intercept and standard comparison charts.

IMPLICATIONS

As mentioned in the Introduction section, the properties of some materials are profoundly influenced by the presence of imperfections; therefore, it is important to have a knowledge about the types of imperfections that exist, and the roles they play in affecting the behavior of materials. Some examples are as follows:

1. Integrated circuit microelectronic devices found in our computers, calculators, and home appliances function because of highly controlled concentrations of specific impurities that are incorporated into small, localized regions of semiconducting materials (Sections 19.11 and 19.14).

2. A knowledge of the role that dislocations play in the plastic deformation process allows us to understand strengthening mechanisms for metals (Chapter 7).

3. The strengths of metals are enhanced as a result of interactions between impurity atoms (in solid solution) and dislocations (Section 7.9).

4. The presence of grain boundaries may affect material properties [e.g., the optical characteristics of normally transparent materials (Figure 1.2)].

5. Mass transport by diffusion involves the motion of vacancies and interstitial impurity atoms (Section 5.2).

IMPORTANT TERMS AND CONCEPTS

Alloy
Atom percent
Atomic vibration
Boltzmann's constant
Burgers vector
Composition
Dislocation line
Edge dislocation
Grain size
Imperfection
Interstitial solid solution
Microscopy
Microstructure
Mixed dislocation
Photomicrograph
Point defect
Scanning electron microscope (SEM)
Screw dislocation
Self-Interstitial
Solid solution
Solute
Solvent
Substitutional solid solution
Transmission electron microscope (TEM)
Vacancy
Weight percent

REFERENCES

ASM Handbook, Vol. 9, *Metallography and Microstructures,* ASM International, Materials Park, OH, 1985.

Moffatt, W. G., G. W. Pearsall, and J. Wulff, *The Structure and Properties of Materials,* Vol. 1, *Structure,* John Wiley & Sons, New York, 1964.

Phillips, V. A., *Modern Metallographic Techniques and Their Applications,* Wiley-Interscience, New York, 1971.

Van Bueren, H. G., *Imperfections in Crystals,* North-Holland Publishing Co., Amsterdam (Wiley-Interscience, New York), 1960.

Vander Voort, G. F., *Metallography, Principles and Practice,* McGraw-Hill Book Co., New York, 1984.

QUESTIONS AND PROBLEMS

4.1 Calculate the fraction of atom sites that are vacant for copper at its melting temperature of 1084°C (1357 K). Assume an energy for vacancy formation of 0.90 eV/atom.

4.2 Calculate the number of vacancies per cubic meter in iron at 850°C. The energy for vacancy formation is 1.08 eV/atom. Furthermore, the density and atomic weight for Fe are 7.65 g/cm^3 and 55.85 g/mol, respectively.

4.3 Calculate the energy for vacancy formation in aluminum, given that the equilibrium number of vacancies at 500°C (773 K) is 7.57 × 10^{23} m^{-3}. The atomic weight and density (at 500°C) for aluminum are, respectively, 26.98 g/mol and 2.62 g/cm^3.

4.4 Below, atomic radius, crystal structure, electronegativity, and the most common valence are tabulated, for several elements; for those that are nonmetals, only atomic radii are indicated.

Element	Atomic Radius (nm)	Crystal Structure	Electro-nega-tivity	Valence
Ni	0.1246	FCC	1.8	2+
C	0.071			
H	0.046			
O	0.060			
Ag	0.1445	FCC	1.9	1+
Al	0.1431	FCC	1.5	3+
Co	0.1253	HCP	1.8	2+
Cr	0.1249	BCC	1.6	3+
Fe	0.1241	BCC	1.8	2+
Pt	0.1387	FCC	2.2	2+
Zn	0.1332	HCP	1.6	2+

Which of these elements would you expect to form the following with nickel:
(a) A substitutional solid solution having complete solubility?
(b) A substitutional solid solution of incomplete solubility?
(c) An interstitial solid solution?

4.5 For both FCC and BCC crystal structures, interstitial sites that may be occupied by impurity atoms are located at the centers of each of the unit cell edges. Compute the radius r of an impurity atom that will just fit into one of these sites for each of the two crystal structures in terms of the atomic radius R of the host atom. For which crystal structure is r larger? Consult Section 3.4.

4.6 Derive the following equations:
(a) Equation 4.7a.
(b) Equation 4.9a.
(c) Equation 4.10a.
(d) Equation 4.11b.

4.7 What is the composition, in atom percent, of an alloy that consists of 30 wt% Zn and 70 wt% Cu?

4.8 What is the composition, in weight percent, of an alloy that consists of 6 at% Pb and 94 at% Sn?

4.9 Calculate the composition, in weight percent, of an alloy that contains 218.0 kg titanium, 14.6 kg of aluminum, and 9.7 kg of vanadium.

4.10 What is the composition, in atom percent, of an alloy that contains 98 g tin and 65 g of lead?

4.11 What is the composition, in atom percent, of an alloy that contains 99.7 lb_m copper, 102 lb_m zinc, and 2.1 lb_m lead?

4.12 What is the composition, in atom percent, of an alloy that consists of 97 wt% Fe and 3 wt% Si?

4.13 Convert the atom percent composition in Problem 4.11 to weight percent.

4.14 Calculate the number of atoms per cubic meter in lead.

4.15 The concentration of carbon in an iron-carbon alloy is 0.15 wt%. What is the concentration in kilograms of carbon per cubic meter of alloy?

4.16 For a solid solution consisting of two elements (designated as 1 and 2), sometimes it is desirable to determine the number of atoms per cubic centimeter of one element in a solid solution, N_1, given the concentration of that element specified in weight percent, C_1. This computation is possible using the following expression:

$$N_1 = \frac{N_A C_1}{\dfrac{C_1 A_1}{\rho_1} + \dfrac{A_1}{\rho_2}(100 - C_1)} \tag{4.17}$$

where

N_A = Avogadro's number
ρ_1 and ρ_2 = densities of the two elements
A_1 = the atomic weight of element 1

Derive Equation 4.17 using Equation 4.2 and expressions contained in Section 4.3.

4.17 Gold forms a substitutional solid solution with silver. Compute the number of gold atoms per cubic centimeter for a silver-gold alloy that contains 10 wt% Au and 90 wt% Ag. The densities of pure gold and silver are 19.32 and 10.49 g/cm^3, respectively.

4.18 Germanium forms a substitutional solid solution with silicon. Compute the number of germanium atoms per cubic centimeter for a germanium-silicon alloy that contains 15 wt% Ge and 85 wt% Si. The densities of pure germanium and silicon are 5.32 and 2.33 g/cm^3, respectively.

4.19 Sometimes it is desirable to be able to determine the weight percent of one element, C_1, that will produce a specified concentration in terms of the number of atoms per cubic centimeter, N_1, for an alloy composed of two types of atoms. This computation is possible using the following expression:

$$C_1 = \frac{100}{1 + \frac{N_A \rho_2}{N_1 A_1} - \frac{\rho_2}{\rho_1}} \quad (4.18)$$

where

N_A = Avogadro's number

ρ_1 and ρ_2 = densities of the two elements

A_1 and A_2 = the atomic weights of the two elements

Derive Equation 4.18 using Equation 4.2 and expressions contained in Section 4.3.

4.20 Molybdenum forms a substitutional solid solution with tungsten. Compute the weight percent of molybdenum that must be added to tungsten to yield an alloy that contains 1.0×10^{22} Mo atoms per cubic centimeter. The densities of pure Mo and W are 10.22 and 19.30 g/cm^3, respectively.

4.21 Niobium forms a substitutional solid solution with vanadium. Compute the weight percent of niobium that must be added to vanadium to yield an alloy that contains 1.55×10^{22} Nb atoms per cubic centimeter. The densities of pure Nb and V are 8.57 and 6.10 g/cm^3, respectively.

4.22 Cite the relative Burgers vector–dislocation line orientations for edge, screw, and mixed dislocations.

4.23 For both FCC and BCC crystal structures, the Burgers vector **b** may be expressed as

$$\mathbf{b} = \frac{a}{2}[hkl]$$

where a is the unit cell edge length and $[hkl]$ is the crystallographic direction having the greatest linear atomic density.
(a) What are the Burgers vector representations for FCC, BCC, and simple cubic crystal structures? See Problems 3.40 and 3.41 at the end of Chapter 3.
(b) If the magnitude of the Burgers vector $|\mathbf{b}|$ is

$$|\mathbf{b}| = \frac{a}{2}(h^2 + k^2 + l^2)^{1/2}$$

determine the values of $|\mathbf{b}|$ for aluminum and tungsten. You may want to consult Table 3.1.

4.24 **(a)** The surface energy of a single crystal depends on the crystallographic orientation with respect to the surface. Explain why this is so.
(b) For an FCC crystal, such as aluminum, would you expect the surface energy for a (100) plane to be greater or less than that for a (111) plane? Why?

4.25 **(a)** For a given material, would you expect the surface energy to be greater than, the same as, or less than the grain boundary energy? Why?
(b) The grain boundary energy of a low-angle grain boundary is less than for a high-angle one. Why is this so?

4.26 **(a)** Briefly describe a twin and a twin boundary.
(b) Cite the difference between mechanical and annealing twins.

4.27 For each of the following stacking sequences found in FCC metals, cite the type of planar defect that exists:
(a) . . . *A B C A B C B A C B A* . . .
(b) . . . *A B C A B C B C A B C* . . .
Now, copy the stacking sequences and indicate the position(s) of planar defect(s) with a vertical dashed line.

4.28 Using the intercept method, determine the average grain size, in millimeters, of the specimen whose microstructure is shown in Figure 4.12*b*; assume that the magnification is 100×, and use at least seven straight-line segments.

4.29 Employing the intercept technique, determine the average grain size for the steel specimen whose microstructure is shown in Figure 9.23*a*; use at least seven straight-line segments.

4.30 **(a)** For an ASTM grain size of 6, approximately how many grains would there be per square inch in a micrograph taken at a magnification of 100×?
(b) Estimate the grain size number for the photomicrograph in Figure 4.12*b*, assuming a magnification of 100×.

4.31 A photomicrograph was taken of some metal at a magnification of 100× and it was determined that the average number of grains per square inch is 10. Compute the ASTM grain size number for this alloy.

5

Diffusion

Photograph of a steel gear that has been "case hardened." The outer surface layer was selectively hardened by a high-temperature heat treatment during which carbon from the surrounding atmosphere diffused into the surface. The "case" appears as the dark outer rim of that segment of the gear that has been sectioned. Actual size. (Photograph courtesy of Surface Division Midland-Ross.)

5.1 Introduction

Many reactions and processes that are important in the treatment of materials rely on the transfer of mass either within a specific solid (ordinarily on a microscopic level) or from a liquid, a gas, or another solid phase. This is necessarily accomplished by **diffusion,** the phenomenon of material transport by atomic motion. This chapter discusses the atomic mechanisms by which diffusion occurs, the mathematics of diffusion, and the influence of temperature and diffusing species on the rate of diffusion.

The phenomenon of diffusion may be demonstrated with the use of a *diffusion couple,* which is formed by joining bars of two different metals together so that there is intimate contact between the two faces, as illustrated for copper and nickel in Figure 5.1, which includes schematic representations of atom positions and composition across the interface. This couple is heated for an extended period at an elevated temperature (but below the melting temperature of both metals), and cooled to room temperature. Chemical analysis will reveal a condition similar to that represented in Figure 5.2, namely, pure copper and nickel at the two extremities of the couple, separated by an alloyed region. Concentrations of both metals vary with position as shown in Figure 5.2*c*. This result indicates that copper atoms have migrated or diffused into the nickel, and that nickel has diffused into copper. This process, whereby atoms of one metal diffuse into another, is termed **interdiffusion,** or **impurity diffusion.**

Interdiffusion may be discerned from a macroscopic perspective by changes in concentration which occur over time, as in the example for the Cu–Ni diffusion couple. There is a net drift or transport of atoms from high to low concentration regions. Diffusion also occurs for pure metals, but all atoms exchanging positions are of the same type; this is termed **self-diffusion.** Of course, self-diffusion is not normally subject to observation by noting compositional changes.

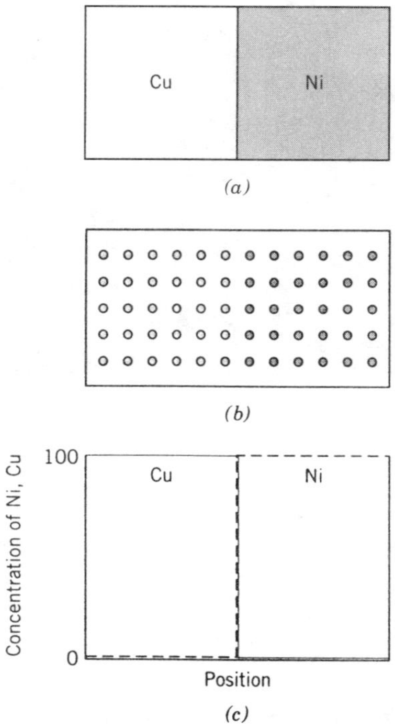

FIGURE 5.1 (*a*) A copper–nickel diffusion couple before a high-temperature heat treatment. (*b*) Schematic representations of Cu (colored circles) and Ni (black circles) atom locations within the diffusion couple. (*c*) Concentrations of copper and nickel as a function of position across the couple.

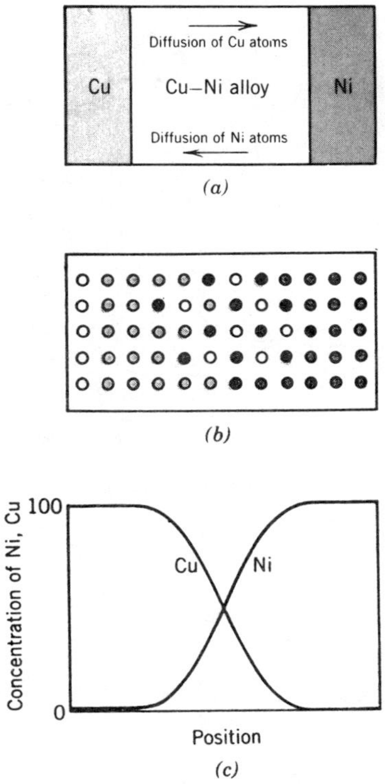

FIGURE 5.2 (*a*) A copper–nickel diffusion couple after a high-temperature heat treatment, showing the alloyed diffusion zone. (*b*) Schematic representations of Cu (colored circles) and Ni (black circles) atom locations within the couple. (*c*) Concentrations of copper and nickel as a function of position across the couple.

5.2 DIFFUSION MECHANISMS

From an atomic perspective, diffusion is just the stepwise migration of atoms from lattice site to lattice site. In fact, the atoms in solid materials are in constant motion, rapidly changing positions. For an atom to make such a move, two conditions must be met: (1) there must be an empty adjacent site, and (2) the atom must have sufficient energy to break bonds with its neighbor atoms and then cause some lattice distortion during the displacement. This energy is vibrational in nature (Section 4.7). At a specific temperature some small fraction of the total number of atoms are capable of diffusive motion, by virtue of the magnitudes of their vibrational energies. This fraction increases with rising temperature.

Several different models for this atomic motion have been proposed; of these possibilities, two dominate for metallic diffusion.

VACANCY DIFFUSION

One mechanism involves the interchange of an atom from a normal lattice position to an adjacent vacant lattice site or vacancy, as represented schematically in Figure 5.3*a*. This mechanism is aptly termed **vacancy diffusion.** Of course, this process necessitates the presence of vacancies, and the extent to which vacancy diffusion can occur is a function of the number of these defects that are present; significant concentrations of vacancies may exist in metals at elevated temperatures (Section 4.2). Since diffusing atoms and vacancies exchange positions, the diffusion of atoms in one direction corresponds to the motion of vacancies in the opposite direction. Both self-diffusion and interdiffusion occur by this mechanism; for the latter, the impurity atoms must substitute for host atoms.

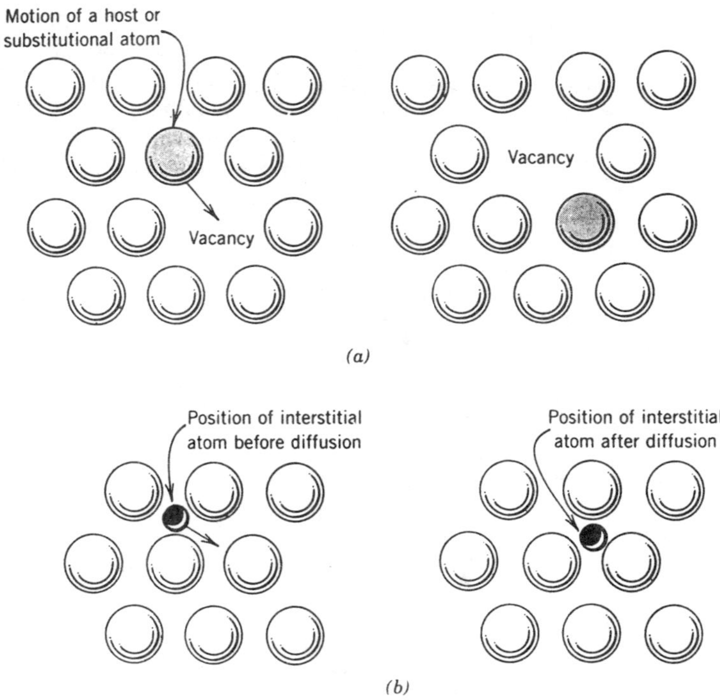

FIGURE 5.3 Schematic representations of (*a*) vacancy diffusion and (*b*) interstitial diffusion.

INTERSTITIAL DIFFUSION

The second type of diffusion involves atoms that migrate from an interstitial position to a neighboring one that is empty. This mechanism is found for interdiffusion of impurities such as hydrogen, carbon, nitrogen, and oxygen, which have atoms that are small enough to fit into the interstitial positions. Host or substitutional impurity atoms rarely form interstitials and do not normally diffuse via this mechanism. This phenomenon is appropriately termed **interstitial diffusion** (Figure 5.3*b*).

In most metal alloys, interstitial diffusion occurs much more rapidly than diffusion by the vacancy mode, since the interstitial atoms are smaller, and thus more mobile. Furthermore, there are more empty interstitial positions than vacancies; hence, the probability of interstitial atomic movement is greater than for vacancy diffusion.

5.3 STEADY-STATE DIFFUSION

Diffusion is a time-dependent process—that is, in a macroscopic sense, the quantity of an element that is transported within another is a function of time. Often it is necessary to know how fast diffusion occurs, or the rate of mass transfer. This rate is frequently expressed as a **diffusion flux** (J), defined as the mass (or, equivalently, the number of atoms) M diffusing through and perpendicular to a unit cross-sectional area of solid per unit of time. In mathematical form, this may be represented as

$$J = \frac{M}{At} \tag{5.1a}$$

where A denotes the area across which diffusion is occurring and t is the elapsed diffusion time. In differential form, this expression becomes

$$J = \frac{1}{A}\frac{dM}{dt} \tag{5.1b}$$

The units for J are kilograms or atoms per meter squared per second (kg/m^2-s or $atoms/m^2$-s).

If the diffusion flux does not change with time, a steady-state condition exists. One common example of **steady-state diffusion** is the diffusion of atoms of a gas through a plate of metal for which the concentrations (or pressures) of the diffusing species on both surfaces of the plate are held constant. This is represented schematically in Figure 5.4*a*.

When concentration C is plotted versus position (or distance) within the solid x, the resulting curve is termed the **concentration profile;** the slope at a particular point on this curve is the **concentration gradient:**

$$\text{concentration gradient} = \frac{dC}{dx} \tag{5.2a}$$

In the present treatment, the concentration profile is assumed to be linear, as depicted in Figure 5.4*b*, and

$$\text{concentration gradient} = \frac{\Delta C}{\Delta x} = \frac{C_A - C_B}{x_A - x_B} \tag{5.2b}$$

For diffusion problems, it is sometimes convenient to express concentration in terms of mass of diffusing species per unit volume of solid (kg/m^3 or g/cm^3).[1]

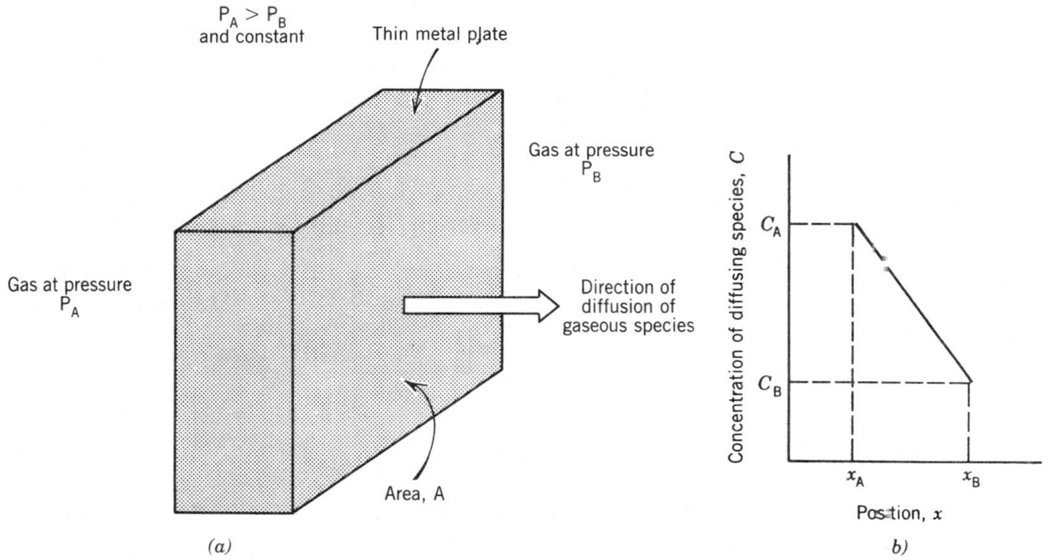

FIGURE 5.4 (*a*) Steady-state diffusion across a thin plate. (*b*) A linear concentration profile for the diffusion situation in (*a*).

[1] Conversion of concentration from weight percent to mass per unit volume (in kg/m^3) is possible using Equation 4.9.

The mathematics of steady-state diffusion in a single (x) direction are relatively simple, in that the flux is proportional to the concentration gradient through the expression

$$J = -D\frac{dC}{dx} \tag{5.3}$$

The constant of proportionality D is called the **diffusion coefficient,** which is expressed in square meters per second. The negative sign in this expression indicates that the direction of diffusion is down the concentration gradient, from a high to a low concentration. Equation 5.3 is sometimes called **Fick's first law.**

Sometimes the term **driving force** is used in the context of what compels a reaction to occur. For diffusion reactions, several such forces are possible; but when diffusion is according to Equation 5.3, the concentration gradient is the driving force.

One practical example of steady-state diffusion is found in the purification of hydrogen gas. One side of a thin sheet of palladium metal is exposed to the impure gas composed of hydrogen and other gaseous species such as nitrogen, oxygen, and water vapor. The hydrogen selectively diffuses through the sheet to the opposite side, which is maintained at a constant and lower hydrogen pressure.

Example Problem 5.1

A plate of iron is exposed to a carburizing (carbon-rich) atmosphere on one side and a decarburizing (carbon-deficient) atmosphere on the other side at 700°C (1300°F). If a condition of steady state is achieved, calculate the diffusion flux of carbon through the plate if the concentrations of carbon at positions of 5 and 10 mm (5×10^{-3} and 10^{-2} m) beneath the carburizing surface are 1.2 and 0.8 kg/m^3, respectively. Assume a diffusion coefficient of 3×10^{-11} m^2/s at this temperature.

Solution

Fick's first law, Equation 5.3, is utilized to determine the diffusion flux. Substitution of the values above into this expression yields

$$J = -D\frac{C_A - C_B}{x_A - x_B} = -(3 \times 10^{-11}\ \text{m}^2/\text{s})\frac{(1.2 - 0.8)\ \text{kg/m}^3}{(5 \times 10^{-3} - 10^{-2})\ \text{m}}$$

$$= 2.4 \times 10^{-9}\ \text{kg/m}^2\text{-s}$$

5.4 Nonsteady-State Diffusion

Most practical diffusion situations are nonsteady-state ones. That is, the diffusion flux and the concentration gradient at some particular point in a solid vary with time, with a net accumulation or depletion of the diffusing species resulting. This is illustrated in Figure 5.5, which shows concentration profiles at three different diffusion times. Under conditions of nonsteady state, use of Equation 5.3 is no longer convenient; instead, the partial differential equation

$$\frac{\partial C}{\partial t} = \frac{\partial}{\partial x}\left(D\frac{\partial C}{\partial x}\right) \tag{5.4a}$$

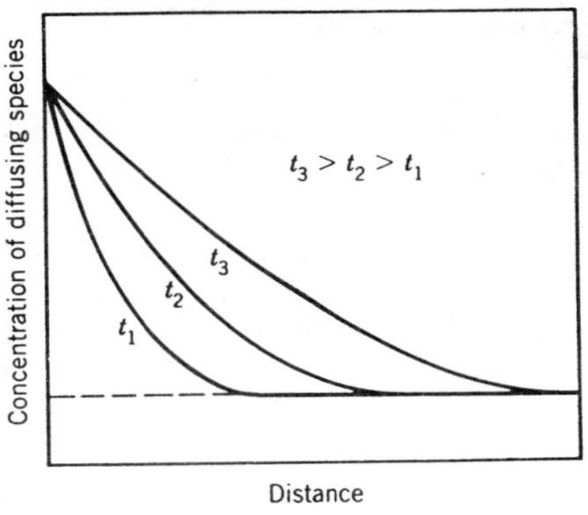

FIGURE 5.5 Concentration profiles for nonsteady-state diffusion taken at three different times, t_1, t_2, and t_3.

known as **Fick's second law,** is used. If the diffusion coefficient is independent of composition (which should be verified for each particular diffusion situation), Equation 5.4a simplifies to

$$\frac{\partial C}{\partial t} = D \frac{\partial^2 C}{\partial x^2} \tag{5.4b}$$

Solutions to this expression (concentration in terms of both position and time) are possible when physically meaningful boundary conditions are specified. Comprehensive collections of these are given by Crank, and Carslaw and Jaeger (see References).

One practically important solution is for a semi-infinite solid[2] in which the surface concentration is held constant. Frequently, the source of the diffusing species is a gas phase, the partial pressure of which is maintained at a constant value. Furthermore, the following assumptions are made:

1. Before diffusion, any of the diffusing solute atoms in the solid are uniformly distributed with concentration of C_0.
2. The value of x at the surface is zero and increases with distance into the solid.
3. The time is taken to be zero the instant before the diffusion process begins.

These boundary conditions are simply stated as

For $t = 0$, $C = C_0$ at $0 \le x \le \infty$

For $t > 0$, $C = C_s$ (the constant surface concentration) at $x = 0$

$C = C_0$ at $x = \infty$

Application of these boundary conditions to Equation 5.4b yields the solution

$$\frac{C_x - C_0}{C_s - C_0} = 1 - \text{erf}\left(\frac{x}{2\sqrt{Dt}}\right) \tag{5.5}$$

[2] A bar of solid is considered to be semi-infinite if none of the diffusing atoms reaches the bar end during the time over which diffusion takes place. A bar of length l is considered to be semi-infinite when $l > 10\sqrt{Dt}$.

Table 5.1 **Tabulation of Error Function Values**

z	$erf(z)$	z	$erf(z)$	z	$erf(z)$
0	0	0.55	0.5633	1.3	0.9340
0.025	0.0282	0.60	0.6039	1.4	0.9523
0.05	0.0564	0.65	0.6420	1.5	0.9661
0.10	0.1125	0.70	0.6778	1.6	0.9763
0.15	0.1680	0.75	0.7112	1.7	0.9838
0.20	0.2227	0.80	0.7421	1.8	0.9891
0.25	0.2763	0.85	0.7707	1.9	0.9928
0.30	0.3286	0.90	0.7970	2.0	0.9953
0.35	0.3794	0.95	0.8209	2.2	0.9981
0.40	0.4284	1.0	0.8427	2.4	0.9993
0.45	0.4755	1.1	0.8802	2.6	0.9998
0.50	0.5205	1.2	0.9103	2.8	0.9999

where C_x represents the concentration at depth x after time t. The expression $\mathrm{erf}(x/2\sqrt{Dt})$ is the Gaussian error function,[3] values of which are given in mathematical tables for various $x/2\sqrt{Dt}$ values; a partial listing is given in Table 5.1. The concentration parameters that appear in Equation 5.5 are noted in Figure 5.6, a concentration profile taken at a specific time. Equation 5.5 thus demonstrates the relationship between concentration, position, and time, namely, that C_x, being a function of the dimensionless parameter $x/\sqrt{Dt}$, may be determined at any time and position if the parameters C_0, C_s, and D are known.

Suppose that it is desired to achieve some specific concentration of solute, C_1, in an alloy; the left-hand side of Equation 5.5 now becomes

$$\frac{C_1 - C_0}{C_s - C_0} = \text{constant}$$

This being the case, the right-hand side of this same expression is also a constant, and subsequently

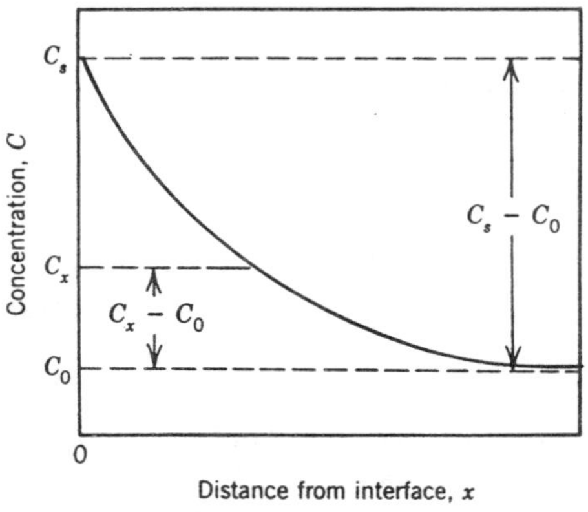

FIGURE 5.6 Concentration profile for nonsteady-state diffusion; concentration parameters relate to Equation 5.5.

[3] This Gaussian error function is defined by

$$\mathrm{erf}(z) = \frac{2}{\sqrt{\pi}} \int_0^z e^{-y^2}\,dy$$

where $x/2\sqrt{Dt}$ has been replaced by the variable z.

$$\frac{x}{2\sqrt{Dt}} = \text{constant} \tag{5.6a}$$

or

$$\frac{x^2}{Dt} = \text{constant} \tag{5.6b}$$

Some diffusion computations are thus facilitated on the basis of this relationship, as demonstrated in Example Problem 5.3.

Example Problem 5.2

For some applications, it is necessary to harden the surface of a steel (or iron-carbon alloy) above that of its interior. One way this may be accomplished is by increasing the surface concentration of carbon in a process termed **carburizing;** the steel piece is exposed, at an elevated temperature, to an atmosphere rich in a hydrocarbon gas, such as methane (CH_4).

Consider one such alloy that initially has a uniform carbon concentration of 0.25 wt% and is to be treated at 950°C (1750°F). If the concentration of carbon at the surface is suddenly brought to and maintained at 1.20 wt%, how long will it take to achieve a carbon content of 0.80 wt% at a position 0.5 mm below the surface? The diffusion coefficient for carbon in iron at this temperature is 1.6×10^{-11} m²/s; assume that the steel piece is semi-infinite.

Solution

Since this is a nonsteady-state diffusion problem in which the surface composition is held constant, Equation 5.5 is used. Values for all the parameters in this expression except time t are specified in the problem as follows:

$$C_0 = 0.25 \text{ wt\% C}$$
$$C_s = 1.20 \text{ wt\% C}$$
$$C_x = 0.80 \text{ wt\% C}$$
$$x = 0.50 \text{ mm} = 5 \times 10^{-4} \text{ m}$$
$$D = 1.6 \times 10^{-11} \text{ m}^2\text{/s}$$

Thus,

$$\frac{C_x - C_0}{C_s - C_0} = \frac{0.80 - 0.25}{1.20 - 0.25} = 1 - \text{erf}\left[\frac{(5 \times 10^{-4} \text{ m})}{2\sqrt{(1.6 \times 10^{-11} \text{ m}^2\text{/s})(t)}}\right]$$

$$0.4210 = \text{erf}\left(\frac{62.5 \text{ s}^{1/2}}{\sqrt{t}}\right)$$

We must now determine from Table 5.1 the value of z for which the error function is 0.4210. An interpolation is necessary, as

z	erf(z)
0.35	0.3794
z	0.4210
0.40	0.4284

$$\frac{z - 0.35}{0.40 - 0.35} = \frac{0.4210 - 0.3794}{0.4284 - 0.3794}$$

or

$$z = 0.392$$

Therefore,

$$\frac{62.5\ \text{s}^{1/2}}{\sqrt{t}} = 0.392$$

and solving for t,

$$t = \left(\frac{62.5\ \text{s}^{1/2}}{0.392}\right)^2 = 25{,}400\ \text{s} = 7.1\ \text{h}$$

Example Problem 5.3

The diffusion coefficients for copper in aluminum at 500 and 600°C are 4.8×10^{-14} and 5.3×10^{-13} m²/s, respectively. Determine the approximate time at 500°C that will produce the same diffusion result (in terms of concentration of Cu at some specific point in Al) as a 10-h heat treatment at 600°C.

Solution

This is a diffusion problem in which Equation 5.6b may be employed. The composition in both diffusion situations will be equal at the same position (i.e., x is also a constant), thus

$$Dt = \text{constant} \qquad (5.7)$$

at both temperatures. That is,

$$(Dt)_{500} = (Dt)_{600}$$

or

$$t_{500} = \frac{(Dt)_{600}}{D_{500}} = \frac{(5.3 \times 10^{-13}\ \text{m}^2/\text{s})(10\ \text{h})}{4.8 \times 10^{-14}\ \text{m}^2/\text{s}} = 110.4\ \text{h}$$

5.5 Factors that Influence Diffusion

Diffusing Species

The magnitude of the diffusion coefficient D is indicative of the rate at which atoms diffuse. Coefficients, both self- and interdiffusion, for several metallic systems are listed in Table 5.2. The diffusing species as well as the host material influence the diffusion coefficient. For example, there is a significant difference in magnitude between self- and carbon interdiffusion in α iron at 500°C, the D value being greater for the carbon interdiffusion (3.0×10^{-21} vs. 2.4×10^{-12} m²/s). This comparison also provides a contrast between rates of diffusion via vacancy and interstitial modes as discussed above. Self-diffusion occurs by a vacancy mechanism, whereas carbon diffusion in iron is interstitial.

Temperature

Temperature has a most profound influence on the coefficients and diffusion rates. For example, for the self-diffusion of Fe in α-Fe, the diffusion coefficient increases approximately six orders of magnitude (from 3.0×10^{-21} to 1.8×10^{-15} m²/s) in rising temperature from 500 to 900°C (Table 5.2). The temperature dependence of diffusion coefficients is related to temperature according to

$$D = D_0 \exp\left(-\frac{Q_d}{RT}\right) \tag{5.8}$$

where

D_0 = a temperature-independent preexponential (m^2/s)

Q_d = the **activation energy** for diffusion (J/mol, cal/mol, or eV/atom)

R = the gas constant, 8.31 J/mol-K, 1.987 cal/mol-K, or 8.62×10^{-5} eV/atom

T = absolute temperature (K)

The activation energy may be thought of as that energy required to produce the diffusive motion of one mole of atoms. A large activation energy results in a relatively small diffusion coefficient. Table 5.2 also contains a listing of D_0 and Q_d values for several diffusion systems.

Taking natural logarithms of Equation 5.8 yields

$$\ln D = \ln D_0 - \frac{Q_d}{R}\left(\frac{1}{T}\right) \tag{5.9a}$$

Or in terms of logarithms to the base 10

$$\log D = \log D_0 - \frac{Q_d}{2.3R}\left(\frac{1}{T}\right) \tag{5.9b}$$

Table 5.2 A Tabulation of Diffusion Data

Diffusing Species	*Host Metal*	$D_0 (m^2/s)$	*Activation Energy Q_d*		*Calculated Values*	
			kJ/mol	*eV/atom*	*T(°C)*	$D (m^2/s)$
Fe	α-Fe (BCC)	2.8×10^{-4}	251	2.60	500	3.0×10^{-21}
					900	1.8×10^{-15}
Fe	γ-Fe (FCC)	5.0×10^{-5}	284	2.94	900	1.1×10^{-17}
					1100	7.8×10^{-16}
C	α-Fe	6.2×10^{-7}	80	0.83	500	2.4×10^{-12}
					900	1.7×10^{-10}
C	γ-Fe	2.3×10^{-5}	148	1.53	900	5.9×10^{-12}
					1100	5.3×10^{-11}
Cu	Cu	7.8×10^{-5}	211	2.19	500	4.2×10^{-19}
Zn	Cu	2.4×10^{-5}	189	1.96	500	4.0×10^{-18}
Al	Al	2.3×10^{-4}	144	1.49	500	4.2×10^{-14}
Cu	Al	6.5×10^{-5}	136	1.41	500	4.1×10^{-14}
Mg	Al	1.2×10^{-4}	131	1.35	500	1.9×10^{-13}
Cu	Ni	2.7×10^{-5}	256	2.65	500	1.3×10^{-22}

Source: E. A. Brandes and G. B. Brook (Editors), *Smithells Metals Reference Book,* 7th edition, Butterworth-Heinemann, Oxford, 1992.

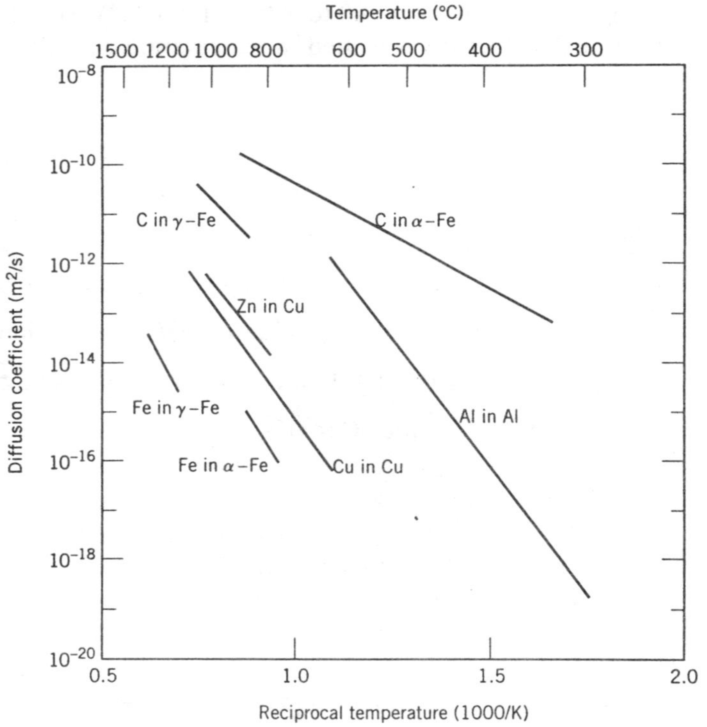

FIGURE 5.7 Plot of the logarithm of the diffusion coefficient versus the reciprocal of absolute temperature for several metals. [Data taken from E. A. Brandes and G. B. Brook, (Editors), *Smithells Metals Reference Book*, 7th edition, Butterworth-Heinemann, Oxford, 1992.]

Since D_0, Q_d, and R are all constants, Equation 5.9b takes on the form of an equation of a straight line:

$$y = b + mx$$

where y and x are analogous, respectively, to the variables log D and $1/T$. Thus, if log D is plotted versus the reciprocal of the absolute temperature, a straight line should result, having slope and intercept of $-Q_d/2.3R$ and log D_0, respectively. This is, in fact, the manner in which the values of Q_d and D_0 are determined experimentally. From such a plot for several alloy systems (Figure 5.7), it may be noted that linear relationships exist for all cases shown.

EXAMPLE PROBLEM 5.4

Using the data in Table 5.2, compute the diffusion coefficient for magnesium in aluminum at 550°C.

SOLUTION

This diffusion coefficient may be determined by applying Equation 5.8; the values of D_0 and Q_d from Table 5.2 are 1.2×10^{-4} m²/s and 131 kJ/mol, respectively. Thus,

$$D = (1.2 \times 10^{-4}\ \text{m}^2/\text{s}) \exp\left[-\frac{(131{,}000\ \text{J/mol})}{(8.31\ \text{J/mol-K})(550 + 273\ \text{K})}\right]$$

$$= 5.8 \times 10^{-13}\ \text{m}^2/\text{s}$$

Example Problem 5.5

In Figure 5.8 is shown a plot of the logarithm (to the base 10) of the diffusion coefficient versus reciprocal of absolute temperature, for the diffusion of copper in gold. Determine values for the activation energy and the preexponential.

Solution

From Equation 5.9b the slope of the line segment in Figure 5.8 is equal to $-Q_d/2.3R$, and the intercept at $1/T = 0$ gives the value of $\log D_0$. Thus, the activation energy may be determined as

$$Q_d = -2.3R\,(\text{slope}) = -2.3R\left[\frac{\Delta(\log D)}{\Delta\left(\frac{1}{T}\right)}\right]$$

$$= -2.3R\left[\frac{\log D_1 - \log D_2}{\frac{1}{T_1} - \frac{1}{T_2}}\right]$$

where D_1 and D_2 are the diffusion coefficient values at $1/T_1$ and $1/T_2$, respectively. Let us arbitrarily take $1/T_1 = 0.8 \times 10^{-3}\ (\text{K})^{-1}$ and $1/T_2 = 1.1 \times 10^{-3}\ (\text{K})^{-1}$. We may now read the corresponding $\log D_1$ and $\log D_2$ values from the line segment in Figure 5.8.

[Before this is done, however, a parenthetic note of caution is offered. The vertical axis in Figure 5.8 is scaled logarithmically (to the base 10); however, the actual diffusion coefficient values are noted on this axis. For example, for $D = 10^{-14}\ \text{m}^2/\text{s}$, the logarithm of D is -14.0 *not* 10^{-14}. Furthermore, this logarithmic scaling affects the readings between decade values; for example, at a location midway between 10^{-14} and 10^{-15}, the value is not 5×10^{-15}, but rather, $10^{-14.5} = 3.2 \times 10^{-15}$].

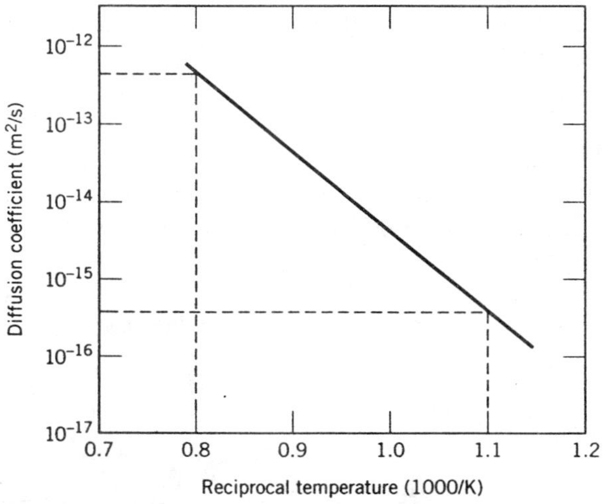

Figure 5.8 Plot of the logarithm of the diffusion coefficient versus the reciprocal of absolute temperature for the diffusion of copper in gold.

Thus, from Figure 5.8, at $1/T_1 = 0.8 \times 10^{-3}$ (K)$^{-1}$, $\log D_1 = -12.40$, while for $1/T_2 = 1.1 \times 10^{-3}$ (K)$^{-1}$, $\log D_2 = -15.45$, and the slope of the line segment in Figure 5.8 is

$$Q_d = -2.3R\left[\frac{\log D_1 - \log D_2}{\dfrac{1}{T_1} - \dfrac{1}{T_2}}\right]$$

$$= -2.3\,(8.31\text{ J/mol-K})\left[\frac{-12.40 - (-15.45)}{0.8 \times 10^{-3}\,(\text{K})^{-1} - 1.1 \times 10^{-3}\,(\text{K})^{-1}}\right]$$

$$= 194{,}000\text{ J/mol} = 194\text{ kJ/mol}$$

Now, rather than trying to make a graphical extrapolation to determine D_0, a more accurate value is obtained analytically using Equation 5.9b, and a specific value of D (or $\log D$) and its corresponding T (or $1/T$) from Figure 5.8. Since we know that $\log D = -15.45$ at $1/T = 1.1 \times 10^{-3}$ (K)$^{-1}$, then

$$\log D_0 = \log D + \frac{Q_d}{2.3R}\left(\frac{1}{T}\right)$$

$$= -15.45 + \frac{(194{,}000\text{ J/mol})(1.1 \times 10^{-3}\,[\text{K}]^{-1})}{(2.3)(8.31\text{ J/mol-K})}$$

$$= -4.28$$

Thus, $D_0 = 10^{-4.28}$ m^2/s $= 5.2 \times 10^{-5}$ m^2/s.

DESIGN EXAMPLE 5.1

The wear resistance of a steel gear is to be improved by hardening its surface. This is to be accomplished by increasing the carbon content within an outer surface layer as a result of carbon diffusion into the steel; the carbon is to be supplied from an external carbon-rich gaseous atmosphere at an elevated and constant temperature. The initial carbon content of the steel is 0.20 wt%, whereas the surface concentration is to be maintained at 1.00 wt%. In order for this treatment to be effective, a carbon content of 0.60 wt% must be established at a position 0.75 mm below the surface. Specify an appropriate heat treatment in terms of temperature and time for temperatures between 900°C and 1050°C. Use data in Table 5.2 for the diffusion of carbon in γ-iron.

SOLUTION

Since this is a nonsteady-state diffusion situation, let us first of all employ Equation 5.5, utilizing the following values for the concentration parameters:

$$C_0 = 0.20\text{ wt\% C}$$

$$C_s = 1.00\text{ wt\% C}$$

$$C_x = 0.60\text{ wt\% C}$$

Therefore

$$\frac{C_x - C_0}{C_s - C_0} = \frac{0.60 - 0.20}{1.00 - 0.20} = 1 - \text{erf}\left(\frac{x}{2\sqrt{Dt}}\right)$$

And thus

$$0.5 = \text{erf}\left(\frac{x}{2\sqrt{Dt}}\right)$$

Using an interpolation technique as demonstrated in Example Problem 5.2 and the data presented in Table 5.1

$$\frac{x}{2\sqrt{Dt}} = 0.4747 \tag{5.10}$$

The problem stipulates that $x = 0.75$ mm $= 7.5 \times 10^{-4}$ m. Therefore

$$\frac{7.5 \times 10^{-4}\text{ m}}{2\sqrt{Dt}} = 0.4747$$

Which leads to

$$Dt = 6.24 \times 10^{-7}\text{ m}^2$$

Furthermore, the diffusion coefficient depends on temperature according to Equation 5.8; and, from Table 5.2 for the diffusion of carbon in γ-iron, $D_0 = 2.3 \times 10^{-5}$ m^2/s and $Q_d = 148{,}000$ J/mol. Hence

$$Dt = D_0 \exp\left(-\frac{Q_d}{RT}\right)(t) = 6.24 \times 10^{-7}\text{ m}^2$$

$$(2.3 \times 10^{-5}\text{ m}^2/\text{s}) \exp\left[-\frac{148{,}000\text{ J/mol}}{(8.31\text{ J/mol-K})(T)}\right](t) = 6.24 \times 10^{-7}\text{ m}^2$$

And solving for the time t

$$t\text{ (in s)} = \frac{0.0271}{\exp\left(-\frac{17{,}810}{T}\right)}$$

Thus, the required diffusion time may be computed for some specified temperature (in K). Below are tabulated t values for four different temperatures that lie within the range stipulated in the problem.

Temperature	*Time*	
(°C)	*s*	*h*
900	106,400	29.6
950	57,200	15.9
1000	32,300	9.0
1050	19,000	5.3

5.6 Other Diffusion Paths

Atomic migration may also occur along dislocations, grain boundaries, and external surfaces. These are sometimes called "*short-circuit*" *diffusion paths* inasmuch as rates are much faster than for bulk diffusion. However, in most situations short-circuit contributions to the overall diffusion flux are insignificant because the cross-sectional areas of these paths are extremely small.

SUMMARY

Solid-state diffusion is a means of mass transport within solid materials by stepwise atomic motion. The term "self-diffusion" refers to the migration of host atoms; for impurity atoms, the term "interdiffusion" is used. Two mechanisms are possible: vacancy and interstitial. For a given host metal, interstitial atomic species generally diffuse more rapidly.

For steady-state diffusion, the concentration profile of the diffusing species is time independent, and the flux or rate is proportional to the negative of the concentration gradient according to Fick's first law. The mathematics for nonsteady state are described by Fick's second law, a partial differential equation. The solution for a constant surface composition boundary condition involves the Gaussian error function.

The magnitude of the diffusion coefficient is indicative of the rate of atomic motion, being strongly dependent on and increasing exponentially with increasing temperature.

IMPLICATIONS

Some properties of materials (e.g., hardness and strength) are subject to alteration and improvement as a result of transformations that involve atomic diffusion; diffusion path lengths are often microscopic in magnitude (i.e., on the order of microns). For these transformations to occur over reasonable time periods (usually on the order of hours), they are ordinarily carried out at elevated temperatures at which diffusion rates are comparatively rapid. An alteration of the microstructure attends many of these transformations, and, having a knowledge of the diffusion phenomenon, is essential in understanding the transformation mechanisms (e.g., see Sections 9.6, 9.7, and 9.14). These high-temperature procedures, often termed *heat treatments,* are utilized at least once during the production of almost all common metallic, ceramic, and polymeric materials. For example, the strength of some steels is reliant on appropriate heat treatments (Chapter 11), as is also the mechanical integrity of many ceramics (Section 14.15).

Furthermore, during the processing of some materials, compositional alterations may occur as a result of mass transport from external sources (e.g., case hardening, Section 8.11). Heat-treating temperatures and times may be predicted using the mathematics of diffusion (i.e., solutions to Fick's second law) in conjunction with appropriate diffusion coefficient values.

IMPORTANT TERMS AND CONCEPTS

Activation energy
Carburizing
Concentration gradient
Concentration profile
Diffusion
Diffusion coefficient
Diffusion flux
Driving force
Fick's first and second laws
Interdiffusion (impurity diffusion)
Interstitial diffusion
Nonsteady-state diffusion
Self-diffusion
Steady-state diffusion
Vacancy diffusion

REFERENCES

Borg, R. J. and G. J. Dienes (Editors), *An Introduction to Solid State Diffusion,* Academic Press, San Diego, 1988.

Brandes, E. A. and G. B. Brook (Editors), *Smithells Metals Reference Book,* 7th edition, Butterworth-Heinemann Ltd., Oxford, 1992.

Carslaw, H. S. and J. C. Jaeger, *Conduction of Heat in Solids,* 2nd edition, Clarendon Press, Oxford, 1986.

Crank, J., *The Mathematics of Diffusion,* 2nd edition, Clarendon Press, Oxford, 1980.

Girifalco, L. A., *Atomic Migration In Crystals,* Blaisdell Publishing Company, New York, 1964.

Shewmon, P. G., *Diffusion in Solids,* McGraw-Hill Book Company, New York, 1963. Reprinted by The Minerals, Metals and Materials Society, Warrendale, PA, 1989.

QUESTIONS AND PROBLEMS

5.1 Briefly explain the difference between self-diffusion and interdiffusion.

5.2 Self-diffusion involves the motion of atoms that are all of the same type; therefore it is not subject to observation by compositional changes, as with interdiffusion. Suggest one way in which self-diffusion may be monitored.

5.3 **(a)** Compare interstitial and vacancy atomic mechanisms for diffusion.

(b) Cite two reasons why interstitial diffusion is normally more rapid than vacancy diffusion.

5.4 Briefly explain the concept of steady state as it applies to diffusion.

5.5 **(a)** Briefly explain the concept of a driving force.

(b) What is the driving force for steady-state diffusion?

5.6 The purification of hydrogen gas by diffusion through a palladium sheet was discussed in Section 5.3. Compute the number of kilograms of hydrogen that pass per hour through a 6-mm-thick sheet of palladium having an area of 0.25 m^2 at 600°C. Assume a diffusion coefficient of 1.7×10^{-8} m^2/s, that the concentrations at the high- and low-pressure sides of the plate are 2.0 and 0.4 kg of hydrogen per cubic meter of palladium, and that steady-state conditions have been attained.

5.7 A sheet of steel 2.5 mm thick has nitrogen atmospheres on both sides at 900°C and is permitted to achieve a steady-state diffusion condition. The diffusion coefficient for nitrogen in steel at this temperature is 1.2×10^{-10} m^2/s, and the diffusion flux is found to be 1.0×10^{-7} kg/m^2-s. Also, it is known that the concentration of nitrogen in the steel at the high-pressure surface is 2 kg/m^3. How far into the sheet from this high-pressure side will the concentration be 0.5 kg/m^3? Assume a linear concentration profile.

5.8 A sheet of BCC iron 2 mm thick was exposed to a carburizing gas atmosphere on one side and a decarburizing atmosphere on the other side at 675°C. After having reached steady state, the iron was quickly cooled to room temperature. The carbon concentrations at the two surfaces of the sheet were determined to be 0.015 and 0.0068 wt%. Compute the diffusion coefficient if the diffusion flux is 7.36×10^{-9} kg/m^2-s. *Hint:* Use Equation 4.9 to convert the concentrations from weight percent to kilograms of carbon per cubic meter of iron.

5.9 Show that Fick's second law (Equation 5.4b) takes on the form of Fick's first law (Equation 5.3) for conditions of steady state, that is,

$$\frac{\partial C}{\partial t} = 0$$

5.10 Show that

$$C_x = \frac{B}{\sqrt{Dt}} \exp\left(-\frac{x^2}{4Dt}\right)$$

is also a solution to Equation 5.4b. The parameter B is a constant, being independent of both x and t.

5.11 Determine the carburizing time necessary to achieve a carbon concentration of 0.30 wt% at a position 4 mm into an iron–carbon alloy that initially contains 0.10 wt% C. The surface concentration is to be maintained at 0.90 wt% C, and the treatment is to be conducted at 1100°C. Use the diffusion data for γ-Fe in Table 5.2.

5.12 An FCC iron–carbon alloy initially containing 0.35 wt% C is exposed to an oxygen-rich and virtually carbon-free atmosphere at 1400 K (1127°C). Under these circumstances the carbon diffuses from the alloy and reacts at the surface with the oxygen in the atmosphere; that is, the carbon concentration at the surface position is maintained essentially at 0 wt% C. (This process of carbon depletion is termed *decarburization.*) At what position will the carbon concentration be 0.15 wt% after a 10-h treatment? The value of D at 1400 K is 6.9×10^{-11} m^2/s.

5.13 Nitrogen from a gaseous phase is to be diffused into pure iron at 675°C. If the surface concentration is maintained at 0.2 wt% N, what will be the concentration 2 mm from the surface after 25 h? The diffusion coefficient for nitrogen in iron at 675°C is 1.9×10^{-11} m^2/s.

5.14 Simplify Equation 5.5 for the situation when C_x is halfway between C_s and C_0.

5.15 For a steel alloy it has been determined that a carburizing heat treatment of 15 h duration will raise the carbon concentration to 0.35 wt% at a point 2.0 mm from the surface. Estimate the time necessary to achieve the same concentration at a 6.0-mm position for an identical steel and at the same carburizing temperature.

5.16 Cite the values of the diffusion coefficients for the interdiffusion of carbon in both α-iron (BCC) and γ-iron (FCC) at 900°C. Which is larger? Explain why this is the case.

5.17 Using the data in Table 5.2, compute the value of D for the diffusion of magnesium in aluminum at 400°C.

5.18 At what temperature will the diffusion coefficient for the diffusion of zinc in copper have a value of 2.6×10^{-16} m^2/s? Use the diffusion data in Table 5.2.

5.19 The preexponential and activation energy for the diffusion of iron in cobalt are 1.1×10^{-5} m^2/s and 253,300 J/mol, respectively. At what temperature will the diffusion coefficient have a value of 2.1×10^{-14} m^2/s?

5.20 The activation energy for the diffusion of carbon in chromium is 111,000 J/mol. Calculate the diffusion coefficient at 1100 K (827°C), given that D at 1400 K (1127°C) is 6.25×10^{-11} m^2/s.

5.21 The diffusion coefficients for nickel in iron are given at two temperatures:

T(K)	D(m^2/s)
1473	2.2×10^{-15}
1673	4.8×10^{-14}

(a) Determine the values of D_0 and the activation energy Q_d.
(b) What is the magnitude of the D at 1300°C (1573 K)?

5.22 The diffusion coefficients for silver in copper are given at two temperatures:

T(°C)	D(m^2/s)
650	5.5×10^{-16}
900	1.3×10^{-13}

(a) Determine the values of D_0 and Q_d.
(b) What is the magnitude of D at 875°C?

5.23 Below is shown a plot of the logarithm (to the base 10) of the diffusion coefficient versus reciprocal of the absolute temperature, for the diffusion of iron in chromium. Determine values for the activation energy and preexponential.

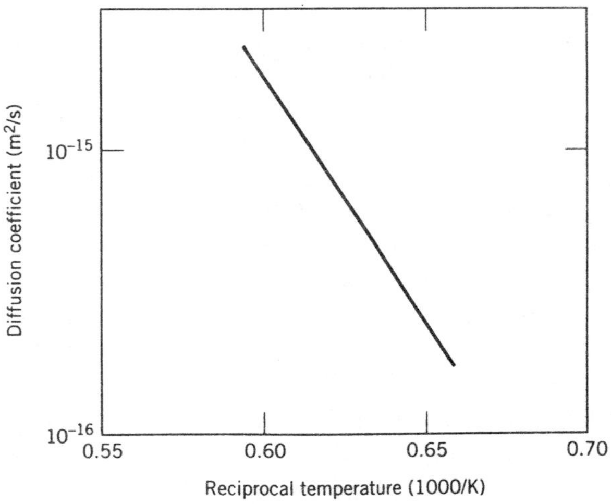

5.24 Carbon is allowed to diffuse through a steel plate 15 mm thick. The concentrations of carbon at the two faces are 0.65 and 0.30 kg C/m^3 Fe, which are maintained constant. If the preexponential and activation energy are

6.2×10^{-7} m^2/s and 80,000 J/mol, respectively, compute the temperature at which the diffusion flux is 1.43×10^{-9} kg/m^2-s.

5.25 The steady-state diffusion flux through a metal plate is 5.4×10^{-10} kg/m^2-s at a temperature of 727°C (1000 K) and when the concentration gradient is -350 kg/m^4. Calculate the diffusion flux at 1027°C (1300 K) for the same concentration gradient and assuming an activation energy for diffusion of 125,000 J/mol.

5.26 At approximately what temperature would a specimen of γ-iron have to be carburized for 4 h to produce the same diffusion result as at 1000°C for 12 h?

5.27 **(a)** Calculate the diffusion coefficient for magnesium in aluminum at 450°C.
(b) What time will be required at 550°C to produce the same diffusion result (in terms of concentration at a specific point) as for 15 h at 450°C?

5.28 A copper-nickel diffusion couple similar to that shown in Figure 5.1*a* is fashioned. After a 700-h heat treatment at 1100°C (1373 K) the concentration of Cu is 2.5 wt% at the 3.0-mm position within the nickel. At what temperature must the diffusion couple need to be heated to produce this same concentration (i.e., 2.5 wt% Cu) at a 2.0 mm-position after 700 h? The preexponential and activation energy for the diffusion of Cu in Ni are given in Table 5.2.

5.29 A diffusion couple similar to that shown in Figure 5.1*a* is prepared using two hypothetical metals A and B. After a 30-h heat treatment at 1000 K (and subsequently cooling to room temperature) the concentration of A in B is 3.2 wt% at the 15.5-mm position within metal B. If another heat treatment is conducted on an identical diffusion couple, only at 800 K for 30 h, at what position will the composition be 3.2 wt% A? Assume that the preexponential and activation energy for the diffusion coefficient are 1.8×10^{-5} m^2/s and 152,000 J/mol, respectively.

5.30 The outer surface of a steel gear is to be hardened by increasing its carbon content. The carbon is to be supplied from an external carbon-rich atmosphere, which is maintained at an elevated temperature. A diffusion heat treatment at 850°C (1123 K) for 10 min increases the carbon concentration to 0.90 wt% at a position 1.0 mm below the surface. Estimate the diffusion time required at 650°C (923 K) to achieve this same concentration also at a 1.0-mm position. Assume that the surface carbon content is the same for both heat treatments, which is maintained constant. Use the diffusion data in Table 5.2 for C diffusion in α-Fe.

5.31 An FCC iron-carbon alloy initially containing 0.20 wt% C is carburized at an elevated temperature and in an atmosphere wherein the surface carbon concentration is maintained at 1.0 wt%. If after 49.5 h the concentration of carbon is 0.35 wt% at a position 4.0 mm below the surface, determine the temperature at which the treatment was carried out.

Design Problem

5.D1 The wear resistance of a steel shaft is to be improved by hardening its surface. This is to be accomplished by increasing the nitrogen content within an outer surface layer as a result of nitrogen diffusion into the steel. The nitrogen is to be supplied from an external nitrogen-rich gas at an elevated and constant temperature. The initial nitrogen content of the steel is 0.002 wt%, whereas the surface concentration is to be maintained at 0.50 wt%. In order for this treatment to be effective, a nitrogen content of 0.10 wt% must be established at a position 0.40 mm below the surface. Specify appropriate heat treatments in terms of temperature and time for temperatures between 475°C and 625°C. The preexponential and activation energy for the diffusion of nitrogen in iron are 3×10^{-7} m^2/s and 76,150 J/mol, respectively, over this temperature range.

INTRODUCTION TO MATERIALS SCIENCE AND ENGINEERING

Kenneth M. Ralls
Department of Mechanical Engineering
The University of Texas at Austin

Thomas H. Courtney
Department of Metallurgical Engineering
Michigan Technological University

John Wulff
Department of Metallurgy and Materials Science
Massachusetts Institute of Technology

JOHN WILEY & SONS

New York • Chichester • Brisbane • Toronto • Singapore

Library of Congress Cataloging in Publication Data:

Ralls, Kenneth M 1938-
Introduction to materials science and engineering.

1. Materials. I. Courtney Thomas H., joint author.
I. Courtney Thomas H., joint author. II. Wulff, John,
1903- joint author. III. Title.
TA403.R354 620.1'12 76-10813
ISBN 0-471-70665-5

Printed in the United States of America

20 19 18 17

12

Diffusion

This chapter introduces some of the useful concepts and ideas concerning diffusion. Many reactions in solids and liquids are diffusion dependent and these will be discussed in subsequent chapters.

12.1 DIFFUSION PHENOMENA

In order for chemical reactions to occur efficiently and effectively, it is usually important that the reactants be well mixed. The mixing of gases or of liquids to form a solution can result from flow due to mechanical agitation such as stirring or due to thermal convection currents. Both of these means are very effective in producing compositional uniformity or homogeneity in gaseous solutions or liquid solutions. Even under quiescent conditions, mixing will proceed by diffusion, in which the thermal motion of individual atoms or molecules leads to homogeneity (Fig. 12.1). Diffusive mixing in liquids is much slower than in gases, and diffusion in solids is even slower because less freedom for atomic motion exists.

Diffusion in solids may be demonstrated experimentally by making a very clean joint, such as that shown in Fig. 12.2*a*, between pure gold and pure nickel. After this couple has been held at an elevated temperature (e.g., 900°C) for a long period of time, the extent of mixing of gold and nickel can be determined by suitable chemical analyses, and a composition profile can be plotted (Fig. 12.2*b*), showing that gold atoms have diffused into the nickel and nickel atoms, into the gold. While inter-diffusion of gold and nickel atoms is occurring, nickel atoms are moving about within the nickel and gold atoms move within the gold also. This phenomenon,

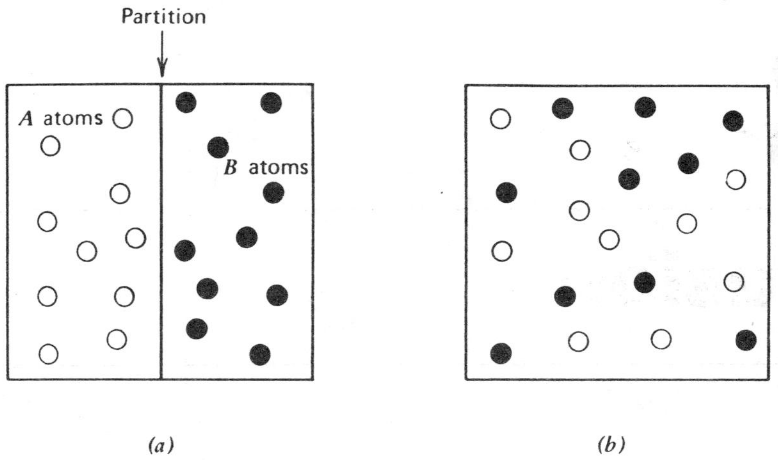

FIGURE 12.1 Mixing of gases by gaseous diffusion. (*a*) Gas atoms of species *A* and *B* are separated by a partition. (*b*) Upon removal of the partition, the gases mix, resulting in a homogeneous distribution.

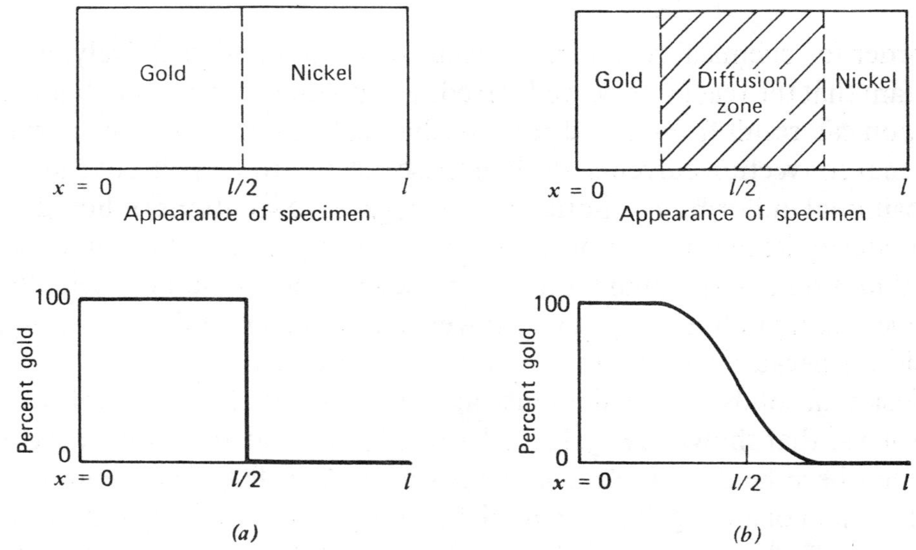

FIGURE 12.2 An Au–Ni diffusion couple. (*a*) Before the diffusion heat treatment, pure gold is on the left-hand side of the couple and pure nickel is on the right-hand side. (*b*) The same couple after a diffusion heat treatment shows that Au atoms have penetrated into the nickel and vice versa.

called self-diffusion, can be demonstrated by depositing a thin layer of radioactive nickel on nonradioactive nickel. After this chemically homogeneous specimen has been given an appropriate diffusion heat treatment, a suitable radiation detector can be used to measure radioactivity as a function of distance into the originally nonradioactive nickel. The penetration plot obtained is shown schematically in Fig. 12.3. Such experiments reveal, for a solid metal held just below its melting point, that over three years are required for an atom to move a distance of one centimeter by self-diffusion.

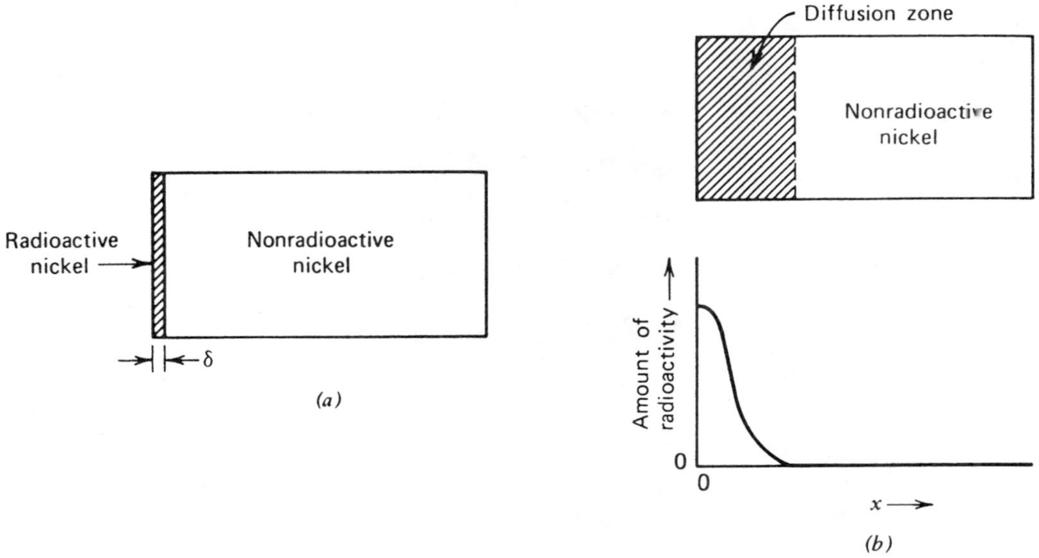

FIGURE 12.3 A self-diffusion experiment. (*a*) A thin layer of radioactive nickel has been deposited on one surface of a nonradioactive nickel specimen. (*b*) A diffusion heat treatment has resulted in the diffusion of radioactive Ni atoms into the initially nonradioactive material.

Atoms are able to move throughout solids because they are not stationary but execute rapid, small-amplitude vibrations about their equilibrium positions. Such vibrations increase with temperature, and at any temperature a very small fraction of atoms has sufficient amplitude to move from one atomic position to an adjacent one. The fraction of atoms possessing this amplitude increases markedly with rising temperature. In jumping from one equilibrium position to another, an atom passes through a higher energy state since atomic bonds are distorted and broken, and the increase in energy (i.e., the activation energy) is supplied by thermal vibrations. As might be expected, defects, especially vacancies, are quite instrumental in affecting the diffusion process in crystalline solids. In a particular material, diffusion depends on the type and number of defects that are present, as well as the thermal vibrations of atoms.

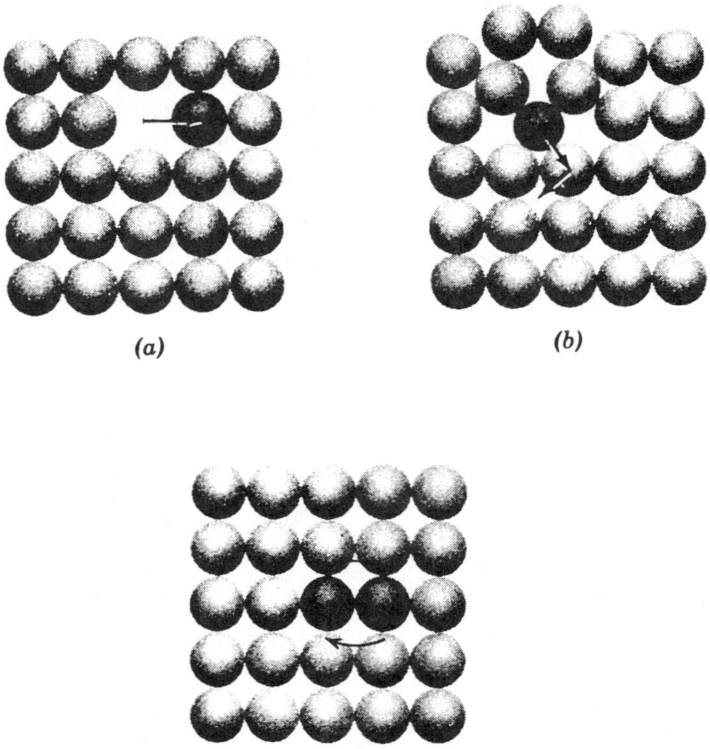

FIGURE 12.4 Possible mechanisms of diffusion. (*a*) The vacancy mechanism, in which an atom and an adjacent vacancy exchange positions, is the mechanism for diffusion in most metals and substitutional solid-solution alloys. The activation energy for self-diffusion by this mechanism is the sum of the energy required to form a vacancy and that required to move it. (*b*) The interstitial mechanism illustrated results in atomic motion since a self-interstitial atom can displace an adjacent atom to an interstitial position. Although the activation energy for such motion is low, self-interstitials occur so infrequently that they do not contribute to diffusion in most metals and substitutional solid-solution alloys. Interstitial impurity atoms and solute atoms in interstitial solid-solution alloys can move fairly readily by this mechanism. (*c*) The direct exchange mechanism, in which two adjacent atoms interchange positions, is highly unlikely because the associated activation energy is extremely high. (Adapted from *The Structure and Properties of Materials,* Vol. II, by J. H. Brophy, R. M. Rose, and J. Wulff, Wiley, New York, 1964.)

12.2 MECHANISMS OF VOLUME DIFFUSION IN METALS

The transfer of a metal atom from one equilibrium position to another is the basic step in the volume diffusion process, that is, mass transport that occurs by the movement of atoms within the bulk of the material. In the case of self-diffusion, there is no net mass transport, but atoms migrate in a random manner throughout the crystal. In interdiffusion, the mass transport almost always occurs so as to minimize compositional differences. Various atomic mechanisms for self-diffusion and interdiffusion have been proposed, and three of them are illustrated in Fig. 12.4. The most energetically favorable process, and one that has been experimentally shown to predominate in most metals, involves an interchange of places by an atom and a neighboring vacancy (Fig. 12.4*a*). For this process, the energy of the atom depends on its position, as shown in Fig. 12.5. The intermediate or activated state, in which the atom is halfway between the initial and final positions, has a much higher energy associated with it, and the increase in energy corresponds to the activation energy necessary to move the atom (or the vacancy). The activation energy for diffusion by a vacancy mechanism is the sum of the energy required to form a vacancy, ΔH_v, (see Sect. 10.3) and that required to move a vacancy from one equilibrium position to another, ΔH_m. That is, diffusion by this mechanism depends not only on the motion of vacancies (and the corresponding motion of atoms) but also on the fraction of vacant sites present.

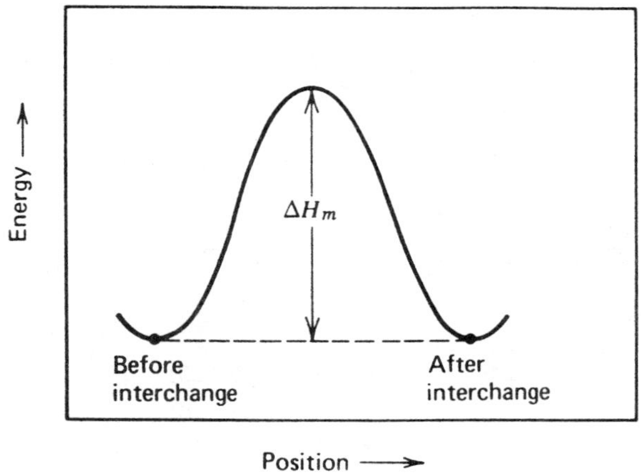

FIGURE 12.5 The energy associated with motion of atoms by a vacancy mechanism (see Fig. 12.4*a*). Halfway between equilibrium positions, the energy of an atom is greatest. ΔH_m represents the activation energy for such atomic motion.

A self-interstitial is more mobile than a vacancy in that a smaller activation energy for motion is encountered as the self-interstitial atom moves to an equilibrium atomic position and simultaneously displaces a neighboring atom into an interstitial site. Nevertheless, the equilibrium number of self-interstitial atoms present at any temperature is negligible in comparison to the number of vacancies, and the activation energy for diffusion by a self-interstitial mechanism (Fig. 12.4*b*) is much higher than that for a vacancy mechanism because the energy to form a self-interstitial is extremely large. Similarly, a direct interchange mechanism (Fig. 12.4*c*), which does not depend upon defects, is untenable because an exceptionally high activation energy would be required.

In alloys where solute atoms are sufficiently small in comparison with host atoms such that the former occupy interstitial sites, the interstitial mechanism predominates for interdiffusion. Thus, hydrogen, carbon, nitrogen, and oxygen diffuse interstitially in most metals, and the activation energy for diffusion is only that associated with motion since the number of unoccupied, adjacent interstitial sites usually is large. As a consequence, interstitial solute atoms diffuse much more rapidly than do substitutional solute atoms in metals.

For volume self-diffusion in a metal, the diffusivity or diffusion coefficient, which provides a measure of the rate at which diffusion occurs, is given by

$$D = D_0 e^{-(\Delta H_v + \Delta H_m)/RT} \tag{12.1a}$$

where D_0 is an experimental constant depending on the metal and $\Delta H_v + \Delta H_m$ is the activation energy for diffusion. In general, the diffusivity can be expressed as

$$D = D_0 e^{-Q/RT} \tag{12.1b}$$

TABLE 12.1 Activation Energies (in kcal/mol)[a] for Diffusion in Metals and Alloys

Increasing Melting Point of Diffusing Substance ⟶ (columns); *Increasing Melting Point of Solvent* ↓ (rows)

Solvent \ *Diffusing Substance*	Hg	Sn	Tl	Zn	Ag	Au	Cu	Mn	Ni	Co	Fe	Cr	Nb
Al				31				29					
Ag	38	39	38	42	$\underline{44}$	48	46		55	60	49		
Au	37				40	$\underline{42}$			42	42			
Cu	44		43	46	47	50	$\underline{48}$	44	57	55	51		
Ni						65	61		$\underline{70}$		55	65	
α-Fe (bcc)						62			59	65	$\underline{57}$		
β-Ti (bcc)		69						65	60	61	61	66	70

Underlined activation energy values are for self-diffusion.

[a] 1 kcal/mol = 4.184 kJ/mol.

Table 12.1 lists some experimentally determined values of the activation energy for diffusion, Q, for several metals and alloys. In self-diffusion, it should be noted (problem 12.9) that Q increases with increasing melting point, indicating that the bonding energy between atoms strongly influences the rate at which diffusion occurs.

12.3 VOLUME DIFFUSION IN IONIC AND COVALENT SOLIDS

Diffusion in most ionic solids occurs by a vacancy mechanism. As a rule, the large anion can move only if anion vacancies are present, and the smaller cation, while in an interstitial position *with respect to the anions*, can diffuse only if cation vacancies are present. However, in certain open crystal structures, such as that of fluorite (CaF_2) or UO_2, anion diffusion does occur by an interstitial mechanism. Imperfections in ionic materials that influence diffusion (see Sects. 10.2 and 10.3) arise in two ways: (1) intrinsic point defects, such as Schottky and Frenkel defects, whose number depends upon temperature, and (2) extrinsic point defects, whose presence is due to impurity ions of different valence than the host ions. The former give rise to a temperature dependence of diffusion similar to that for self-diffusion in metals, and the latter result in a temperature dependence of diffusion which is similar to that for interstitial solute diffusion in metals.

The diffusivity of Na^+ cations in pure NaCl is comparable to self-diffusivities found in metals because Schottky defects are formed relatively easily in NaCl. In extremely pure stoichiometric metal oxides, on the other hand, the energy associated with intrinsic point defects is so high that their concentration becomes sufficient for significant diffusion only at very high temperatures (Table 12.2). A small

TABLE 12.2 Activation Energies for Diffusion in Some Ionic Materials

Diffuser	*Q (kcal/mol)*[a]
Fe in FeO	23
Na in NaCl	41
O in UO_2	36
U in UO_2	76
Co in CoO	25
Fe in Fe_3O_4	48
Cr in $NiCr_2O_4$	76
Ni in $NiCr_2O_4$	65
O in $NiCr_2O_4$	54
Mg in MgO	83
Ca in CaO	77

[a] 1 kcal/mol = 4.184 kJ/mol.

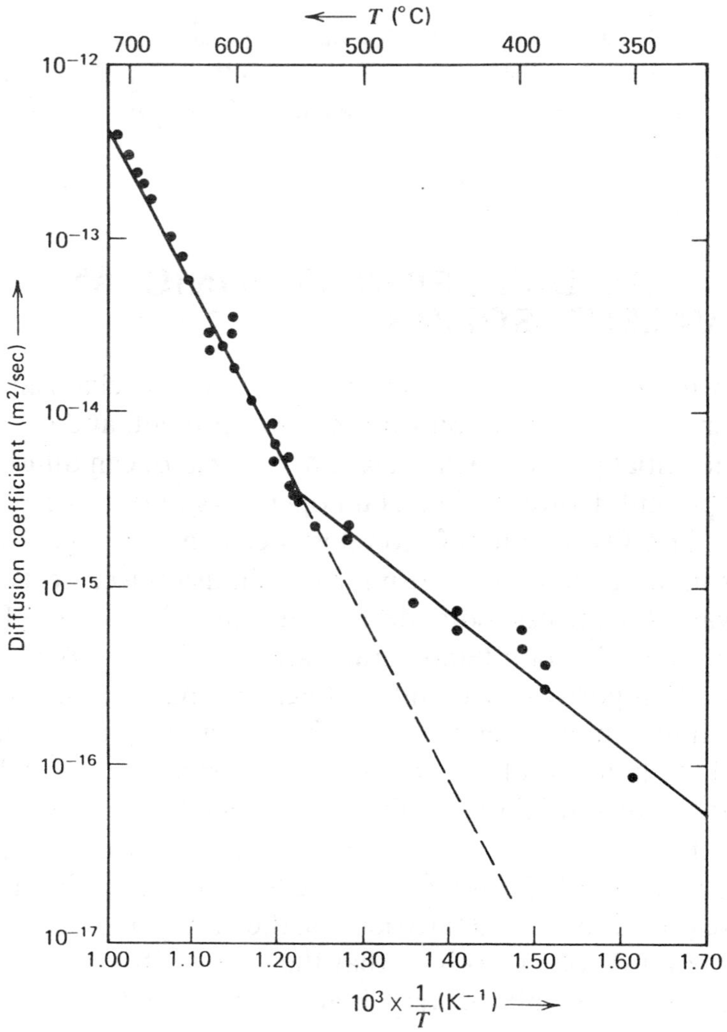

FIGURE 12.6 Self-diffusion coefficient of Na^+ in NaCl containing a small amount of dissolved $CdCl_2$. At high temperatures, the number of Na^+ vacancies associated with Schottky defects is much larger than the number associated with Cd^{2+} ions, and intrinsic diffusion dominates. At low temperatures, the reverse is true, and the vacancies resulting from the presence of Cd^{2+} ions enhance the diffusion of Na^+ ions. The extrapolated dotted line represents the diffusivity of Na^+ ions in the absence of Cd^{2+} ions. [After D. E. Mapother, H. N. Crooks, and R. J. Maurer, *J. Chem. Phys., 18,* 1231 (1950).]

amount of impurities can greatly enhance diffusion at moderate temperatures. An experimental example of this effect is provided by NaCl containing a trace of Cd^{2+} as an impurity (Fig. 12.6). At low temperatures where the number of Na^+ cation vacancies equals the number of Cd^{2+} cation impurities, the activation energy for Na^+ diffusion is associated with motion alone and the diffusivity is proportional to the impurity content. At high temperatures, the activation energy for Na^+ diffusion is larger since it involves the formation of Schottky defects in addition to the motion of Na^+ cations. It is of interest to note that the electrical conductivity of an ionic solid is directly related to the diffusion coefficient because ions are the charge carriers and electrical conduction corresponds to preferential ionic diffusion because of an applied voltage. For such materials, diffusivities can be obtained from electrical conductivity measurements.

Although most covalent solids have relatively open crystal structures (due to directional bonding) and thus larger sites for self-interstitials than metals and most ionic solids, the vacancy mechanism still predominates for self-diffusion and interdiffusion. In the diamond cubic structure (Fig. 3.2), for example, the self-interstitial sites have about the same volume as the atomic sites. Nevertheless, self-interstitials are unfavorable energetically because the covalent bond geometry of directed bonding orbitals cannot be fulfilled. Because of the directional bonding, the activation energies for self-diffusion in covalent solids generally are higher than in metals with comparable melting temperatures; Q for self-diffusion in germanium, for example, is 290 kJ/mol (69 kcal/mol) as compared to 186 kJ/mol (44 kcal/mol) for self-diffusion in silver, even though the melting points of Ag and Ge are within several degrees Celsius of each other.

12.4 OTHER TYPES OF DIFFUSION

In addition to diffusion through the bulk of a solid, atoms may migrate along external or internal paths that afford lower energy barriers to motion. Thus, diffusion can occur along dislocations, grain boundaries, or external surfaces. The rates of diffusion along such *short-circuit* paths are significantly higher than for volume diffusion since the associated activation energies are much lower than for volume diffusion. It is physically plausible that atoms should be most mobile on a free surface, and the atomic disarray at internal line or surface defects also results in relatively high atomic mobility. Nevertheless, most cases of mass transport are due to volume diffusion because the effective cross-sectional areas encountered in short-circuit processes are much smaller than those for volume diffusion. Exceptions to this general rule do occur, however. In fine-grained metals at relatively low temperatures, grain boundary diffusion is more important than volume diffusion (Fig. 12.7). This is so because grain boundary diffusivity, with a lower activation energy, varies less with temperature than does volume diffusivity,

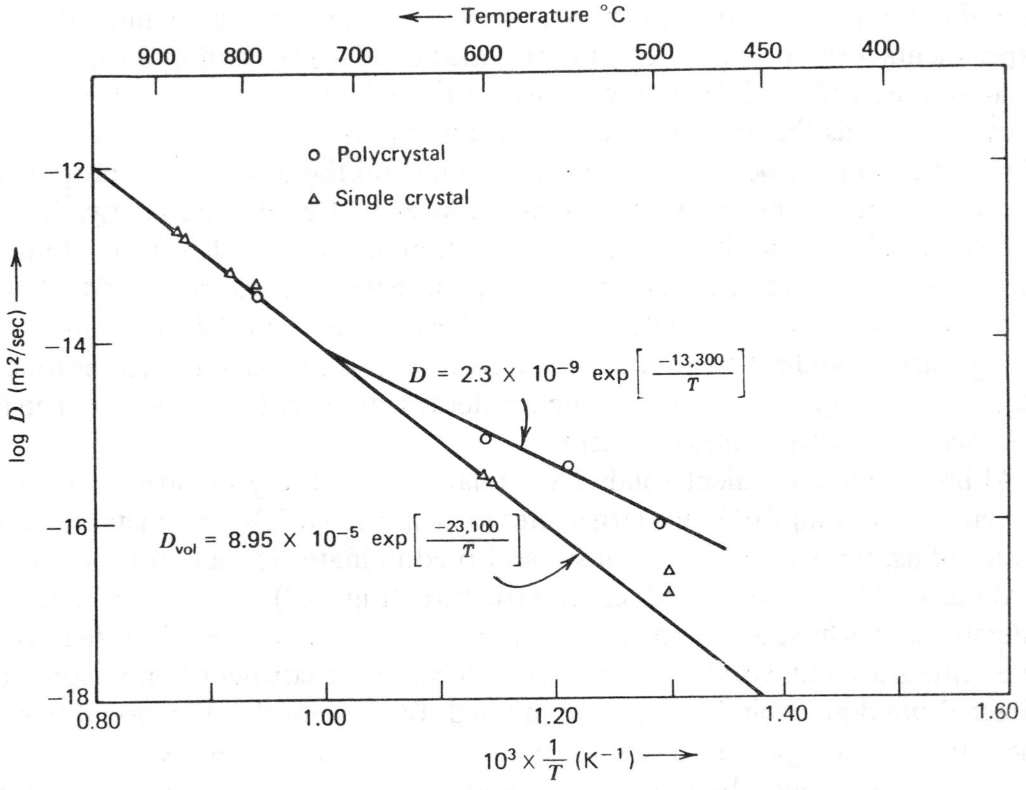

FIGURE 12.7 Self-diffusion coefficient in single and polycrystalline silver. At low temperatures, diffusion is faster in the polycrystalline material because the grain boundaries act as "short-circuit" paths for atomic motion. The activation energy is lower for grain boundary diffusion than it is for volume diffusion, which predominates at high temperatures. (Reproduced by permission from *Atom Movements,* American Society for Metals, 1951.)

with a higher activation energy. Furthermore, in certain powder processes involving sintering of metals or ceramics, the high surface-to-volume ratio of fine powder particles favors surface diffusion.

12.5 DIFFUSION IN NONCRYSTALLINE SOLIDS

Long-chain polymers, which are characterized by strong covalent bonds within molecules and weaker secondary bonds between molecules, exhibit sluggish diffusion because of their large molecular size. Self-diffusion in such materials involves the motion of molecular chain segments and is closely related to their viscous flow behavior. A greater degree of polymerization, with correspondingly larger molecules, results in lower diffusion rates. This can be observed experimentally when a polymer is dissolved in a solvent and interdiffusion is studied.

The more technologically important case of diffusion in polymers is that of foreign molecules, for this relates to the permeability and absorption characteristics displayed by polymers. During absorption, smaller molecules enter into the polymer causing swelling and, perhaps, chemical reactions, both of which can alter mechanical and physical properties. During permeation, smaller molecules diffuse through the polymer. Small molecules diffuse much more rapidly than do larger molecules, and only those atoms and molecules that are soluble yet remain essentially inert with respect to the polymer can diffuse readily. The diffusion path is almost invariably through noncrystalline regions within the polymer since crystalline regions present a much larger barrier to the migration of small foreign molecules. The rate of diffusion depends not only on the diffusing species but also on the state of the polymer. Below the glass transition temperature, diffusion is much less rapid than above it.

Somewhat analogous considerations hold for diffusion in inorganic glasses. In silicate glasses, the silicon atoms are so strongly bonded to their oxygen neighbors that their diffusivity remains low even at high temperatures, where the SiO_4 unit actually migrates. The rather large holes in the silicate network allow small atoms such as hydrogen or helium to permeate through glass quite readily. In addition, their chemical inertness with respect to the constituents of glass enhances their diffusivity. Such considerations explain the apparent *transparency* of glass to hydrogen and helium atoms and indicate the limited usefulness of glass for certain high-vacuum applications. Sodium and potassium ions also diffuse through glass with relative ease because of their small sizes. Their rates of diffusion, however, are considerably lower than those for hydrogen and helium since the cations experience a peripheral electrostatic attraction to the oxygen atoms in the Si—O network. This interaction is, nevertheless, much less restrictive than that sustained by silicon atoms.

12.6 MATHEMATICAL DESCRIPTION OF DIFFUSION

Diffusional processes can be classified as steady state or nonsteady state. In steady state diffusion the net number of atoms crossing a unit area perpendicular to a given direction per unit time is constant with time. In nonsteady state diffusion this quantity, called the flux, varies with time. Steady state diffusion is described by Fick's first law, which states that the flux, J, is proportional to the concentration gradient and the diffusion coefficient. For the one-dimensional case illustrated in Fig. 12.8, Fick's first law is given by

$$J_x = -D\frac{\Delta c}{\Delta x} = -D\frac{dc}{dx} \tag{12.2}$$

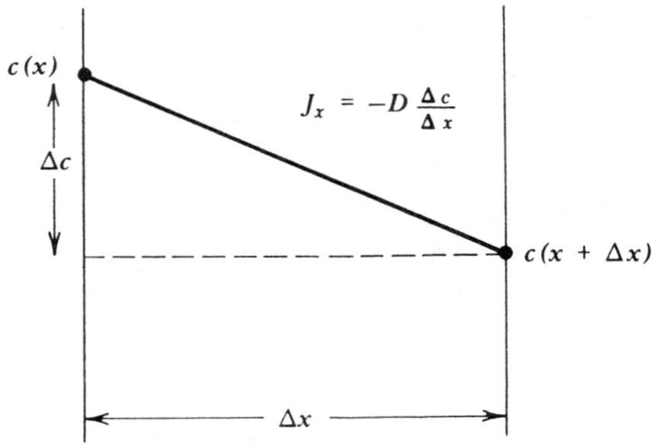

FIGURE 12.8 Steady state diffusion. If the concentration profile of the diffusing species remains constant with time, then steady state diffusion will occur. For the linear concentration gradient illustrated, the net number of atoms of the diffusing species that crosses a unit area per unit time (i.e., the flux) is given by Fick's first law, $J_x = -D\Delta c/\Delta x$. According to Fick's first law, atoms diffuse down a concentration gradient.

where $\Delta c/\Delta x$ (or dc/dx) is the concentration gradient. For diffusion considerations, convenient concentration units are atoms/cm^3 or g/cm^3 (either referred to one atomic species, for example, B atoms/cm^3), and the corresponding flux units are atoms/cm$^2 \cdot$ sec or g/cm$^2 \cdot$ sec, respectively. In both cases, the diffusion coefficient D has units of cm^2/sec. Equation 12.2 indicates that atoms tend to flow *down* a chemical concentration gradient. Equations analogous to Eq. 12.2 are used to describe steady state heat fluxes due to temperature gradients and steady state electrical currents due to electric fields (or potential gradients). An example of steady state diffusion is provided by the permeation of hydrogen atoms through a sheet of palladium with different imposed hydrogen gas pressures on either side of the slab. This process can be used to purify hydrogen gas since palladium is impermeable to other gases such as nitrogen, oxygen, and water vapor.

Most interesting cases of diffusion are not steady state, since the concentration at a given position changes with time and, therefore, the flux changes with time also. To treat such situations, a mass balance is applied to the diffusing species, and this gives rise to Fick's second law, which is used to analyze nonsteady state diffusion. In one dimension, Fick's second law is expressed as:

$$\frac{dc}{dt} = \frac{d}{dx}\left(D\frac{dc}{dx}\right) \tag{12.3}$$

where dc/dt is the time rate of change of concentration at a particular position x. If D is assumed to be constant (i.e., independent of concentration), then Fick's second law becomes

$$\frac{dc}{dt} = D\frac{d^2c}{dx^2} \tag{12.4}$$

Solutions to this equation have been obtained for a large number of boundary conditions and initial conditions. For example, in the case of a radioactive tracer deposited on the surface of a metal, the solution to Eq. 12.4 gives the concentration of the radioactive species in the originally nonradioactive metal as a function of time and position, x, measured from the original interface. Thus, for the particular case illustrated in Fig. 12.3, $c(x, t)$ is given by

$$c(x, t) = \frac{M}{\sqrt{\pi Dt}} e^{-(x^2/4Dt)} \tag{12.5}$$

where M is the mass of radioactive material originally deposited per unit area. When ln $c(x, t)$ is plotted as a function of x^2 after a given diffusion time at a constant heat treatment temperature, the slope equals $-1/4Dt$, and from this D can be determined. Concentration as a function of distance (Eq. 12.5) is plotted for two diffusion times in Fig. 12.9. It is noteworthy that to double the penetration distance effectively requires that the diffusion time be quadrupled. This arises from the exponent $x^2/4Dt$ in Eq. 12.5. It is generally found, regardless of the initial conditions and boundary conditions or of the exact form of the solution to Eq. 12.4, that the ratio x^2/Dt is the important parameter in determining the extent of diffusion. Accordingly, the order of magnitude of the effective diffusion distance in time t is given by $\sqrt{Dt}$, and the order of magnitude of time necessary for diffusion over a distance x is given by x^2/D. Thus, temperature has a large influence on diffusion distance and diffusion time by way of the diffusivity.

Brief comment on interdiffusion in a binary or two-component mixture is warranted because each component may migrate by the same mechanism, yet one component may diffuse more rapidly than the other. In the case of interdiffusion between gold and nickel, for example, gold atoms typically move faster than nickel atoms. One consequence of this is that the interdiffusion coefficient must depend upon the intrinsic diffusivities in binary alloys as well as the relative fractional amounts of each type of atom. For interdiffusion, the diffusion coefficient appearing in the Fick's law expressions (Eqs. 12.2 and 12.3) is actually the interdiffusion coefficient,

$$\tilde{D} = X_B D_A + X_A D_B \tag{12.6}$$

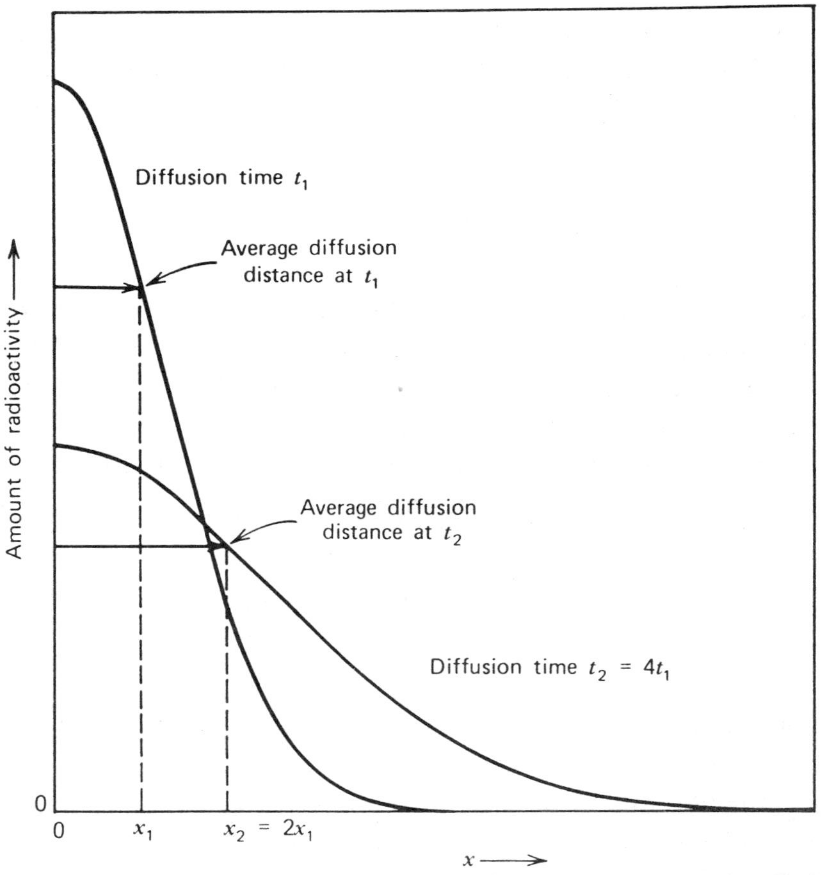

FIGURE 12.9 Solutions to Fick's second law for the self-diffusion experiment shown in Fig. 12.3. In this example of nonsteady state diffusion, it is necessary to quadruple the diffusion time, at a given temperature, in order to double the average diffusion distance of radioactive atoms into the nonradioactive material.

where D_A and D_B are the intrinsic diffusivities associated with the diffusion of A atoms and B atoms, respectively, in an A-B substitutional solid solution, and X_A and X_B are the respective mole fractions. Clearly, if D_A and D_B differ, then $\tilde{D}$ depends on composition. In most actual cases, D_A and D_B also depend on composition. It is important to note that, for interdiffusion in a dilute solution (i.e., $X_A \approx 1$ and $X_B \approx 0$), the intrinsic diffusivity of the dilute component gives the interdiffusion coefficient (i.e., $\tilde{D} \approx D_B$). Similarly, if one component is much more mobile than the other (i.e., $D_B \gg D_A$), this component determines the interdiffusion coefficient in alloys (i.e., $\tilde{D} \approx X_A D_B$, providing $X_A D_B \gg X_B D_A$). In the interdiffusion of an interstitial solute and a metal, each component diffuses by a different mechanism, and the diffusion coefficient in Fick's laws is that of the interstitial, since its diffusivity is so much greater than that of the substitutional atom.

Although Fick's first law (Eq. 12.2) indicates that the driving force for interdiffusion is a concentration gradient, it is more correct to consider the reduction in total free energy as the driving force. This coincides with equalization of the free energy throughout a phase, which corresponds to equalization of concentration. In most cases, elimination of concentration gradients does reduce the free energy; however, in some cases, diffusion occurs up, rather than down, a concentration gradient. Such uphill diffusion can be illustrated by the simple experiment shown in Fig. 12.10, which depicts carbon diffusion in a (Fe-Si)-steel diffusion couple Here, more carbon accumulates on the steel side than would be expected if the concentration gradient were the driving force for diffusion. The presence of dissolved silicon on one side of the couple alters the equilibrium relationships, and, from a free energy point of view, carbon is more welcome in the steel than in the silicon iron.

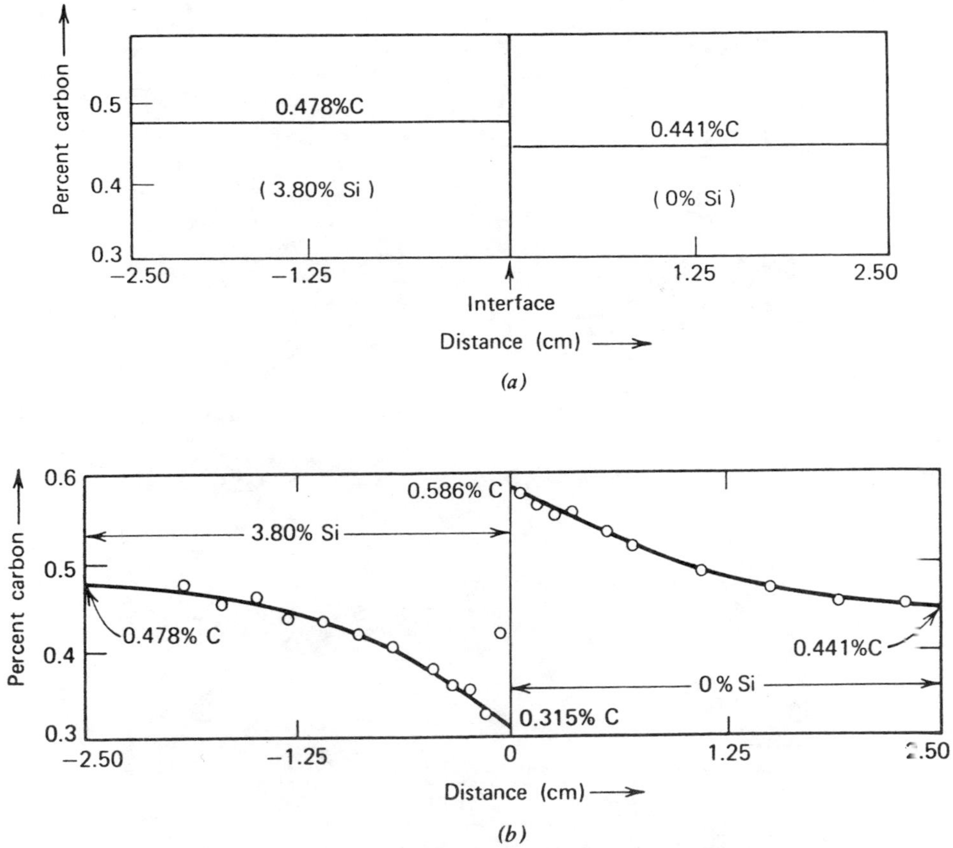

FIGURE 12.10 An example of uphill diffusion. (*a*) The initial carbon distribution is shown for a diffusion couple consisting of a steel with silicon and one without silicon. (*b*) After a diffusion heat treatment at 1050°C for 13 days, carbon has segregated preferentially into the steel that does not contain silicon. Thus, uphill diffusion has occurred. [After L. S. Darken, *Trans. AIME, 180*, 430 (1949).]

12.7 SOLID STATE SINTERING

Interparticle bonding and densification of powder compacts fired in the solid state depend on solid state diffusion. When fine oxide powders are compacted in steel dies at room temperature, between 25 and 60% porosity by volume remains; however, metal powders like copper or silver can deform during compaction and their compacts contain less porosity. A sintering treatment, conducted at elevated temperatures where solid state diffusion proceeds readily, causes pores to become smaller in volume and more spherical in shape. This leads to an increased density of the body (*densification*). The rate of densification increases at higher sintering temperatures because the diffusion coefficient increases.

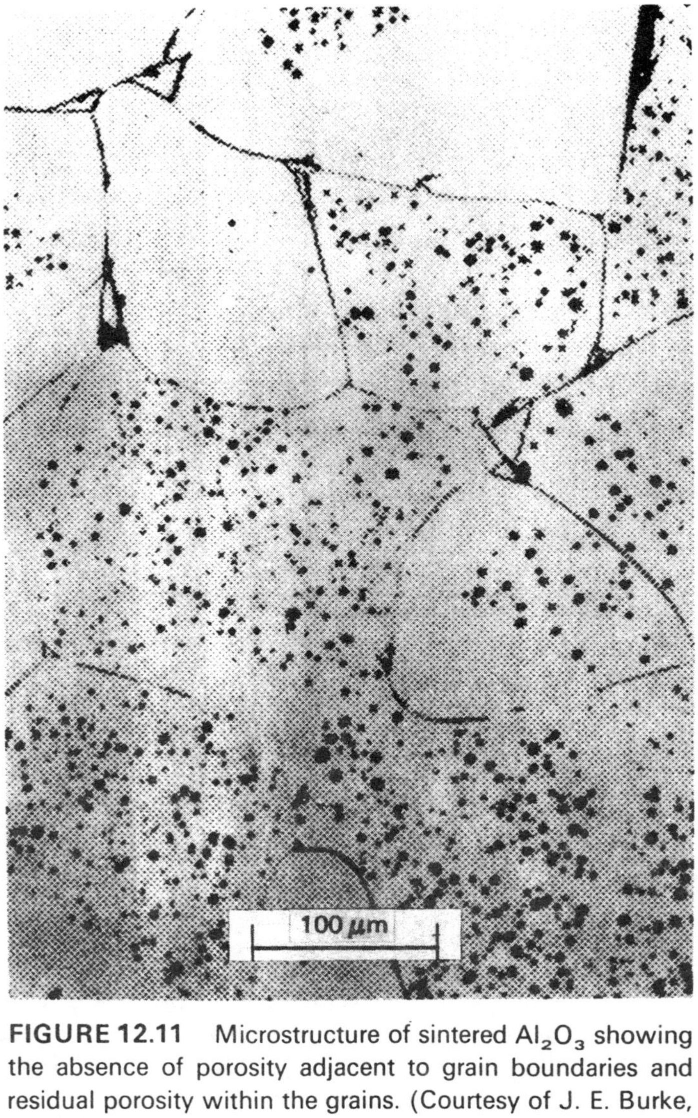

FIGURE 12.11 Microstructure of sintered Al_2O_3 showing the absence of porosity adjacent to grain boundaries and residual porosity within the grains. (Courtesy of J. E. Burke, General Electric Co.)

Although the mechanism of densification during solid state sintering is solid state diffusion, the driving force is the free energy decrease that accompanies the reduction in total surface area (see Sect. 11.8). Thus, for powder compacts of very fine initial particle size, the driving force is large and a high rate of densification can be achieved. Initially, the interparticle interfaces become grain boundaries that serve as sinks for vacancies originating at the pores. As long as grain boundaries intersect each pore, the pore volume decreases fairly rapidly with increasing sintering time. However, when grain growth takes place, grain boundaries move away from pores leaving them trapped within grains, and further densification becomes insignificant because volume diffusion, rather than grain boundary diffusion, must occur. As shown in Fig. 12.11, pure sintered Al_2O_3 has little porosity adjacent to grain boundaries but exhibits considerable porosity in the grain interiors.

Conventionally sintered products usually contain about 5% residual porosity by volume. Since residual porosity adversely affects mechanical strength, it is desirable to achieve complete densification. This requires more expensive processing procedures, however. One technique involves the application of mechanical pressure at the sintering temperature (termed *hot pressing*). Hot pressing is restricted to bodies of relatively simple shape and is limited by die materials. Another technique involves the addition of certain soluble substances that segregate to grain boundaries or the addition of very fine inert particles to the starting powder. These serve to inhibit grain boundary motion and, thus, restrict grain growth so that a fully dense, porefree, and fine-grained solid is produced by sintering.

REFERENCES

1. Girifalco, L. A. *Atomic Migration in Crystals*, Blaisdell, New York, 1964.
2. Shewmon, P. G. *Diffusion in Solids*, McGraw-Hill, New York, 1963.

QUESTIONS AND PROBLEMS

12.1 Calculate the diffusion coefficient for self-diffusion in copper at 1000°C if $Q = 48{,}000$ cal/mol and $D_0 = 0.2$ cm^2/sec.

12.2 Consider a *random walk* problem by assuming a forward step is taken every time you throw a head in a head-tails process and a backward step every time a tail is thrown. Assume one second lapses for every time a step is taken. Take a coin and throw 20 flips and determine where you have walked to after 20 seconds, that is, if 11 heads and 9 tails are thrown your distance is +2, if 8 heads and 12 tails are thrown your distance is −4. Repeat this for a total of 200 flips and after each 20 flips determine your new position, $\bar{x}$. After you are all through plot the position, $(\bar{x})^2$ versus time. Do your results approximate a straight line? Such an experiment reveals the random nature of diffusion and illustrates how an atom wanders about in a crystal.

12.3 The diffusivities of carbon in α iron (bcc) and γ iron (fcc) are given by

$$D = 0.0079 \exp\left[-\frac{20{,}000 \text{ cal/mol}}{RT}\right] \text{cm}^2/\text{sec}$$

$$D = 0.21 \exp\left[-\frac{33{,}800 \text{ cal/mol}}{RT}\right] \text{cm}^2/\text{sec}$$

Calculate the respective diffusion coefficients at 800°C and explain the difference.

12.4 Make a schematic plot of ln D vs. $1/T$ for volume diffusion and grain boundary diffusion assuming $Q_{gb} \cong \frac{1}{2}Q_{\text{vol}}$. At which temperature regimes does grain boundary diffusion predominate over volume diffusion. (Your answer illustrates the general principle that high activation energy processes dominate at high temperatures and low activation energy ones at low temperatures.)

12.5 By considering a mass balance per unit time in a slab of thickness Δx and recognizing that the input of atoms per unit time per unit area is $J(x)$ and the corresponding output is $J(x + \Delta x) = J(x) + dJ/dx \cdot \Delta x$, derive Fick's second law.

12.6 Explain why, in Fig. 12.10*b*, there has been little or no net transfer of silicon from the left-hand side of the diffusion couple to the right-hand side. Sketch what you expect the concentration of silicon and carbon to be after diffusing for a very long time at 1200°C.

12.7 The diffusivity of hydrogen in fcc iron is three orders of magnitude greater than that of carbon in fcc iron at 1100 C. Explain.

12.8 What is the thermodynamic driving force for the mixing of gases illustrated in Fig. 12.1? For the mixing of radioactive and nonradioactive metals in Fig. 12.3?

12.9 Using the activation energies for self-diffusion in Table 12.1 and those supplied below, plot activation energy for diffusion vs. melting temperature in K. Discuss your results. *Data*: Self-diffusion activation energies (kcal/mol): Na(10), Nb(105), Cd(19), Pb(24), Cr(73), Ge(69), Co(68).

12.10 The activation energies for carbon, nitrogen, and hydrogen diffusion in bcc iron are 20, 18, and 3 kcal/mol, respectively. Explain the variation.

12.11 The activation energies for diffusion of Co in CoO and Fe in FeO are anomalously low (Table 12.2). Explain why. (*Hint*. Both Fe and Co are multivalent.)

16

Phase Diagrams

An understanding of phase equilibria and of ways to represent phase equilibria is very important for comprehending many materials systems. In this chapter maps are used to indicate the phases present in a material at equilibrium.

16.1 SINGLE COMPONENT SUBSTANCES

A pure substance, under equilibrium conditions, may exist as vapor, liquid, or crystalline solid, depending upon the conditions of temperature and pressure. Phase diagrams provide a convenient way of representing which state of aggregation is stable for a particular set of conditions. Moreover, a phase diagram is a map that shows which *phase* is stable and not just the state of aggregation. It is useful, at this point, to recall that a phase is a structurally homogeneous portion of matter. There is only one vapor phase no matter how many constituents make it up. Similarly, for a pure substance, there is only one liquid phase; however, there may be more than one solid phase (i.e., allotropes or polymorphs) because of differences in crystal structure.

Pure substances such as H_2O, NaCl, CH_4, and Cu all may be regarded as one-component substances. A phase diagram for a pure substance, called a unary equilibrium diagram, shows which phases exist as a function of temperature and pressure. A portion of the unary phase diagram for H_2O (Fig. 16.1*a*) indicates that at 1 atm pressure ice is stable below 0°C ,water is stable between 0°C and 100°C, and vapor is stable above 100°C. The temperatures separating the single-phase regions are fixed points (i.e., invariants) at a given pressure, and they represent the

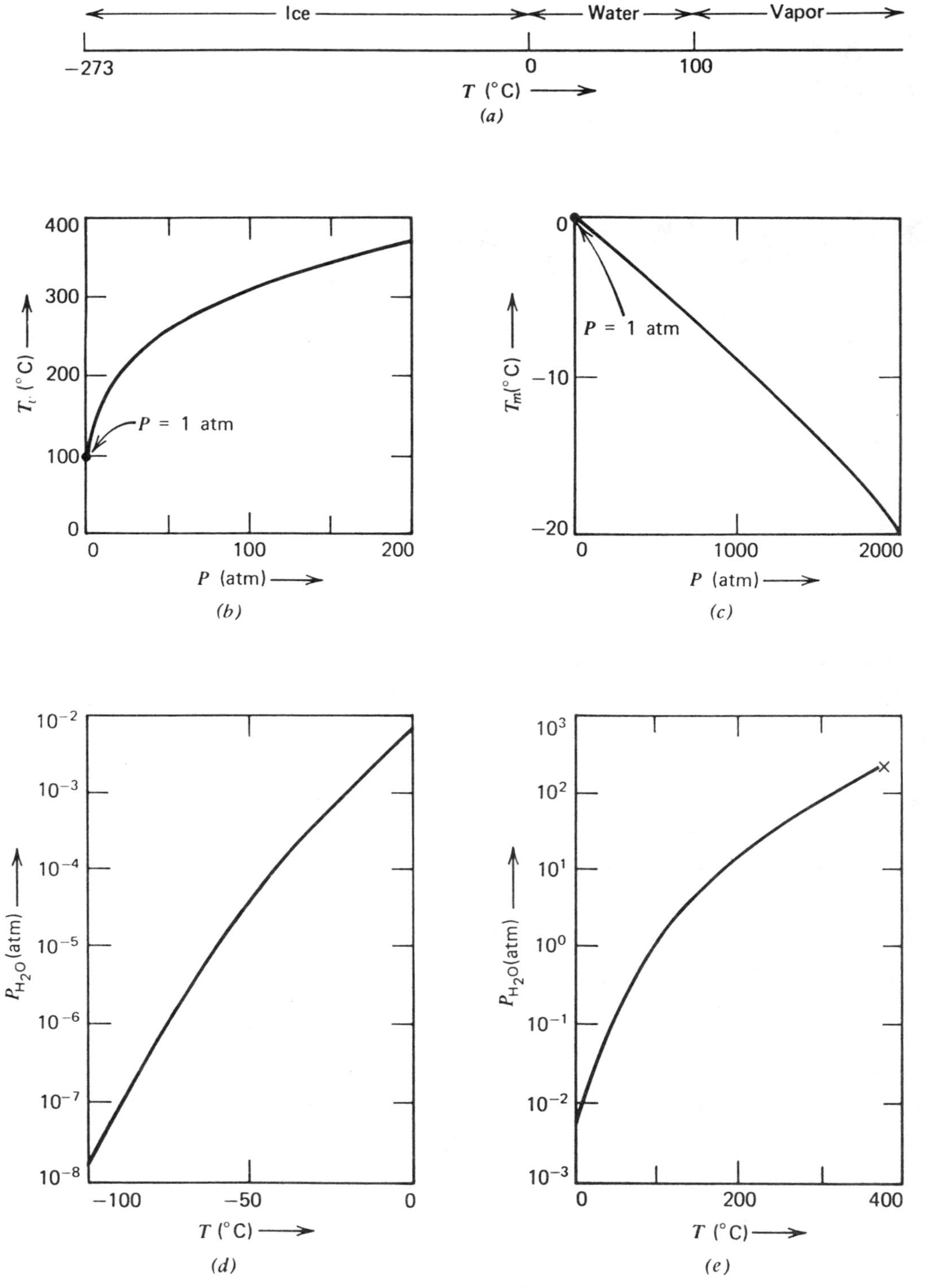

FIGURE 16.1 Phase relationships for H_2O. (*a*) At a pressure of 1 atm, ice, water, and vapor are stable over different temperature ranges. (*b*) The boiling point of water is a function of pressure. (*c*) The melting point of ice is a function of pressure. (*d*) The vapor pressure of ice is a function of temperature. (*e*) The vapor pressure of water is a function of temperature.

conditions of two-phase coexistence. Thus, ice and water coexist in equilibrium at 0°C and 1 atm, and water and vapor coexist in equilibrium at 100°C and 1 atm; at either point, the free energies of the two coexisting phases are equal (see Fig. 1.6).

It is well-known that the boiling point of water increases with increasing pressure (Fig. 16.1*b*); also, the melting point of ice decreases with increasing pressure (Fig. 16.1*c*). Similarly, water will vaporize or ice will sublimate if pressure is reduced sufficiently (i.e., so as to reach the vapor pressure of the phase) at a given temperature (Figs. 16.1*d* and *e*). All of the above are features of the *T–P* diagram for H_2O (Fig. 16.2), which is a unary phase diagram having temperature and pressure as variables. In such a diagram there are single-phase fields where one phase has the lowest free energy, lines along which two phases coexist (i.e., bounda-

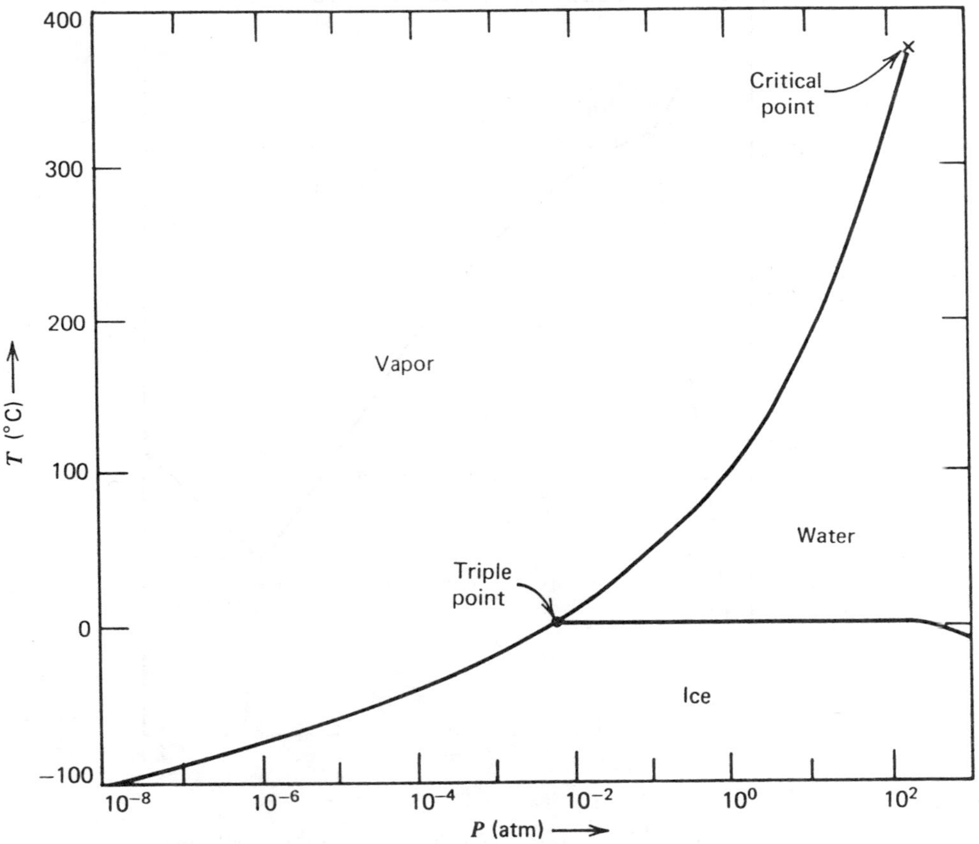

FIGURE 16.2 The *T–P* diagram for H_2O. The equilibrium unary phase diagram, as a function of temperature and pressure, incorporates the separate information presented in Fig. 16.1. Boundaries between single-phase fields represent two-phase coexistence. For example, the boiling point of water as a function of pressure (which is identical to the vapor pressure of water as a function of temperature) separates the liquid (i.e., water) and vapor fields. This boundary terminates at critical values of temperature and pressure (i.e., the critical point), above which liquid can be converted to vapor or vice versa without a distinct or sharp change in phase being observed.

ries between single-phase fields) where two phases have the same free energy, and one or more distinct points at which three phases coexist. These triple points are said to be invariants of the system, for each occurs at a definite, fixed combination of temperature and pressure for a given substance. Triple points provide absolute reference values for both temperature and pressure.

At moderate and low pressures, other one-component substances possess unary phase diagrams which are qualitatively similar to that for water; however, the melting point of most substances increases as pressure increases because most solids are more dense than their liquids. Melting temperature as a function of pressure and vapor pressure as a function of temperature (or, equivalently, sublimation temperature as a function of pressure) represent the extreme limits of

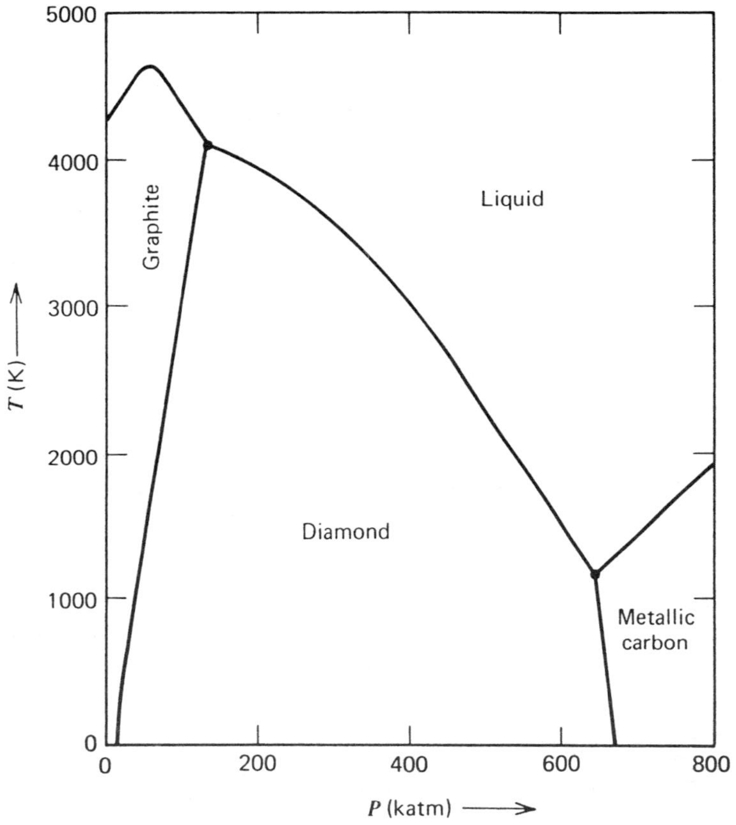

FIGURE 16.3 Unary phase diagram for carbon. At normal pressures graphite is the stable solid phase; at high pressures diamond is the stable solid phase. Thus, production of synthetic diamonds requires very high pressures. Note that metallic carbon can exist only at very high pressures. Phase equilibrium features for normal atmospheric pressure and reduced pressures are not portrayed on this diagram. [After G. C. Suits, *Amer. Scientist,* **52**, 395 (1964). Reproduced by permission, *The American Scientist,* journal of Sigma Xi, the Scientific Research Society of North America.]

usefulness of a crystalline solid for most engineering purposes. That is, if a crystalline solid begins to melt or vaporize, it loses mechanical integrity.

Changes in temperature and pressure can cause allotropic or polymorphic transformations, and such transformations occur at high pressures for many substances. High-pressure phase diagram studies have been rather limited, however, because of difficult experimental conditions. Nevertheless, such studies are important because they provide information about the state of matter in the earth's core and about phases that can be produced only at high pressures. As an example of the latter, Fig. 16.3 shows the unary phase diagram for carbon. It is apparent that graphite is the stable solid phase at atmospheric pressure, whereas diamond is stable at high pressures. Diamond is extremely valuable for cutting tool purposes and for gem purposes because it is very hard; however, its occurrence in nature is rare. Consequently, the current production of synthetic diamonds at high pressures and elevated temperatures represents a significant contribution to technology.

When more than one component is present, phase diagrams become more complex since temperature, pressure, and composition are variables. Because most engineering materials consist of more than one component but are used at pressures near atmospheric pressure, it is important to examine the phase equilibrium relationships that may exist in binary or two-component systems at constant pressure.

16.2 COMPLETE SOLID SOLUBILITY IN BINARY SYSTEMS

An important example of a binary system that exhibits complete solid solubility is that of copper-nickel alloys at 1 atm pressure (Fig. 16.4). The coordinates are temperature and composition, and in this case the latter is expressed as weight percent nickel. It is also common to use atom (or mole) fraction or atomic (or mole) percent as the measure of composition. For most practical purposes, the weight percent of a component is more useful, whereas the atomic percent of a component is more important from a fundamental standpoint. The composition coordinate for the Cu–Ni system (Fig. 16.4) extends from pure Cu on the left to pure Ni on the right.

In a simple view, any phase diagram can be considered as a map. If the alloy composition and temperature are specified, then the phase diagram allows determination of the phase or phases that will be present under equilibrium conditions. In Fig. 16.4, three regions are shown: a solid or α field, a liquid field, and a liquid plus solid two-phase region. If the temperature and composition correspond to point A, the alloy is a single-phase solid; at point B, it is a two-phase mixture of solid and liquid, and at point C, a single-phase liquid. Complete solid

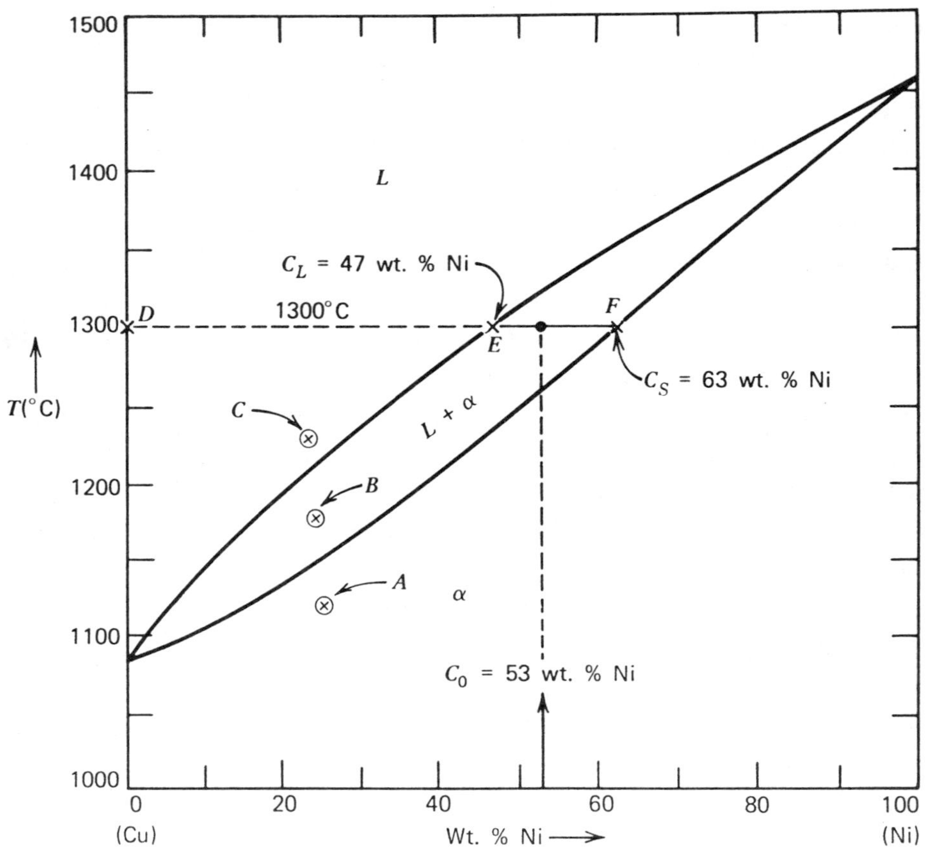

FIGURE 16.4 The copper–nickel binary phase diagram (at $P = 1$ atm). Complete liquid solubility or miscibility and complete solid solubility or miscibility occur because Cu and Ni are compatible elements. Cu–Ni solid solutions melt (or solidify) over a range of temperatures rather than at a fixed temperature. The temperature–composition points A, B, and C correspond to solid, solid and liquid, and liquid, respectively, in equilibrium.

In the experiment described in the text, copper is heated to 1300°C and nickel is slowly added, changing the composition along the line DE. At 1300°C the liquid becomes saturated with nickel when the Ni content reaches 47 wt. % Ni (point E); the addition of more nickel results in the appearance of a solid (α) phase containing 63 wt. % Ni (point F).

solubility is possible only when the two pure components have the same crystal structure and form a substitutional solid solution in all proportions.

The significance of the features of the Cu–Ni phase diagram may be illustrated in part by a simple experiment in which copper is heated above its melting point but below that of pure nickel, say 1300°C. If particles of pure Ni are added little by little to the molten copper, the composition of the resulting liquid alloy changes along the line DE in Fig. 16.4. At 1300°C it is found that Ni dissolves in molten Cu, producing a homogeneous liquid solution until the alloy composition reaches

47 wt. % Ni, whereupon the liquid solution becomes saturated with nickel. Further addition of Ni leads to the formation of a nickel-rich solid solution whose composition differs from that of the saturated liquid solution with which it co-exists. The composition of this solid solution (63 wt. % Ni at 1300°C) is obtained by extending the line *DE* to point *F*, the boundary between the solid and solid plus liquid regions. The above considerations are rather analogous to the dissolution of sugar in hot tea. At a given tea temperature, sugar dissolves up to a certain amount, and addition of more sugar results in a sugar-rich solid that sinks to the bottom of the sugar-saturated tea.

For the Cu–Ni system at 1300°C, increasing the overall Ni content above 47 wt. % Ni increases the amount of Ni-rich solid and decreases the relative amount of saturated liquid, but the compositions of the two phases, given by the intersections of the isothermal line (tie line) with the boundaries of the two-phase field, remain the same. Since the compositions of the two coexisting phases are fixed at this temperature, it is possible to determine the relative amount of each phase if the alloy composition is known. For example, consider an alloy of composition $C_0 = 53$ wt. % Ni at 1300°C. Letting W_α and W_L be the fractional amounts by weight of solid and liquid, respectively, two conservation of mass equations must be satisfied. First, the sum of the fractional amounts must equal unity,

$$W_\alpha + W_L = 1 \qquad (16.1)$$

since the alloy consists of a two-phase solid plus liquid mixture. Second, the mass of Ni distributed between the two phases must equal the mass of Ni in the overall alloy, and this can be expressed as

$$W_\alpha C_s + W_L C_L = C_0 \qquad (16.2)$$

(Consideration of the mass of Cu would give an identical equation.) Simultaneous solution of Eqs. 16.1 and 16.2 gives the fractional amount of liquid by weight

$$W_L = \frac{C_s - C_0}{C_s - C_L} \qquad (16.3a)$$

and the fractional amount of solid by weight,

$$W_\alpha = \frac{C_0 - C_L}{C_s - C_L} \qquad (16.3b)$$

For the example under consideration ($C_0 = 53$ wt. % Ni, $C_s = 63$ wt. % Ni, and $C_L = 47$ wt. % Ni), we have

$$W_L = \frac{63 - 53}{63 - 47} = 0.625 \tag{16.4}$$

That is, 62.5 % of the alloy mass is liquid, and 37.5 % is solid.

Equations 16.3a and b are referred to as the lever rule equations and can be used to determine the relative amounts of phases present in *any* two-phase region of a binary phase diagram, providing the alloy composition and temperature are known. For example, where two-phase equilibrium exists between phases α and β, the relative amount of α at a designated temperature is obtained by measuring the length of an isothermal line between the alloy composition (C_0) and the *opposite* phase-field boundary (C_β), and then dividing this by the total length of tie line within the two-phase region [i.e., $W_\alpha = (C_\beta - C_0)/(C_\beta - C_\alpha)$].

The type of experiment carried out with Cu and Ni at 1300°C can be repeated at other temperatures between 1084.5°C (T_m for Cu) and 1455°C (T_m for Ni), and a pair of composition points (C_L and C_s), representing the liquid and solid compositions for two-phase equilibrium, will be obtained at each temperature. The curved lines generated by connecting the C_L vs. T points and the C_s vs. T points are called the liquidus and solidus lines, respectively, and are important

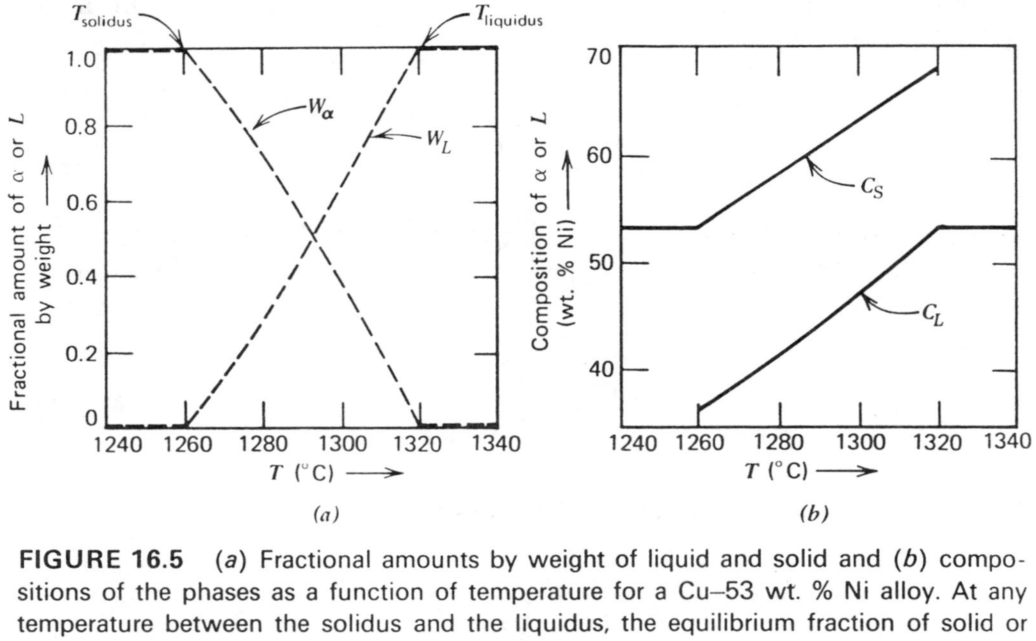

FIGURE 16.5 (*a*) Fractional amounts by weight of liquid and solid and (*b*) compositions of the phases as a function of temperature for a Cu–53 wt. % Ni alloy. At any temperature between the solidus and the liquidus, the equilibrium fraction of solid or liquid can be obtained with the lever rule.

features of the phase diagram since they define the limits of the two-phase region. In addition, the solidus and liquidus lines give the temperatures at which melting starts and is completed, respectively, for an alloy of fixed composition. Thus, if a solid alloy of composition C_0 is heated, melting begins when the solidus temperature for the alloy is reached. The melting process continues, as temperature is raised through the two-phase field, until all solid has been converted to liquid at the liquidus temperature for the alloy. For this binary alloy, the fractional amounts of liquid and solid vary continuously between zero and unity and between unity and zero, respectively, as temperature is raised from the solidus to the liquidus value (Fig. 16.5). This, of course, corresponds to the continuous change in the composition of each coexisting phase, given by the solidus or liquidus line as a function of temperature. The characteristic of melting over a range of temperatures or, conversely, of solidifying over a range of temperatures, which is common in

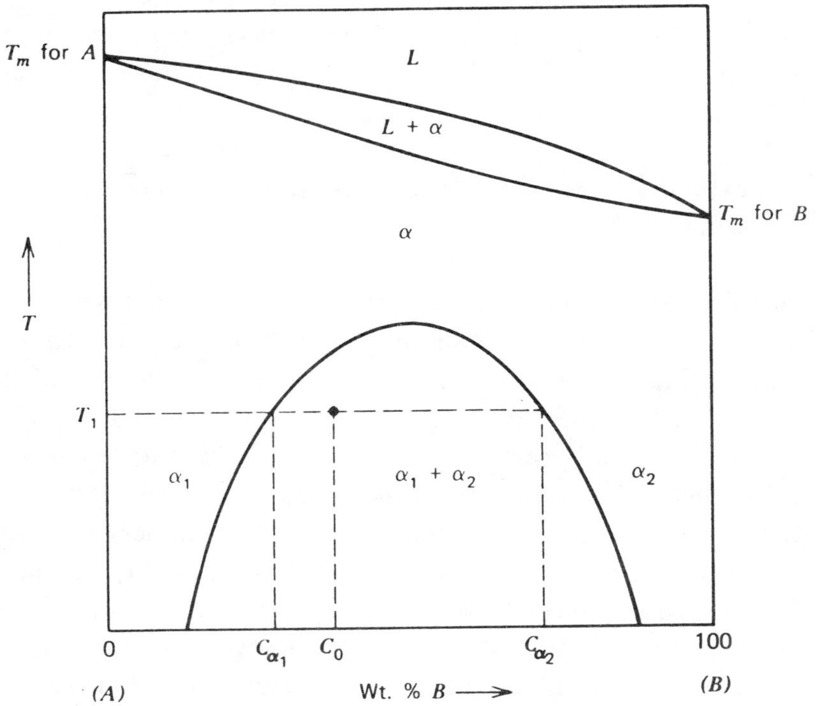

FIGURE 16.6 A solid state miscibility gap in a binary diagram. This diagram is similar to that of Cu–Ni at high temperatures, but on cooling the solid phase separates into two solid phases, α_1 and α_2, having the same crystal structure but different compositions. (Subscripts are used to distinguish between the solid phases in this case.) At temperature T_1, an alloy of composition C_0 consists of two phases coexisting in equilibrium and having compositions C_{α_1} and C_{α_2}. The lever rule can be used to determine the relative amounts of these phases.

binary systems, is quite distinct from the fixed-temperature melting or freezing of a single-component substance.

Cu and Ni exhibit complete solid solubility, but in many alloys only a certain amount of one component can dissolve into the solid form of the other component and vice versa. This is necessarily the case if the two pure components have different crystal structures. Even when they have the same crystal structure, differences in relative atomic size and in chemical nature often lead to limited solid solubility. An example is shown in Fig. 16.6, where complete solid solubility occurs at elevated temperatures, but immiscibility (or a miscibility gap) develops at lower temperatures. Thus, on cooling an alloy of composition C_0, the high-temperature α solid solution separates into two distinct solid phases, designated α_1 and α_2, which have the same crystal structure but different compositions. Since the lever rule may be used in any two-phase region, it is possible to calculate the relative amounts of α_1 and α_2 at a particular temperature. For the alloy C_0 at temperature T_1 (Fig. 16.6), the two coexisting solid phases have compositions C_{α_1} and C_{α_2}, and their fractional amounts by weight are $W_{\alpha_1} = (C_{\alpha_2} - C_0)/(C_{\alpha_2} - C_{\alpha_1})$ and $W_{\alpha_2} = (C_0 - C_{\alpha_1})/(C_{\alpha_2} - C_{\alpha_1})$. Liquid-state miscibility gaps also are found in certain binary systems.

16.3 THERMAL ANALYSIS AND PHASE DIAGRAMS

Before proceeding to other features of binary systems, it is instructive to outline another experimental procedure which, in principle, can be used to determine the boundaries in a binary phase diagram. The hypothetical set of experiments suggested in the previous section could be used to delineate the Cu–Ni phase diagram; however, in actual practice, it is more convenient to utilize an alternative technique called thermal analysis. With reference to Fig. 16.7*a*, consider an alloy of composition C_0 that has been heated well into the single-phase liquid region. After equilibration at the elevated temperature, heat is slowly extracted from the system at a constant rate, and the temperature is measured as a function of time. A typical cooling curve obtained in this manner is shown in Fig. 16.7*b*. The temperature initially decreases with time in an approximately linear manner (see Sect. 1.4) until solidification begins at the liquidus temperature. As liquid is converted to solid during cooling through the two-phase region, evolution of the heat of fusion decreases the rate at which temperature falls as compared to cooling through a single-phase region. This is reflected by a change in slope of the cooling curve at the liquidus temperature. When the solidus temperature is reached, solidification is complete, and the slope of the cooling curve becomes steeper again. Thus, for a given alloy, the liquidus and solidus temperatures can be determined by noting where the cooling curve displays discrete changes in slope.

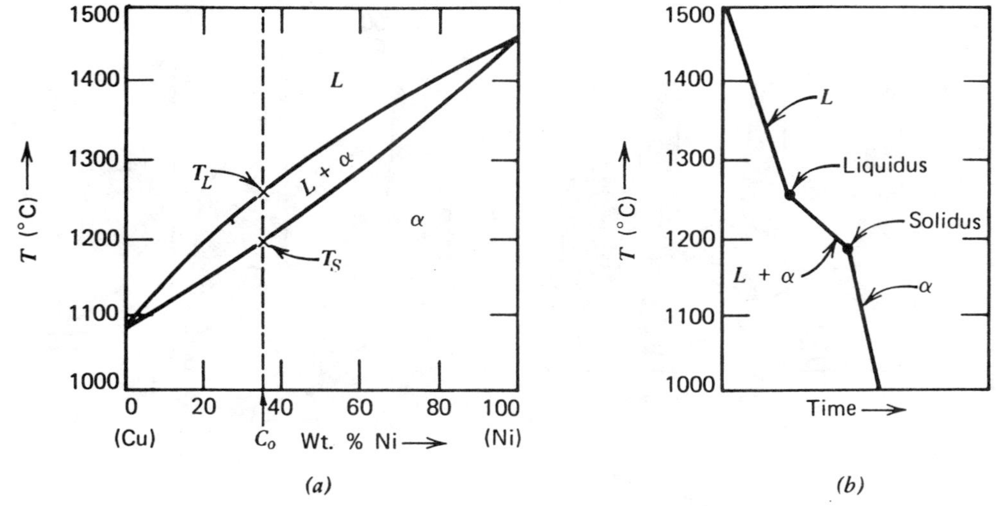

FIGURE 16.7 An alternate way of determining the liquidus and solidus curves. (*a*) An alloy of composition C_0 is heated into the liquid region (to 1500°C), and heat is slowly extracted. (*b*) The cooling curve (temperature vs. time) enables determination of the liquidus and solidus temperatures for this alloy because slope discontinuities occur at these points.

Repetition of this procedure with different alloys enables determination of the complete phase diagram as shown in Fig. 16.8. It should be noted that the liquidus and solidus temperatures coincide at the melting point of a pure component, and a *thermal arrest* results at T_m because liquid and solid can coexist in equilibrium only at this temperature (see Sect. 1.4). Cooling curve thermal arrests can also occur for alloys in many binary systems that are somewhat more complex than those discussed previously.

16.4 BINARY EUTECTIC SYSTEMS

A very large number of two-component substances consist of solid two-phase aggregates rather than a single solid solution phase. An especially important type of phase diagram in which two-phase solids are encountered is a simple eutectic system (Fig. 16.9). In this case, addition of B to pure A results in a substance that melts at temperatures lower than T_m for A, and addition of A to pure B results in decreased melting temperatures as well. Furthermore, there are certain compositions for which complete melting occurs at temperatures less than T_m for either pure component. Such behavior is important in the case of alloys used for soldering or brazing. It is also related to the action of permanent antifreeze when added to water, since the ethylene glycol-water system is a simple eutectic.

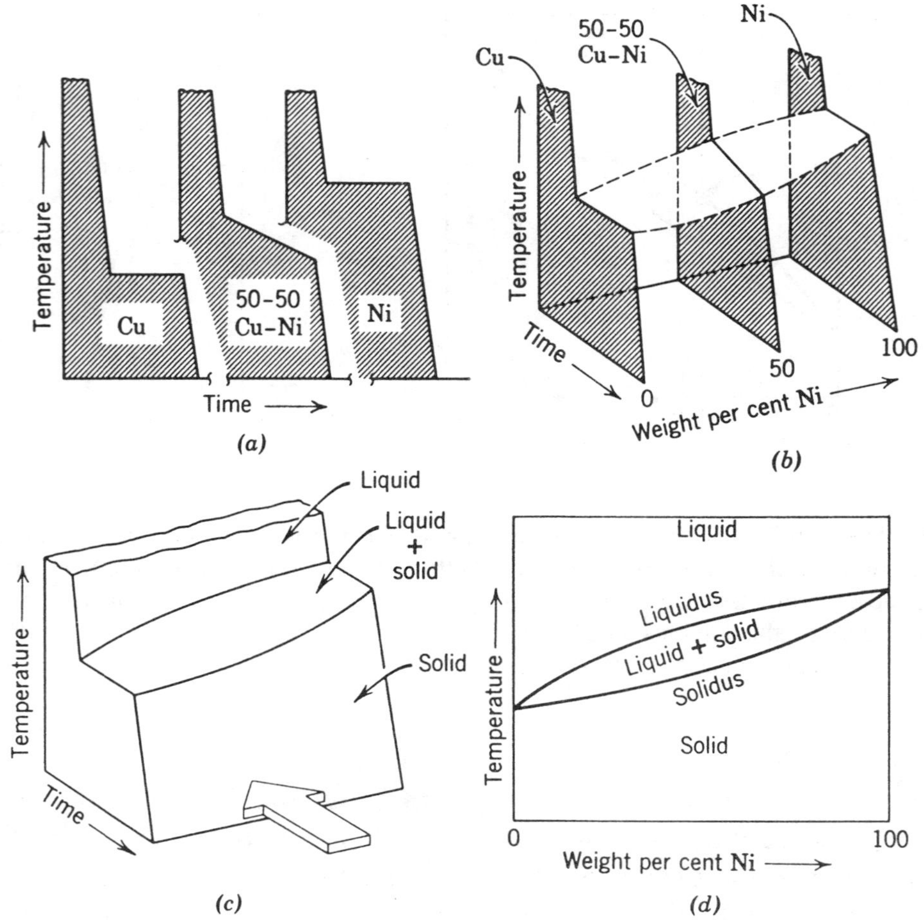

FIGURE 16.8 (*a*) A series of cooling curves for Cu–Ni alloys. (*b*) The cooling curves of (*a*) on time-temperature-composition coordinates. (*c*) The surfaces generated by cooling curves for all possible Cu–Ni alloys. (*d*) The Cu–Ni phase diagram, which is (*c*) viewed in the direction indicated by the arrow. (From *The Structure and Properties of Materials*, Vol. I, by W. G. Moffatt, G. W. Pearsall, and J. Wulff, Wiley, New York, 1964.)

Three different two-phase regions are found in a simple eutectic phase diagram. The unique features of such a diagram, however, are the eutectic temperature, T_E, and the eutectic composition, C_E. The latter corresponds to the composition at which the $L/L + \alpha$ and $L/L + \beta$ liquidus lines intersect with each other and with the horizontal line at T_E, called the eutectic invariant line. Any alloy in equilibrium at the eutectic temperature and having a composition lying on the eutectic invariant line consists of three coexisting phases, and these three phases (α, β, and L) have definite, fixed compositions corresponding to C_{α_E}, C_{β_E}, and C_E, respectively (Fig. 16.9). The compositions of the phases and the temperature for three-phase equilibrium in a binary system at constant pressure are invariants of the system, just as the melting point of a pure substance at constant pressure is invariant.

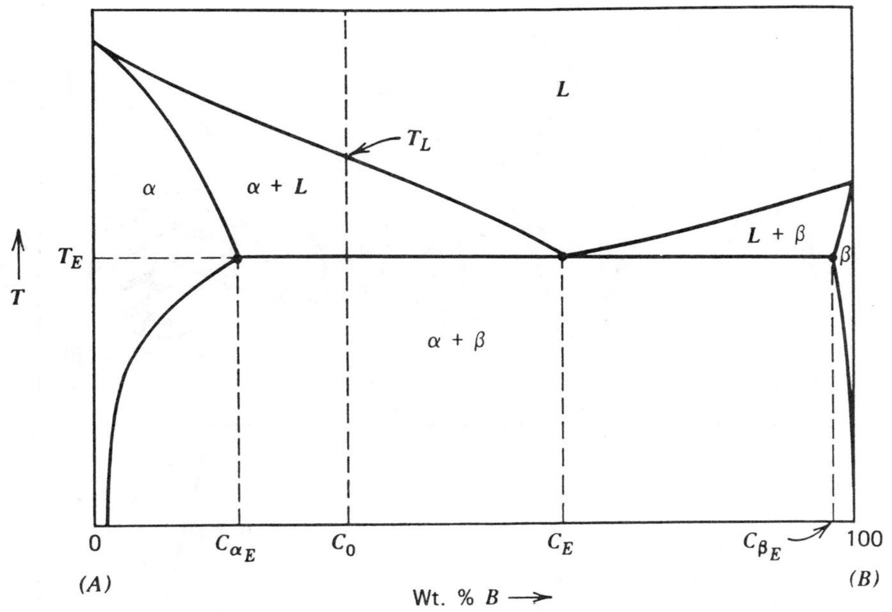

FIGURE 16.9 A hypothetical binary eutectic diagram. This diagram is characterized by limited solubility for each solid phase and by melting point depression with respect to each pure component. The eutectic invariant reaction is the most important feature of this system, and equilibrium coexistence of α, β, and L (having compositions C_{α_E}, C_{β_E}, and C_E) can occur only at the eutectic temperature T_E. Note that melting begins at the eutectic temperature for a wide range of alloy compositions.

A cooling curve for an alloy of the eutectic composition is represented schematically in Fig. 16.10. The form of this curve is identical to that for a pure substance because a thermal arrest occurs at the solidification temperature, T_E; however, the process of solidification differs in these two cases. Note that the alloy is completely liquid at a temperature infinitesimally above T_E but is a solid two-phase mixture of α and β at a temperature infinitesimally below T_E. At the eutectic temperature, solidification proceeds according to the reaction

$$L(C_E) \xrightarrow{\text{cooling at } T_E} \alpha(C_{\alpha_E}) + \beta(C_{\beta_E}) \qquad (16.5)$$

This equation is a shorthand way of representing the eutectic invariant reaction; it specifies that liquid of composition C_E decomposes, on cooling, at T_E into two solid phases (α and β) having compositions C_{α_E} and C_{β_E}. Evolution of heat of fusion accompanies the eutectic reaction, and since the three phases can coexist only at the eutectic temperature, a thermal arrest occurs. On heating, the exact

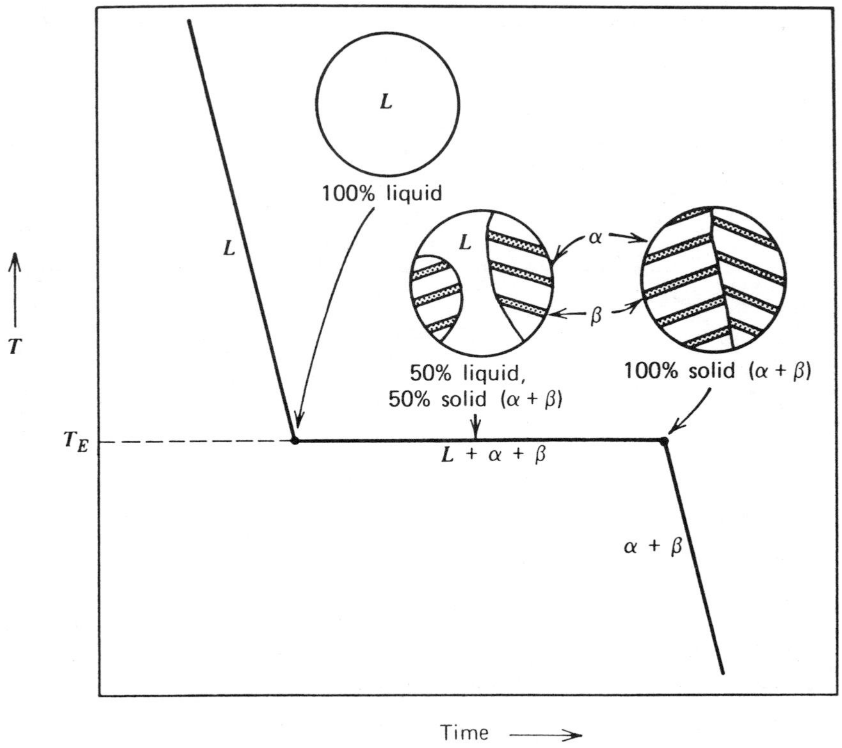

FIGURE 16.10 Cooling curve for the eutectic alloy (composition C_E in Fig. 16.9). A thermal arrest is observed at the eutectic temperature because equilibrium three-phase coexistence can occur only at this temperature. Two distinct solid phases form simultaneously from the liquid, and the heat of fusion that is evolved must be removed isothermally.

opposite occurs, and the solid alloy of composition C_E completely melts at T_E (i.e., Eq. 16.5 proceeds in the reverse direction).

Microstructures of the eutectic alloy before, during, and after solidification are represented schematically in Fig. 16.10. The distribution and morphology of phases in the eutectic solid are of considerable technological importance. Since α and β form simultaneously from the melt, they invariably are intermixed on a very intimate scale. In many eutectics, the arrangement is a lamellar array with alternating layers of α and β, as represented in Fig. 16.10. The intimate two-phase mixture in a eutectic solid is a consequence of the necessity of diffusion during the eutectic reaction, since the three phases involved have different compositions. The interlamellar spacing and the thicknesses of α and β lamellae depend upon cooling rate. A faster solidification rate (i.e., more rapid extraction of heat) imposes a limit on diffusion that results in a finer eutectic structure (i.e., smaller interlamellar spacing).

For alloys with compositions other than C_E, the phase diagram not only provides information about the solidification process but also information about the resulting microstructure. Consider an alloy of composition C_0 such that $C_{\alpha_E} < C_0 < C_E$ (Fig. 16.9). This is called a hypoeutectic alloy. On cooling between the liquidus and eutectic temperatures, the fractional amount of α increases monotonically, and the compositions of α and L follow the solidus and liquidus lines, so that just above T_E the alloy consists of α with composition C_{α_E} and liquid with composition C_E (Fig. 16.9). The relative proportions of α and L in this two-phase mixture are given by

$$W_\alpha = \frac{C_E - C_0}{C_E - C_{\alpha_E}} \tag{16.6a}$$

and

$$W_L = \frac{C_0 - C_{\alpha_E}}{C_E - C_{\alpha_E}} \tag{16.6b}$$

Since the liquid has reached the eutectic composition, it undergoes the eutectic reaction (Eq. 16.5) at T_E. The cooling curve for this hypoeutectic alloy exhibits a slope change at the liquidus temperature and a thermal arrest at T_E (Fig. 16.11). For a fixed mass of alloy, the duration of the thermal arrest varies from a maximum when $C_0 = C_E$ to zero when $C_0 = C_{\alpha_E}$ because the amount of liquid that undergoes the eutectic reaction varies with alloy composition according to Eq. 16.6b.

During the eutectic reaction, any α which had formed above the eutectic temperature, termed proeutectic or primary α, remains unaffected. Thus, the microstructure of a completely solidified hypoeutectic alloy consists of a mixture of primary α and the two-phase $(\alpha + \beta)$ eutectic solid (Fig. 16.11). These morphologically distinct entities (i.e., primary α and eutectic solid), called microconstituents, are important because the properties of a hypoeutectic alloy often depend more upon the relative amounts of microconstituents than upon the relative amounts of phases. In this case, the fractional amounts of the microconstituents are identical to the fractional amounts of the two phases present just prior to the start of the eutectic invariant reaction:

$$W_{\text{primary } \alpha} = \frac{C_E - C_0}{C_E - C_{\alpha_E}} \quad (\equiv W_\alpha \text{ at } T_E + \Delta T) \tag{16.7a}$$

$$W_{\text{eutectic solid}} = \frac{C_0 - C_{\alpha_E}}{C_E - C_{\alpha_E}} \quad (\equiv W_L \text{ at } T_E + \Delta T) \tag{16.7b}$$

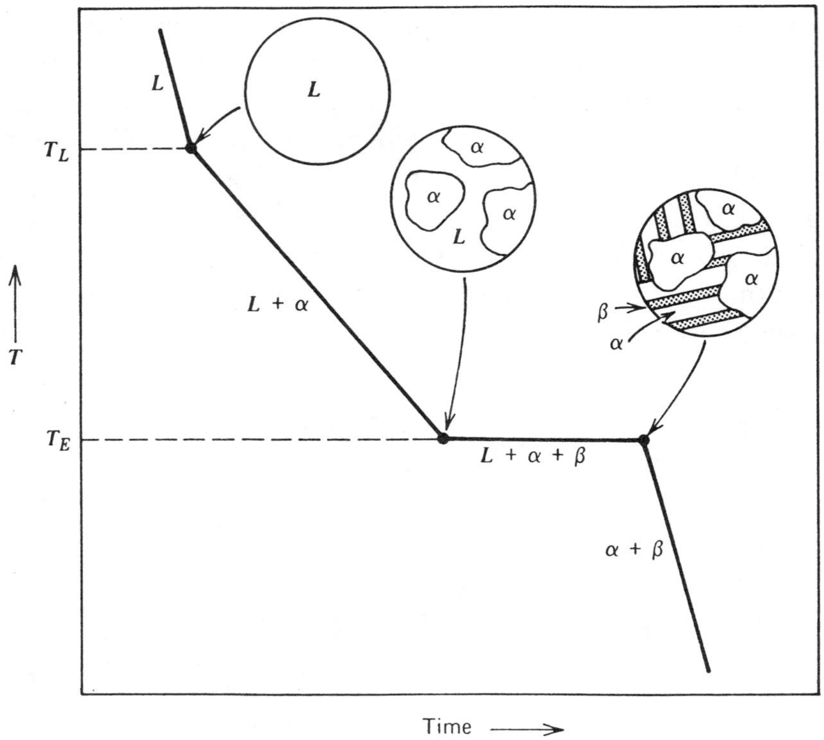

FIGURE 16.11 Cooling curve for a hypoeutectic alloy (composition C_0 in Fig. 16.9). Primary or proeutectic α begins to crystallize at the liquidus temperature where the cooling curve displays a slope change. Just above the eutectic temperature, liquid coexists with a maximum amount of primary α. At the eutectic temperature, this liquid (having the eutectic composition) undergoes the eutectic reaction with a corresponding thermal arrest. Once the eutectic reaction is completed, the solidified alloy consists of a mixture of primary α and eutectic solid, which is a mixture of α and β formed by the eutectic reaction.

On the other hand, the fractional amount of total α in the solid (i.e., primary α plus α in the eutectic solid) is given by

$$W_\alpha = \frac{C_{\beta_E} - C_0}{C_{\beta_E} - C_{\alpha_E}} \tag{16.8}$$

which is obviously greater than the fractional amount of primary α.

For an alloy whose composition lies between C_E and C_{β_E}, termed a hypereutectic alloy, the same considerations discussed above apply, but the final microstructure will contain primary β and eutectic solid as microconstituents. A complete set of thermal analysis experiments with alloys having different compositions facilitates determination of a simple eutectic phase diagram. Typical results and the corresponding phase diagram are shown in Fig. 16.12.

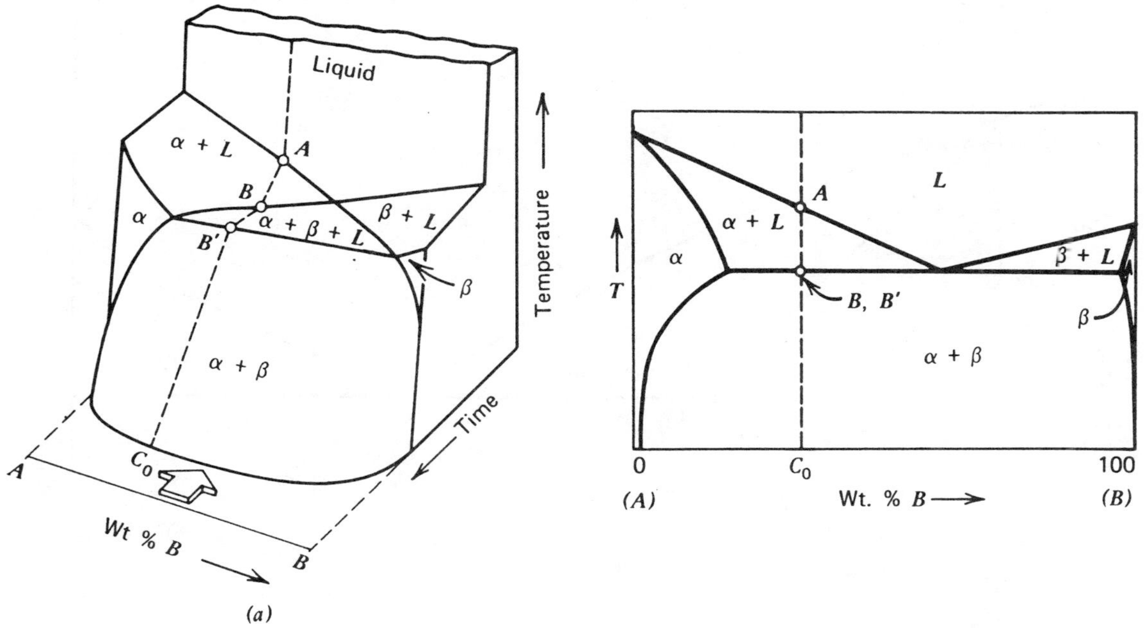

FIGURE 16.12 (*a*) The results of a series of thermal analysis experiments for alloys in the system shown in Fig. 16.9. The cooling curves delineate the liquidus, solidus, and eutectic temperatures as well as the boundaries (solvus lines) between the single-phase solid fields and the two-phase solid regions. The diagram in (*b*) is obtained by viewing (*a*) in the direction noted by the arrow.

16.5 OTHER THREE-PHASE REACTIONS IN BINARY SYSTEMS

The eutectic reaction is but one of a number of possible three-phase invariant reactions in binary systems. In the solid-state analog of a eutectic reaction, called a eutectoid reaction, one solid phase having the eutectoid composition decomposes on cooling to two different solid phases. A particularly important eutectoid reaction occurs in the Fe–Fe_3C system, which is shown in Fig. 16.13. At the eutectoid temperature (723°C), the fcc γ phase (austenite) decomposes on cooling to form the bcc α phase (ferrite) and Fe_3C (cementite), according to the reaction:

$$\gamma(0.80 \text{ wt. } \%\text{C}) \xrightarrow{\text{cooling at } 723^\circ\text{C}} \alpha(0.02 \text{ wt. } \%\text{C}) + \text{Fe}_3\text{C}(6.69 \text{ wt. } \%\text{C}) \tag{16.9}$$

The eutectoid decomposition product, whose microstructure is shown in Fig. 16.14*a*, is called pearlite and is a microconstituent consisting of alternating ferrite (α) and cementite (Fe_3C) lamellae. Pearlite is the only microconstituent present in a

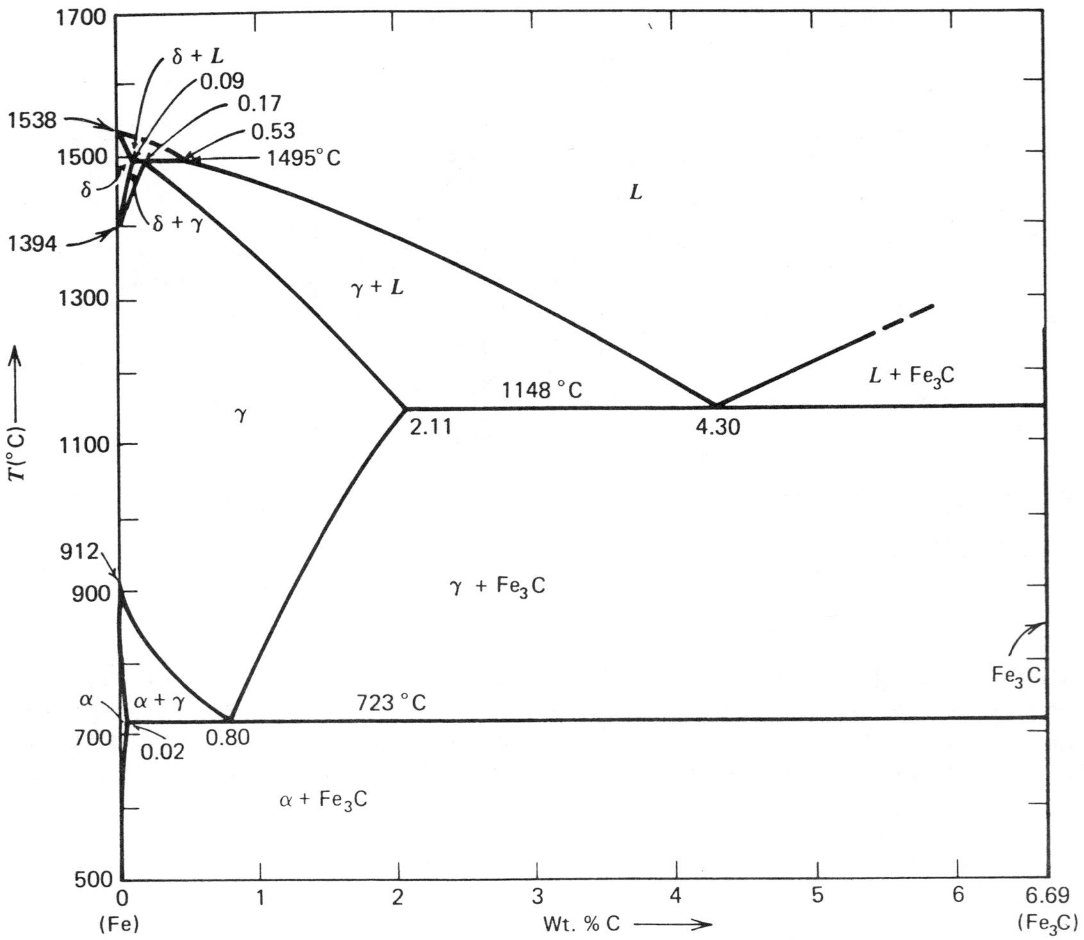

FIGURE 16.13 The Fe–Fe_3C system. In this important binary system, four solid phases participate in three invariant reactions (peritectic at 1495°C, eutectic at 1148°C, and eutectoid at 723°C).

slowly cooled alloy having the eutectoid composition. Alloys with compositions less than or greater than 0.80 wt. % C develop different microstructures. For example, when a hypoeutectoid alloy (e.g., Fe—0.5 wt. % C) cools from the austenite (γ) region into the $\alpha + \gamma$ region, ferrite begins to nucleate and grow at austenite grain boundaries. This process, which is similar to the formation of the primary microconstituent in a eutectic system, results in an increasing amount of ferrite and a decreasing amount of austenite that becomes enriched in carbon content. Just above the eutectoid temperature, the austenite approaches the eutectoid composition (0.80 wt. % C), and all of the remaining γ undergoes the eutectoid reaction at 723°C. The final microstructure contains two microconstituents, proeutectoid ferrite and pearlite (Fig. 16.14*b*), whose relative amounts may be determined with equations analogous to Eqs. 16.7a and b. Such iron-

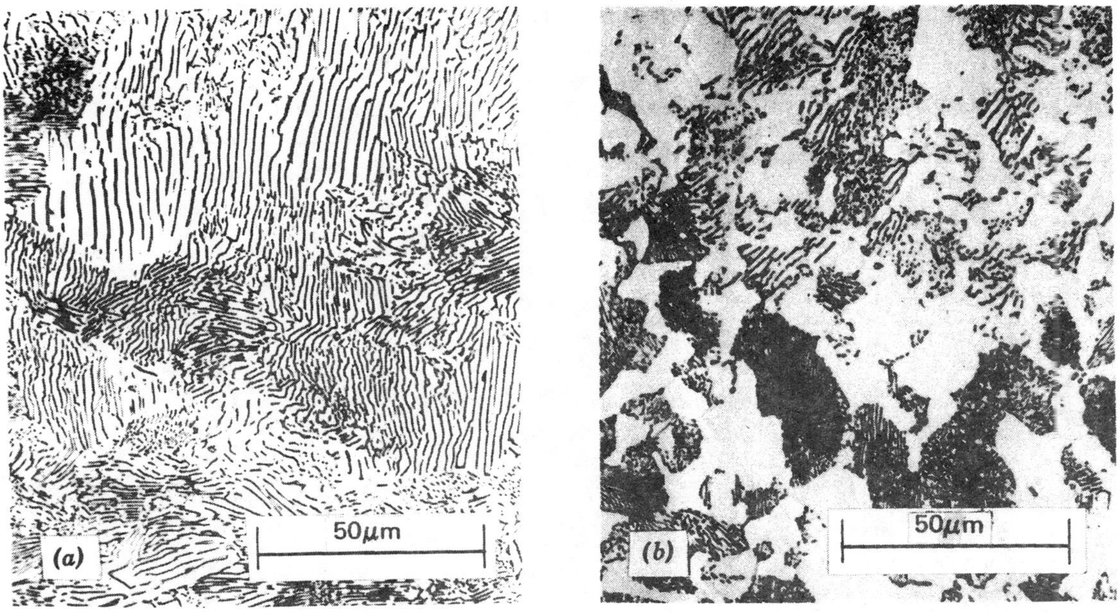

FIGURE 16.14 (*a*) Photomicrograph of a eutectoid steel (0.80 wt. % C). Shown is pearlite, a microconstituent consisting of ferrite (α) and cementite (Fe_3C) that formed by eutectoid decomposition of austenite (γ). This lamellar microconstituent is important in many steels. (*b*) Photomicrograph of a hypoeutectoid steel (0.5 wt. % C). This alloy contains two microconstituents: proeutectoid ferrite (formed prior to the eutectoid reaction) and pearlite (formed by the eutectoid reaction). (Photomicrographs courtesy of United States Steel Corp.)

carbon alloys are one form of plain carbon steels, the strength of which increases almost linearly with the fractional amount of pearlite present.

The Fe–Fe_3C system also contains a peritectic invariant reaction at 1495°C. In this case, a solid phase decomposes on heating into a liquid and another solid phase, and the reverse occurs on cooling. This peritectic reaction is

$$\delta(0.09 \text{ wt. } \%\text{C}) + L(0.53 \text{ wt. } \%\text{C}) \xrightarrow{\text{cooling at } 1495^\circ\text{C}} \gamma(0.17 \text{ wt. } \%\text{C}) \quad (16.10)$$

It is worth noting that many chemical compounds are said to decompose rather than melt at a specific temperature, and often this occurs by means of a peritectic invariant reaction. The solid-state analog of the peritectic reaction, called a peritectoid reaction, involves three different solid phases instead of a liquid and two solid phases. Peritectic and peritectoid reactions do not give rise to microconstituents as the eutectic and eutectoid reactions do.

The three-phase invariant reactions represented in Eqs. 16.5, 16.9, and 16.10 have been written for cooling processes. On heating, each of these reactions

TABLE 16.1 Types of Three-Phase Reactions Occurring Most Commonly in Condensed Systems

Name of Reaction	*Equation*	*Phase Diagram Characteristic*
Monotectic	$L_I \xrightarrow{\text{cooling}} \alpha + L_{II}$	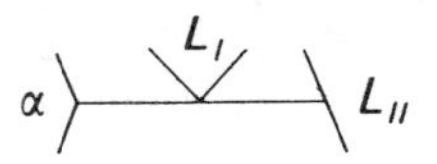
Monotectoid	$\alpha_1 \xrightarrow{\text{cooling}} \alpha_2 + \beta$	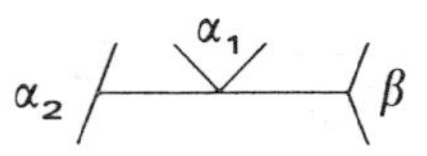
Eutectic	$L \xrightarrow{\text{cooling}} \alpha + \beta$	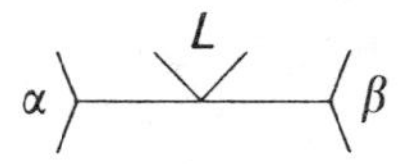
Eutectoid	$\alpha \xrightarrow{\text{cooling}} \beta + \gamma$	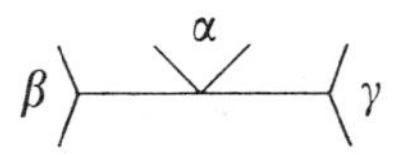
Syntectic	$L_I + L_{II} \xrightarrow{\text{cooling}} \alpha$	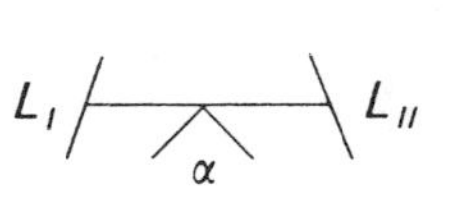
Peritectic	$\alpha + L \xrightarrow{\text{cooling}} \beta$	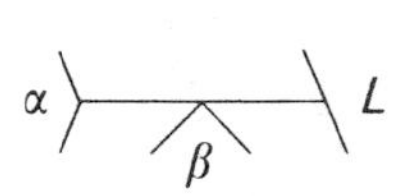
Peritectoid	$\alpha + \beta \xrightarrow{\text{cooling}} \gamma$	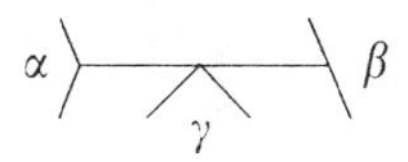

proceeds in the reverse direction. This is also true for other three-phase reactions in binary systems that may involve vapor, liquid, and solid phases. Although a large number of three-phase reactions are possible, those involving condensed phases usually are of more practical significance in binary metallic and ceramic systems. The most important of these are summarized in Table 16.1.

16.6 INTERMEDIATE PHASES

It was mentioned in Sect. 16.2 that limited solid solubility is more common than complete solid solubility. Accordingly, in most cases, only a finite amount of one component will dissolve in another pure component. Such a solid phase, based on a pure component and extending to certain finite compositions into a binary phase diagram, is called a terminal solid solution, and the line representing the solubility limit of a terminal solid solution with respect to a two-phase solid region is called a solvus line. Many phase diagrams contain intermediate phases whose occurrence cannot be readily predicted from the nature of the pure components.

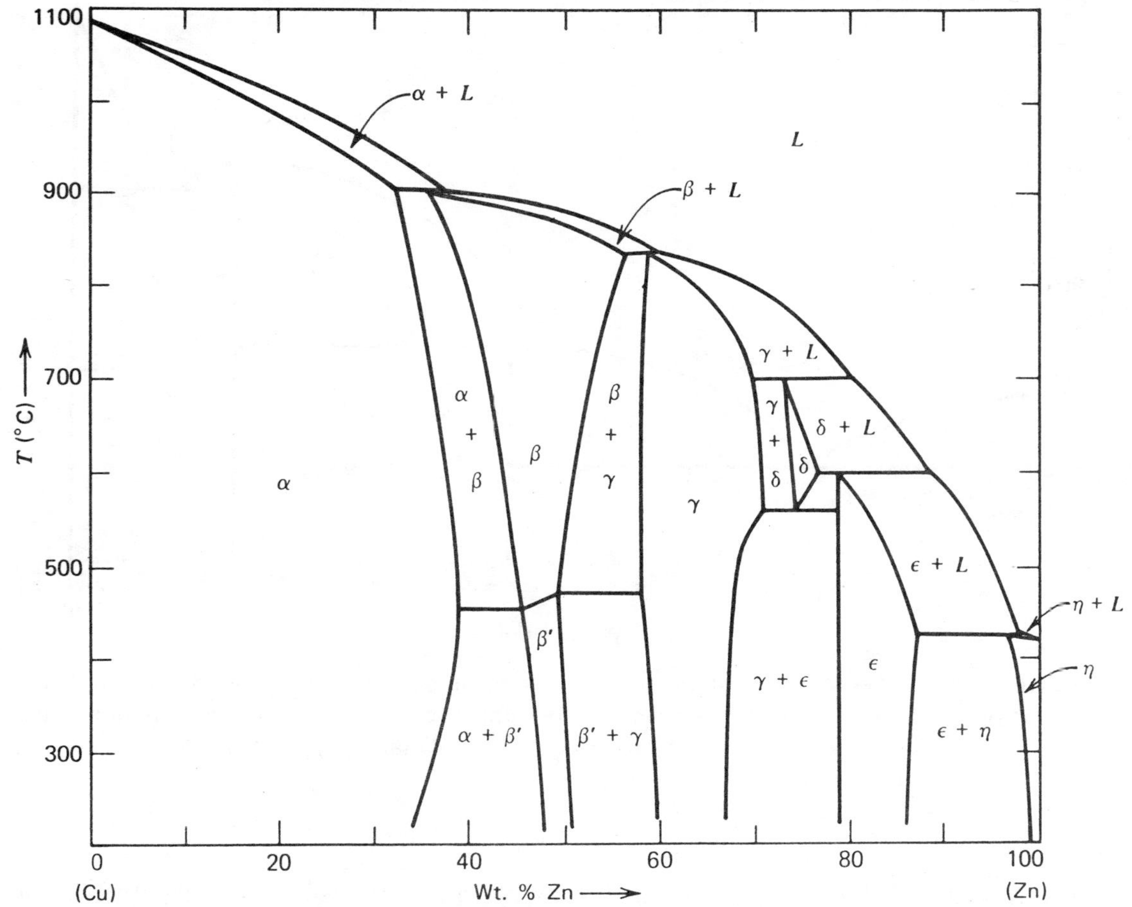

FIGURE 16.15 The Cu–Zn system. This system contains a number of intermediate phases (intermediate solid solutions) and a number of invariant reactions. Copper-rich alloys in this system constitute the important technological alloys known as brasses.

An intermediate phase may exist over a range of compositions (intermediate solid solution) or only at a relatively fixed composition (a compound, if there is a stoichiometric relationship between the components). The Cu–Zn system displays a number of intermediate solid solutions (Fig. 16.15). Intermediate solid solutions often have higher electrical resistivities and hardnesses than either of the two components. Examples of compounds are found in the Mg–Ni system (Fig. 16.16). Here, both Mg_2Ni and $MgNi_2$ have very narrow composition ranges and are designated intermetallic compounds. Intermetallic compounds differ from common chemical compounds in that the bonding is primarily metallic rather than ionic or covalent, as would be found with compounds in certain metal–nonmetal systems or ceramic systems. Some metal–nonmetal compounds, such as Fe_3C, are metallic in character, whereas others, such as MgO, are ceramic phases.

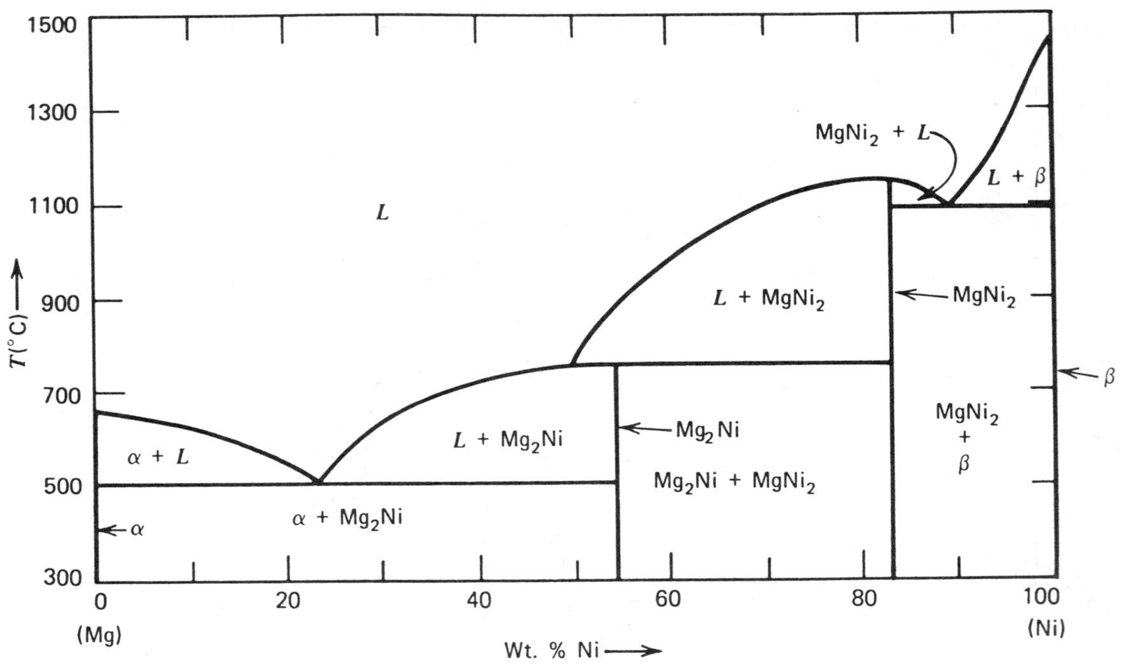

FIGURE 16.16 The Mg–Ni system. In this system, intermetallic compounds (having fixed compositions and definite stoichiometries) occur. Unlike covalent or ionic compounds, intermetallic compounds often have stoichiometries that are dictated by relative atomic sizes and atomic packing considerations.

Intermediate phases may undergo polymorphic transformations, and some may melt at a fixed temperature (e.g., $MgNi_2$). These are termed congruent transformations, in which one phase changes to another phase of the same composition at a definite temperature. Thus, $MgNi_2$ is said to be a congruently melting phase, whereas Mg_2Ni melts incongruently since it undergoes peritectic decomposition. A congruently melting compound can serve as a pure component in a binary system. For example, the Mg–Ni system (Fig. 16.16) can be subdivided into the Mg–$MgNi_2$ and $MgNi_2$–Ni systems. Congruent transformations also are observed at specific alloy compositions for some binary solid solutions. The Ti–Zr system (Fig. 16.17) contains two examples. The 50 wt. % Ti–50 wt. % Zr alloy melts congruently at 1537°C (minimum melting point), and the 34 wt. % Ti–66 wt. % Zr alloy undergoes a congruent solid state transformation at about 535°C.

16.7 MULTICOMPONENT SYSTEMS

Most commercially important alloys and ceramic materials contain more than two components. Although in some cases the proportion of the third or additional components is small, they can have a large effect on the properties of the material.

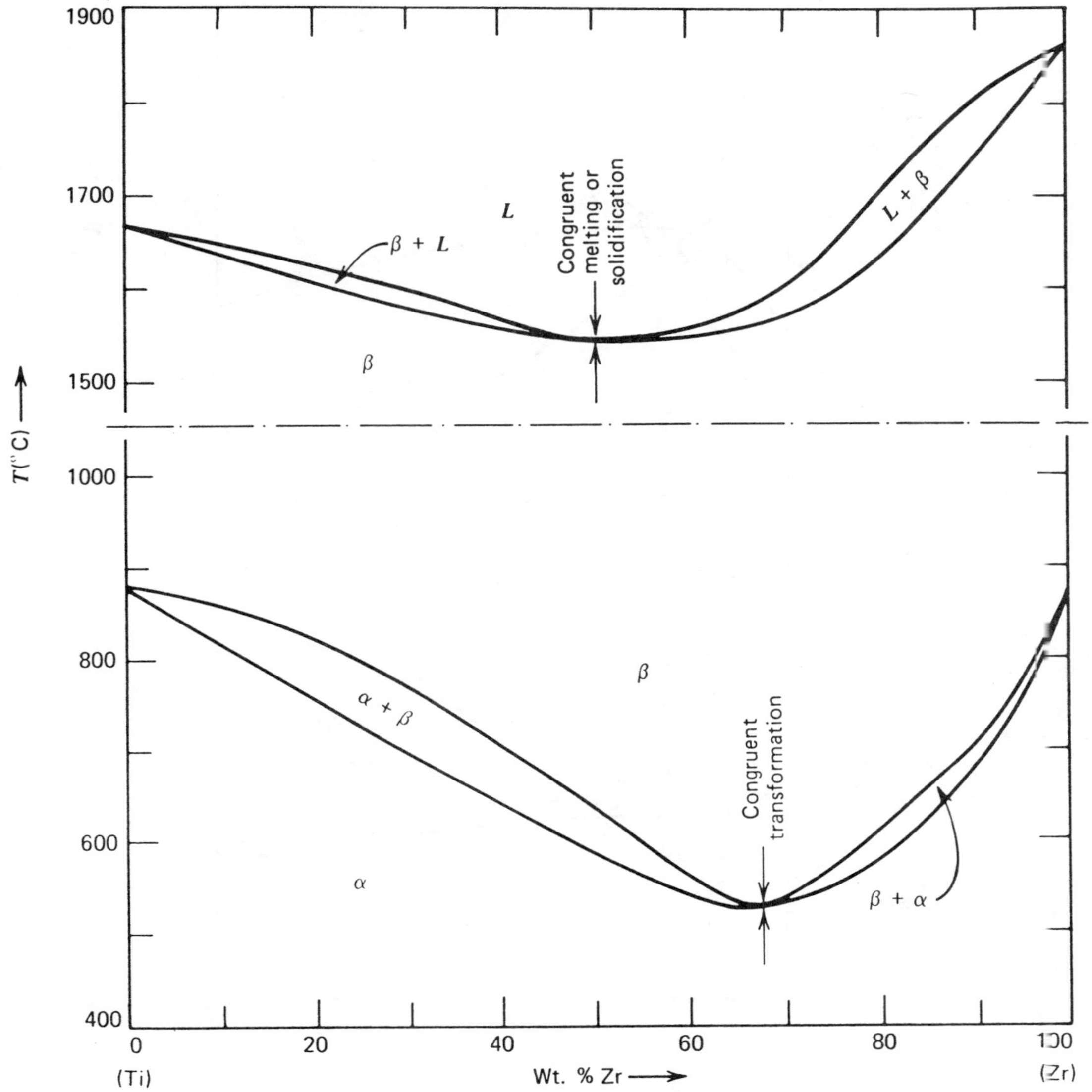

FIGURE 16.17 The Ti–Zr system. Titanium and zirconium are isomorphous (i.e., have the same crystal structure) at both high and low temperatures. This leads to a rather unique miscibility in the low-temperature (hcp) form as well as in the high-temperature (bcc) form. An alloy containing 50 wt. % Zr melts congruently at 1537°C and an alloy containing 66 wt. % Zr undergoes a solid state congruent transformation at 535°C.

Since it is difficult to delineate phase relationships for even a ternary system at constant pressure without recourse to a three-dimensional model, two-dimensional maps often are utilized. In such a case, one of two variables is usually fixed—either the temperature or the percentage of one of the components. For our purposes, it is sufficient to note that addition of a third component not only alters the composition of a particular phase in a binary system but also raises or lowers the temperatures at which phase changes take place. This is demonstrated in the plot

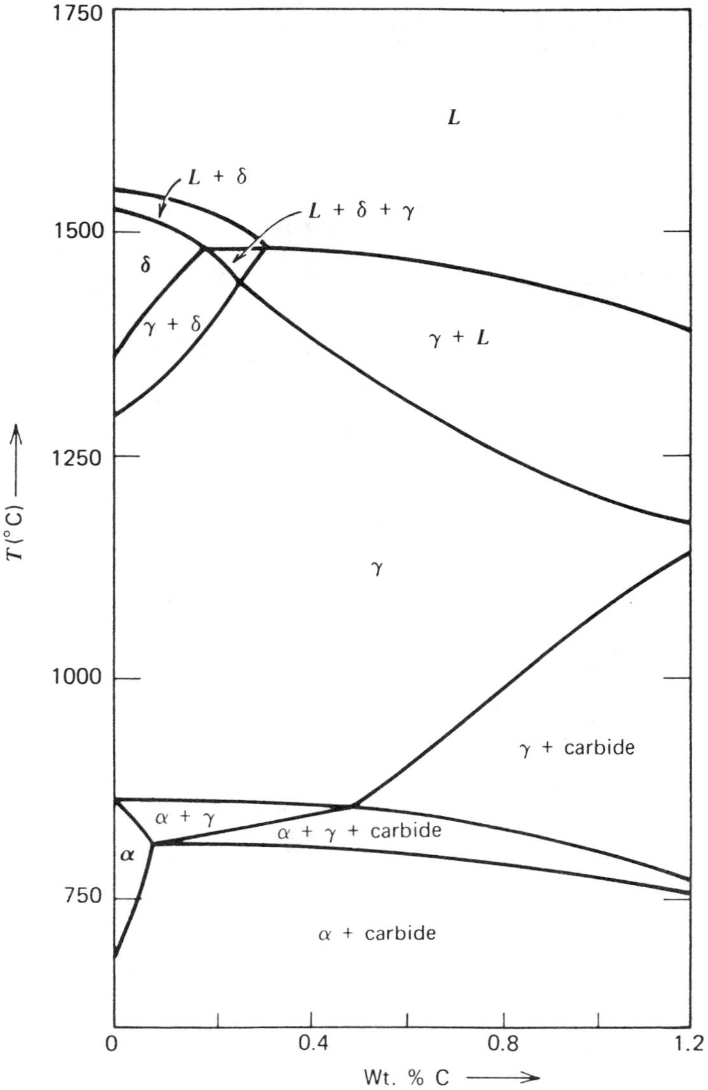

FIGURE 16.18 Phase diagram of the Fe–C system containing 5% Cr. In this "pseudobinary" diagram, the phase relationships between iron and carbon have been altered by the presence of chromium. Note that three phases can be present in a region of this diagram, unlike the case of a binary diagram. (Adapted from L. H. Van Vlack, *Materials Science for Engineers*, 1970, Addison-Wesley, Reading, Mass.)

that shows the effect of 5% Cr on the Fe–Fe_3C system (Fig. 16.18). Furthermore, invariant reactions in multicomponent systems are more complex than in binary systems, for example, three distinct solid phases form from the eutectic liquid in a ternary eutectic reaction.

16.8 THE THERMODYNAMICS OF PHASE EQUILIBRIA

Concepts relating to the occurrence of phases or phase stability are essentially chemical in nature. It is the province of crystal chemistry to explain and predict extensive or restricted solid solubility and the occurrence of intermediate phases. Such predictions are rather limited currently, but two underlying chemical factors are apparent: atomic size and electronic structure. If these factors are similar for two pure components, then changes in enthalpy upon solid solution formation will be small, and the increased entropy due to increased disorder in a solid solution will favor extensive solid solubility. That is, the total free energy will be lowered by solid solution formation. If two components interact unfavorably because of size differences or differences in electronic structure, solid solubility usually will be restricted or negligible, but intermediate phases may or may not occur. Truly unfavorable interaction occurs when the component atoms do not bond well with each other, a situation that disfavors the formation of intermediate phases and solid solutions. If component atoms do bond with each other, intermediate phases may be favored. A simple thermodynamic approach can provide some useful insight into binary systems.

The criterion for equilibrium at constant temperature and pressure is a minimum in the free energy of the system. This was considered previously for a pure substance at constant pressure (see Chapter 1). With binary substances, such as alloys, the free energy is a function of composition as well as temperature and often is lowest when a mixture of two phases of different compositions coexist. This is amply demonstrated by the large number of two-phase regions in binary phase diagrams. To understand the thermodynamic basis for binary equilibrium diagrams, it is necessary to develop expressions for the free energy of a phase. This can be done in terms of expressions for enthalpy and entropy.

When two substances that form a solid solution are mixed together, there invariably is a decrease in free energy that reflects both a change in enthalpy because of bonding differences and a change in entropy because of the increased disorder. The enthalpy change may be positive or negative, but it is dominated by the increase in entropy. The molar enthalpy of a solid solution at some temperature can be represented as

$$H = X_A H_A^\circ + X_B H_B^\circ + \Delta H_{\text{mix}} \tag{16.11}$$

where H_A° and H_B° are the standard state enthalpies of the pure components, $X_A (= 1 - X_B)$ is the mole fraction of A in solution, X_B is the mole fraction of B in solution, and ΔH_{mix} is the enthalpy of mixing. Similarly, the molar entropy of a solid solution at some temperature can be represented as

$$S = X_A S_A^\circ + X_B S_B^\circ + \Delta S_{\text{mix}} \tag{16.12}$$

A combination of Eqs. 16.11 and 16.12 provides the free energy of a solid solution:

$$\begin{aligned} G &= X_A(H_A^\circ - TS_A^\circ) + X_B(H_B^\circ - TS_B^\circ) + \Delta H_{\text{mix}} - T\,\Delta S_{\text{mix}} \\ &= X_A G_A^\circ + X_B G_B^\circ + \Delta G_{\text{mix}} \end{aligned} \tag{16.13}$$

Since this equation affords no information about the chemical nature of the solid solution, it is useful to examine ΔH_{mix} and ΔS_{mix} more closely.

In certain cases, the enthalpy of mixing can be approximated by

$$\Delta H_{\text{mix}} \approx X_A X_B V \tag{16.14}$$

where V is an interaction energy. If $V < 0$, an A atom bonds more strongly with B atoms than with other A atoms, and a B atom bonds more strongly with A atoms; that is, unlike nearest neighbors are favored. If $V > 0$, like nearest neighbors are favored, since like atoms bond more strongly than do unlike atoms. If $V = 0$, unlike and like neighbors are equally favored, and a truly random solid solution should occur.

An approximate form for the entropy of mixing, on a molar basis, is

$$\Delta S_{\text{mix}} \approx -R(X_A \ln X_A + X_B \ln X_B) \tag{16.15}$$

where R is the universal gas constant. Since X_A and X_B must be smaller than or equal to unity, ΔS_{mix} as given by this equation necessarily will be positive. This result is largely independent of bonding, depending on randomness considerations alone. Substitution of the physically plausible Eqs. 16.14 and 16.15 into Eq. 16.13 gives

$$G \approx X_A G_A^\circ + X_B G_B^\circ + X_A X_B V + RT(X_A \ln X_A + X_B \ln X_B) \tag{16.16}$$

(Comparison of this equation, with $V = 0$, should be made with Eq. 13.3.) Equation 16.16 provides two important results. First, a small amount of B added to A (or vice versa) causes a decrease in the free energy. Second, if $V \leq 0$, the free energy curve will always have a positive curvature and, accordingly, exhibit a single minimum. Features similar to those described above also pertain to liquid solutions. The case of intermediate phases is only slightly more complex, although the

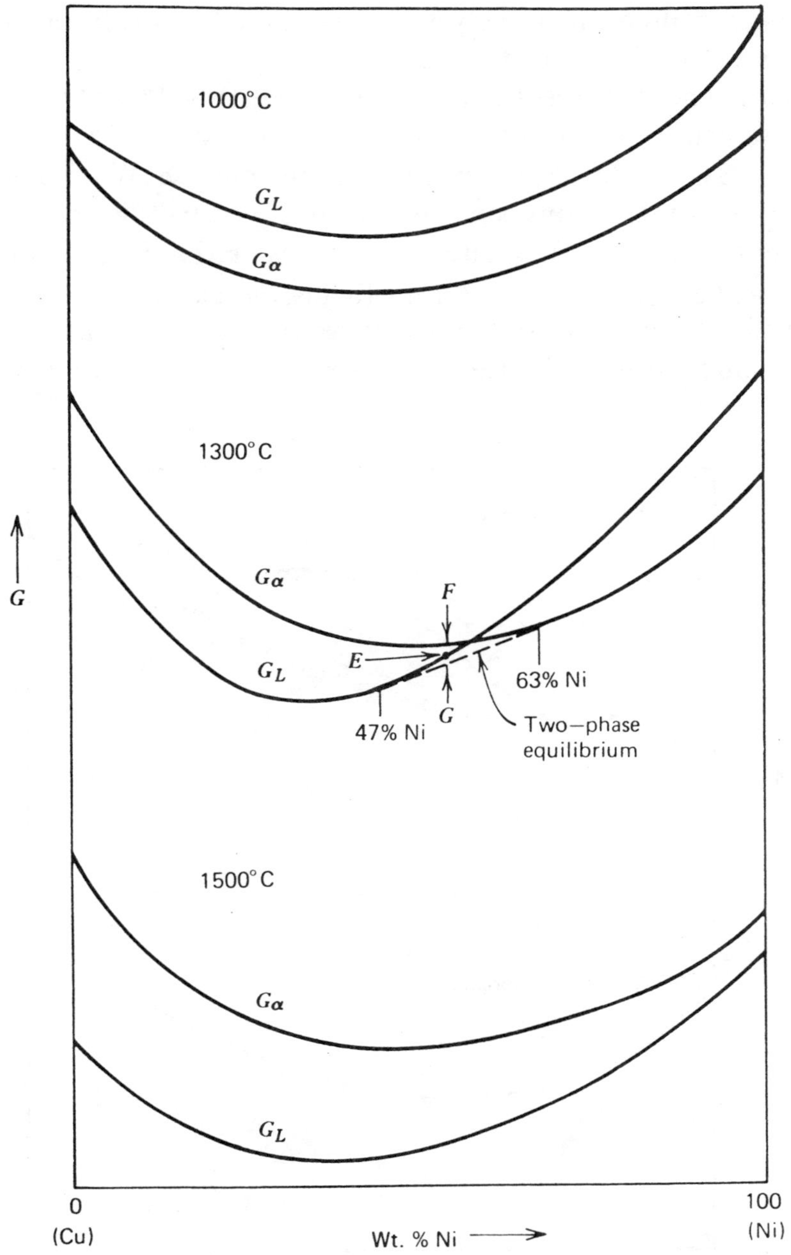

FIGURE 16.19 Schematic free energy vs. composition curves at various temperatures for the Cu–Ni system (see Fig. 16.4). For any composition, the lowest free energy represents stable equilibrium. When the free energy curves for two phases intersect, the lowest free energy (for a certain composition range) occurs for a two-phase mixture; this is represented by a common tangent line between the two free energy curves.

enthalpy of mixing almost invariably is negative, and the entropy of mixing may be very small for a stoichiometric or ordered phase.

Schematic free energy curves for the Cu–Ni system (Fig. 16.4) at various temperatures are presented in Fig. 16.19. When $T > T_m$ for Ni, the liquid is stable at all compositions, having a lower free energy than the phase α. When $T < T_m$ for Cu, α is stable at all compositions, since its free energy curve lies below that of the liquid. [Note that the standard state free energies used in representing the molar free energy of a phase (Eq. 16.13 or 16.16)—that is, the end points of the α free energy curves—are the free energies of the respective pure components existing as that phase.] At a temperature intermediate between the melting points of Cu and Ni,

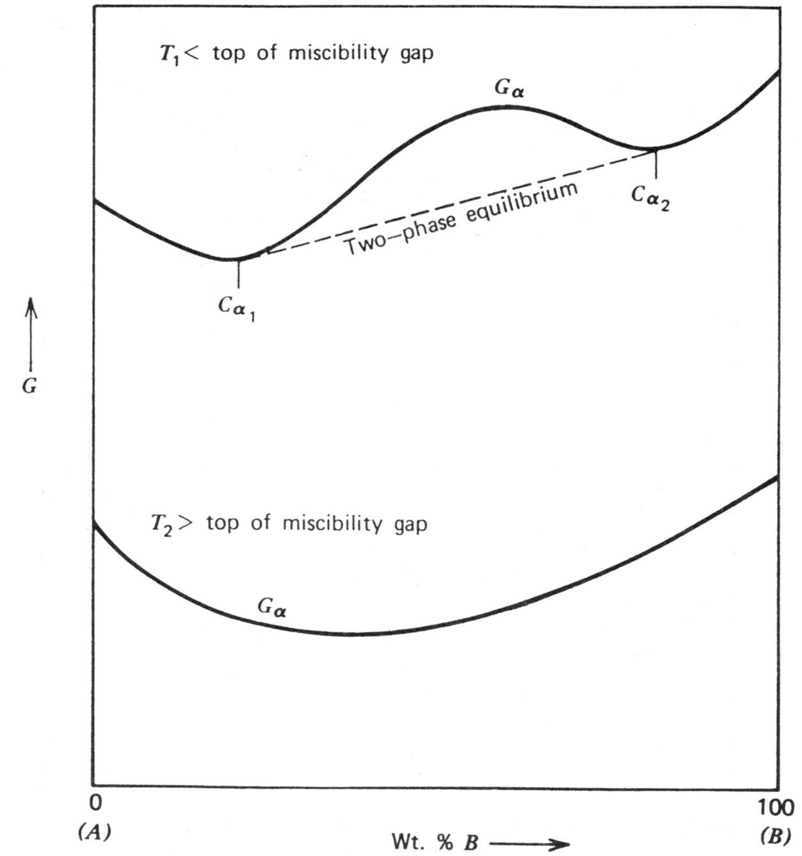

FIGURE 16.20 Schematic free energy vs. composition curves for the solid phase in a system that contains a solid state miscibility gap (see Fig. 16.6). At a temperature below the top of the miscibility gap (T_1), the free energy curve has two minima and a maximum because the enthalpy of mixing is positive and, as a consequence, two-phase equilibrium occurs over a certain range of compositions. At a temperature above the top of the miscibility gap (T_2), the free energy curve has only one minimum and a single phase exists at all compositions.

the liquid and α free energy curves intersect, with one being lower for certain compositions and the other being lower for other compositions. At 1300°C and an alloy composition of 53 wt. % Ni, the liquid (point *E*) is more stable than α (point *F*); however, the free energy of the alloy is lowest at point *G* on a common tangent line between the two free energy curves; that is, the points on the tangent line represent the free energy of a mixture of the α and liquid phases, and this, corresponds to two-phase equilibrium. The discrete points of common tangency define the compositions of the two coexisting phases (47 wt. % Ni and 63 wt. % Ni). Because

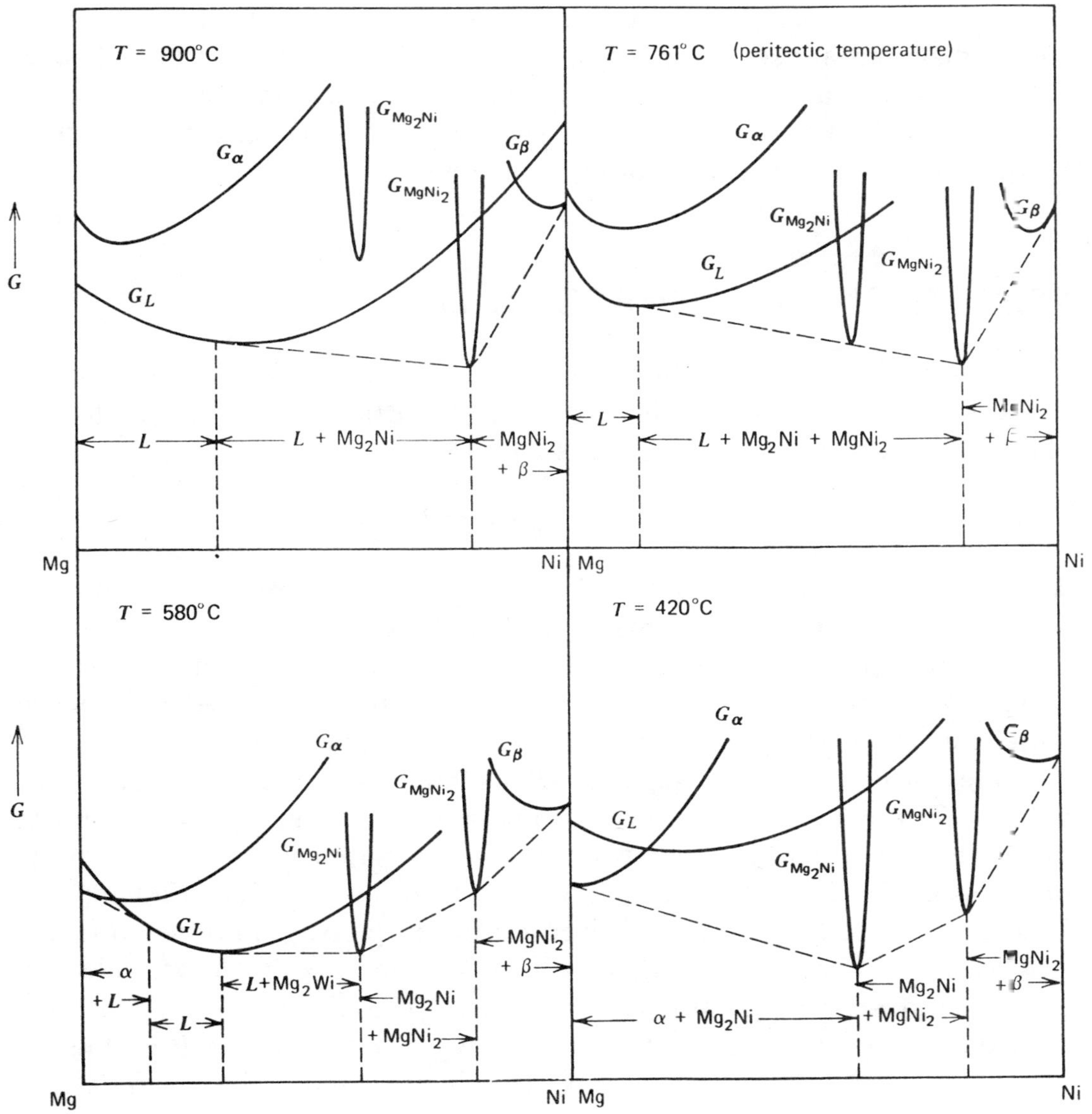

FIGURE 16.21 Schematic free energy vs. composition curves for the Mg–Ni system (Fig. 16.16). Intermediate phases or intermetallic compounds have discrete free energy curves.

only one common tangent line is possible, it should be apparent that α and L coexisting in equilibrium at a given temperature will necessarily have fixed compositions regardless of their relative amounts.

As another example, the binary phase diagram shown in Fig. 16.6 represents a case in which the enthalpy of mixing (or the interaction energy V) is positive for the solid phase (Fig. 16.20). Since $V > 0$, the free energy curve for the solid phase undergoes a change of shape from a positive curvature only and one minimum at higher temperatures to two minima and a maximum below a critical temperature. The latter is responsible for the development of a miscibility gap, since a common tangent can be drawn between two points on this single free energy curve.

When intermediate phases exist, as in the Mg–Ni system (Fig. 16.16), free energy diagrams are still straightforward (Fig. 16.21). Note that the free energy curve for a compound has a very sharp minimum and that three-phase coexistence (e.g., at the peritectic temperature) corresponds to simultaneous common tangency between the free energy curves for three phases.

16.9 THE GIBBS PHASE RULE

The thermodynamic conditions for phase equilibria lead to a simple equation that can be used to ascertain the number of coexisting phases. This is the Gibbs phase rule:

$$p + f = c + n \tag{16.17}$$

where p designates the number of phases in a materials system, c the number of components, n the number of noncompositional variables (e.g., T and P), and f the number of degrees of freedom. The latter is defined as the number of variables (temperature, pressure, and composition) that can be changed independently without changing the number of phases existing at equilibrium.

In the case of a unary system, the T–P diagram (e.g., Fig. 16.2) can be examined with the Gibbs phase rule. Here, $c = 1$ and $n = 2$, so that $p + f = 3$. In a single-phase field $p = 1$, and both temperature and pressure can be changed independently since $f = 2$. Along a two-phase coexistence line $p = 2$, and if temperature is changed, there must be a prescribed change in pressure in order to maintain two-phase equilibrium. At a triple point $p = 3$, and $f = 0$. No variable can be altered if three-phase equilibrium is to be maintained; $f = 0$ defines an invariance.

In the case of a simple binary eutectic at constant pressure (e.g., Fig. 16.9), $c = 2$ and $n = 1$, since temperature is the only noncompositional variable. Thus, $p + f = 3$, and three-phase coexistence between α, β, and L represents an invariant for which each phase has a definite composition and the temperature is fixed.

In the $\alpha + L$ two-phase region $p = 2$ and $f = 1$. Accordingly, a change in temperature must be accompanied by corresponding changes in the composition of each phase in accordance with the solidus and liquidus lines.

The Gibbs phase rule serves as a mnemonic device that allows easy computation of the maximum number of equilibrium phases in a materials system. Furthermore, it can be used to analyze a nonequilibrium situation, for example, the existence of three phases in the microstructure of a binary substance at constant pressure over a range of temperatures. Such situations often occur because phase transformations are limited kinetically by diffusion rates, a topic that will be discussed in the next chapter.

REFERENCES

1. Van Vlack, L. H. *Elements of Materials Science and Engineering*, 3rd edition, Addison-Wesley, Reading, Mass., 1975.
2. Guy, A. G., and Hren, J. J. *Elements of Physical Metallurgy*, 3rd edition, Addison-Wesley, Reading, Mass., 1975.

QUESTIONS AND PROBLEMS

16.1 Pure iron melts at 1538°C. Body-centered cubic iron is stable between 1538°C and 1394°C and also below 912°C. Face-centered cubic iron is stable between 1394°C and 912°C

(a) Sketch the cooling curve expected under equilibrium, for pure Fe cooled from 1600°C to room temperature.

(b) Sketch schematically the free energy curves as a function of temperature over the same temperature range for each phase.

16.2 It can be shown that the total differential of internal energy is given by

$$dE = T\,dS - P\,dV$$

for a phase of a pure substance.

(a) Using the definitions of enthalpy and free energy (Eqs. 1.5 and 1.7), show that $dG = -S\,dT + V\,dP$.

(b) At constant pressure, how does G vary with T? At constant temperature, how does G vary with P?

(c) For a pure substance, two-phase coexistence occurs when each phase has the same free energy on a molar basis. Alternatively, the differentials of their respective free energies must be equal if equilibrium exists. Based on this and using the expression in part (a), show that the slope of a phase field boundary in a unary diagram is

$$\frac{dT}{dP} = \frac{\Delta V_{\text{trans}}}{\Delta S_{\text{trans}}} = \frac{T_{\text{trans}}\,\Delta V_{\text{trans}}}{\Delta H_{\text{trans}}}$$

16.3 When a pure substance undergoes a phase change on heating at constant pressure, there is a discrete increase in enthalpy (i.e., $\Delta H_{trans} > 0$ for heating); however, the volume may increase or decrease, and this determines the sign of the slope of a boundary in a unary diagram [see relation in part (c) of problem 16.2].

(a) Demonstrate that this is so by considering the S/L and L/V boundaries for H_2O (Fig. 16.2).

(b) α-Fe, stable at 912°C and below, is bcc and has a lattice parameter of $a = 0.2904$ nm at 912°C; γ-Fe, stable at 912°C and above, is fcc and has a lattice parameter of $a = 0.3646$ nm at 912°C. At high pressures, will the α–γ transformation occur at higher or lower temperatures than 912°C? Explain.

(c) On heating, α-Ti transforms to β-Ti with a relative volume change of -0.55%. How does the α/β boundary vary as a function of pressure?

16.4 Describe in detail the process of equilibrium solidification in the case of a 50 wt. % Cu–50 wt. % Ni alloy (Fig. 16.4). Sketch the compositions of the liquid and solid as a function of temperature.

16.5 Consider the phase diagram shown in Fig. 16.6. For an alloy containing 40 wt. % B, calculate the fractional amounts (by weight) of α_1 and α_2 existing at T_1, T_2, and T_3 (where $T_1 > T_2 > T_3$).

T	C_{α_1} (wt. % B)	C_{α_2} (wt. % B)
T_1	48	52
T_2	36	64
T_3	12	88

16.6 Can the lever rule be applied at the temperature of a three-phase invariant reaction in a binary system? Why or why not?

16.7 The most convenient way to specify compositions in a materials system is either in terms of weight percent of each component or in terms of atomic (or mole) percent of each component (which is 100 times the mole fraction).

(a) For a binary alloy containing C_0 wt. % B, set up general expressions for at. % A and for at. % B in terms of C_0 and the atomic weights of each component.

(b) What at. % C is there in cementite (6.69 wt. % C)? What is the maximum at. % C that can dissolve in ferrite (at 723°C)?

(c) Suggest why compositions in terms of weight percent are more useful from a practical point of view than those in terms of atomic percent.

16.8 One eutectic reaction in the Mg–Ni system (Fig. 16.16) is

$$L\ (23.5\ \text{wt. \% Ni}) \xrightleftharpoons{507^\circ\text{C}} \alpha\ (0\ \text{wt. \% Ni}) + Mg_2Ni\ (54.6\ \text{wt. \% Ni})$$

Consider two alloys of composition C_1 and C_2 containing less Ni and more Ni, respectively, than the eutectic composition. The fractional amount of primary microconstituent by weight is the same in each alloy, but the fractional amount of total α in alloy C_1 is 2.5 times the fractional amount of total α in alloy C_2. Calculate the compositions C_1 and C_2 in terms of wt. % Ni.

16.9 Identify and completely write out all three-phase invariant reactions occurring in the Cu–Zn system (Fig. 16.15).

16.10 Part of the water-cane sugar ($C_{12}H_{22}O_{11}$) system is shown below.

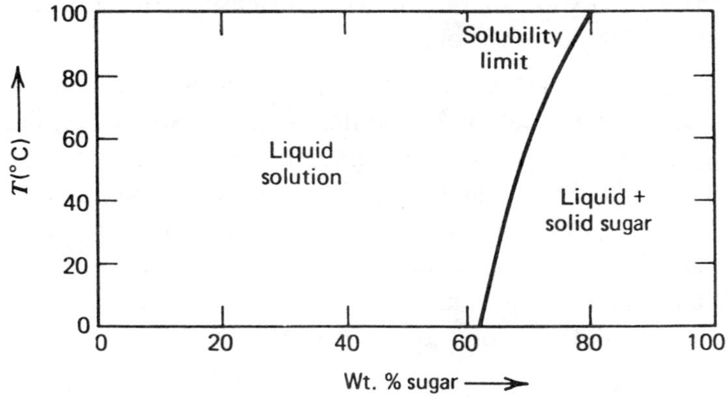

(a) What is the maximum amount of sugar that can be dissolved in boiling water at 100°C? Give both wt. % sugar and mole % sugar.

(b) If the above solution is cooled to 20°C, what will be the composition of the water solution? What will be the fractional amounts (by weight) of saturated water and solid sugar at 20°C?

16.11 The formation of substitutional solid solutions by pairs of metals usually is disfavored if (i) the solvent and solute atoms have atomic radii that differ by more than ±15% and (ii) the electronegativities of the respective elements differ by more than ±0.4 (Table 3.5). The size factor often plays a dominant role in precluding substitutional solid solution formation.

(a) Solely on the basis of information provided below, indicate which of the following pairs of metals would *not* be likely to form a continuous series of solid solutions: Ta–W, Pt–Pb, Co–Ni, Co–Zn, and Ti–Ta.

Metal	*Elemental Atomic Radius (nm)*	*Crystal Structure*
Ti	0.1461	hcp ($T < 883$°C); bcc ($T > 883$°C)
Co	0.1251	hcp ($T < 427$°C); fcc ($T > 427$°C)
Ni	0.1246	fcc
Zn	0.1332	hcp
Ta	0.1430	bcc
W	0.1370	bcc
Pt	0.1387	fcc
Pb	0.1750	fcc

(b) Consult *Metals Handbook*, 8th edition, Volume 8, and check your predictions.

16.12 Explain why complete mutual solubility can occur between the two components of a substitutional solid solution but not for an interstitial solid solution.

16.13 The cation-to-anion radius ratios for MgO, Al_2O_3, and Cr_2O_3 are 0.47, 0.36, and 0.40, respectively. Al_2O_3 and Cr_2O_3 form a continuous series of solid solutions.
(a) Is this a surprising result? Why or why not?
(b) Would you expect to find limited or extensive solid solubility in the MgO–Cr_2O_3 system? Why or why not?

16.14 (a) Using free energy curves for the solid phases of a binary system based on two metallic components having different crystal structures, illustrate (i) the case in which there is very limited solid solubility in each terminal solid solution and (ii) the case in which there is extensive solid solubility in each terminal solid solution. (Assume that no intermediate phases exist.)
(b) What conclusions can you draw from part (a)?
(c) What effect does an intermediate phase have on the solid solubility limit of a terminal solid solution?

16.15 Cu (atomic radius, 0.1278 nm) melts at 1084.5°C. Bismuth (atomic radius, 0.1535 nm) melts at 271.4°C. Complete liquid miscibility exists in the Cu–Bi system, and a three-phase reaction takes place at 270°C. Sketch, in as much detail as you can, the expected phase diagram.

16.16 How much ferrite, austenite, and cementite by weight are in 0.1 kg of an Fe–C alloy containing 0.5 wt. % C at (i) 1000°C, (ii) 724°C, and (iii) room temperature?

16.17 How much pearlite by weight is there in 1.0 kg of an Fe–C alloy containing 0.4 wt. % C at 722°C?

16.18 For plain carbon steels (i.e., Fe–C alloys) that have been cooled slowly from 1000°C to room temperature, plot the fractional amounts by weight of (i) proeutectoid ferrite and pearlite and (ii) ferrite and cementite as a function of carbon content between 0.02 wt. % C and 0.8 wt. % C.

16.19 Draw schematic cooling curves for Fe—0.4 wt. % C and Fe—0.8 wt. % C cooled slowly from 1000°C to room temperature. Sketch the microstructures at selected temperatures, and identify phases and microconstituents.

16.20 Sketch schematic free energy vs. composition curves at various temperatures for the eutectic system shown in Fig. 16.9. Be sure to include the eutectic temperature.

16.21 (a) Sketch schematic free energy vs. wt. % C curves for Fe–Fe_3C alloys at various temperatures below 1200°C.
(b) Fe_3C is a metastable phase; that is, its free energy curve lies above the common tangent lines between the free energy curves of liquid and graphite, austenite and graphite, and ferrite and graphite. (The iron-graphite system is stable and the iron-cementite system is metastable.) If L, γ, and α, respectively, coexisted with graphite rather than Fe_3C, how would the eutectic and eutectoid temperatures be altered and how would the solubility limit of C in γ and of C in α be altered?

16.22 Sketch schematic free energy vs. composition curves at various temperatures, including 1537°C and 535°C, for the Ti–Zr system (Fig. 16.17).

X-RAY STRUCTURE DETERMINATION

A PRACTICAL GUIDE

Second Edition

GEORGE H. STOUT

LYLE H. JENSEN

Department of Biological Structure
University of Washington
Seattle, Washington

WILEY

A Wiley-Interscience Publication

JOHN WILEY & SONS

New York • Chichester • Brisbane • Toronto • Singapore

Library of Congress Cataloging in Publication Data:

Stout, George H., 1932–
X-ray structure determination.

"A Wiley-Interscience publication."
Includes bibliographical references and index.
1. X-ray crystallography. I. Jensen, Lyle H.
II. Title.
QD945.S8 1989 548'.83 88-27931
ISBN 0-471-60711-8

Printed in the United States of America

10 9 8 7

CHAPTER 1

X-RAYS

Although most crystallographers are only indirectly concerned with X-rays themselves, an understanding of the origins and properties of X-rays is necessary for their proper use in crystallographic studies. The information contained in this chapter provides a background for the application of X-ray methods to structural problems.

1.1. ORIGIN[1]

X-rays lie in the electromagnetic spectrum between ultraviolet light and gamma radiation and have an approximate range of wavelengths of 0.1–100 Å.[2] They are usually produced by rapidly decelerating fast-moving electrons and converting their energy of motion into a quantum of radiation. The wavelengths produced will depend on the energy of the electrons; we shall be concerned with X-rays having a wavelength of about 1 Å. X-rays are also emitted by certain radioactive isotopes, for example, ^{55}Fe. Although such sources are convenient for testing and calibration, they have not been used for diffraction purposes.

To generate X-rays, electrons are accelerated by an electric field and directed against a metal target, which slows them rapidly by multiple

[1] *International Tables*, Vol. III, pp. 71–78.

[2] Although the *Ångstrom unit* (1 Å = 10^{-8} cm) is not a standard SI unit, angstroms are extremely useful for work in the range of molecular dimensions since bond lengths then have single-digit values. They are still more commonly used by crystallographers than the nearest SI equivalent, the nanometer (1 Å = 0.1 nm).

collisions. Under the usual conditions most of the electrons are not brought to a full stop by a single collision, and a continuum of radiation is formed (Fig. 1.1). The minimum wavelength of this *white radiation* is determined by the accelerating voltage and can be calculated from

$$\lambda_{\text{min}} = \frac{12{,}398}{V_{\text{acc}}}\ \text{Å} \tag{1.1}$$

The greatest intensity occurs at a somewhat longer wavelength. As the voltage is increased, not only are the cutoff and peak intensity moved to shorter, more penetrating wavelengths, but also the total intensity increases even though the electron current remains the same.

While the distribution of intensity in the white radiation depends primarily on the accelerating voltage and only to a small extent on the nature of the target material, X-ray spectra show in addition a number of sharp spikes of high intensity whose positions change from one material to another (Fig. 1.2). These peaks are the *characteristic lines* for the element of which the target is made.[3] When the electrons bombarding the target reach certain critical energies (*threshold potentials*) they are capable of knocking electrons out of their atomic orbitals. In particular, at energies of about 10,000 eV (for elements with atomic number ~30) they can remove electrons from the innermost (K) shell. The vacancy in the K shell is then filled by the descent of an electron from the next higher shell (L) or the one above that (M). The decrease in potential energy in going from the higher level to the lower appears as radiation, and as the energies of the shells are

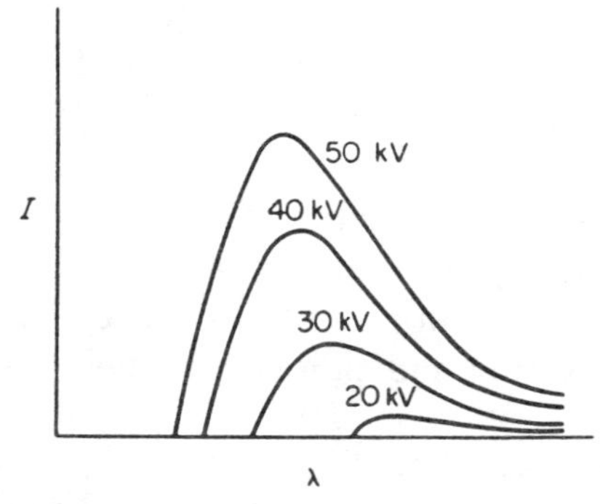

Figure 1.1. Continuous X-ray spectra as a function of accelerating voltage.

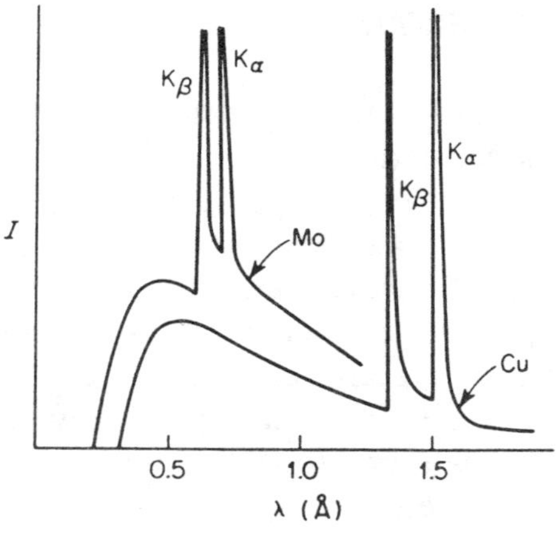

Figure 1.2. X-ray spectra with characteristic peaks: Mo K_α, 50 kV; Cu K_α, 35 kV.

[3]For a complete list of wavelengths, see *International Tables*, Vol. IV, pp. 5–43.

well defined, each transition gives a nearly monochromatic line. The principal peaks are

$$K_{\alpha 1}, K_{\alpha 2} \qquad L \rightarrow K$$

$$K_{\beta 1}, K_{\beta 2} \qquad M \rightarrow K$$

Because the difference in energy between L and K is less than that between M and K, K_α is always at a longer wavelength than K_β. The lines are close doublets because transitions can occur from two possible electronic configurations, which differ slightly in energy. $K_{\alpha 1}$ is twice as intense as $K_{\alpha 2}$ and about three to six times as strong as $K_{\beta 1}$. $K_{\beta 2}$ is usually so weak that it is ignored.

As the atomic number (Z) of the target element increases, the characteristic lines shift to shorter wavelengths, and one can, in principle, select a target to give almost any desired value for the K_α line. In practice, however, one is limited to materials that are conductive, solid, dense, and high-melting, that is, to metals. Fortunately, the transition elements of the first and second long periods ($Z = 21$–30 and 39–48) meet these requirements and have characteristic radiation in the region that is most useful for crystal structure analysis.

1.2. ABSORPTION AND FILTERING[4]

For reasons that will become clear later, the radiation used for most diffraction work should be as nearly monochromatic as possible. The K_α lines fulfill this requirement, but the presence of the accompanying K_β is a nuisance. Fortunately, selective filters may be found that will remove the K_β to any desired extent, with a relatively much smaller loss of K_α.

The absorption of X-rays by a solid follows, like so many other absorption phenomena, the equation

$$I/I_0 = e^{-\mu\tau} \tag{1.2}$$

where μ is the linear absorption coefficient and τ is the path length through the solid. If one plots μ against λ for a given element, one finds a set of curves of the shape $\mu = k\lambda^3$ that are connected by sharp jumps (Fig. 1.3). These discontinuities are ***absorption edges*** and occur at the wavelength at which the incident X-ray quantum is just energetic enough to knock an electron out of an atomic orbital. In particular, the K absorption edge of an element lies slightly to the short-wavelength side of the K_β lines for that element. Like the characteristic lines, the absorption edge shifts to longer wavelengths with decreasing Z, and the magnitude of this shift is such that

[4] *International Tables*, Vol. III, pp. 71–78.

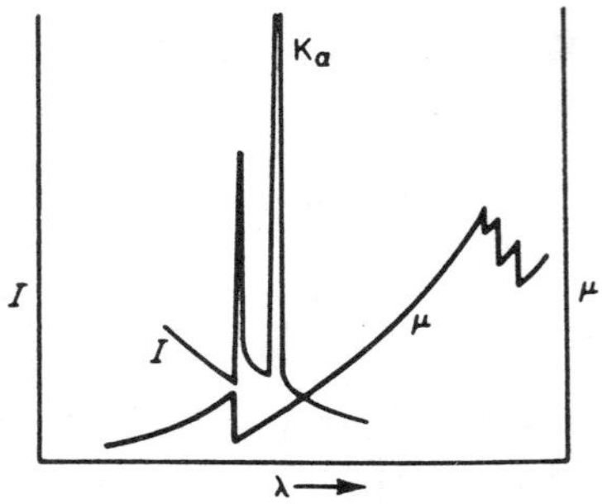

Figure 1.3. X-ray spectrum showing characteristic peaks (I curve) and absorption coefficient (μ curve) for the same element as a function of wavelength λ.

the edge for an element of atomic number $Z-1$ falls between the K_α and K_β lines of the element with an atomic number one higher, Z.[5] Consequently an element can be used as a selective filter to remove the K_β line from the spectrum of the next higher element. Figure 1.4 shows the effect of niobium ($Z=41$) as a filter for molybdenum ($Z=42$) radiation.

For targets chosen from the second long period, $Z-1$ and $Z-2$ are both possible K_β filters. Either is acceptable, and in practice considerations of availability and convenient physical form will decide. By going one or two atomic numbers lower, it is possible to find filters that will remove the K_α radiation as well, a technique (the *balanced filter method*[6]) that is occasionally used for obtaining accurate measurements of the effects of background. Table 1.1 gives filters suitable for both purposes as well as the thickness of filter needed to reduce K_β to $0.01K_\alpha$.

An alternative method of obtaining monochromatic X-rays is by the use of a crystal monochromator.[7] In this case the direct beam from the X-ray tube is reflected (diffracted) from a large single crystal of a suitable material before being used. Because of the nature of X-ray diffraction (see Chapter

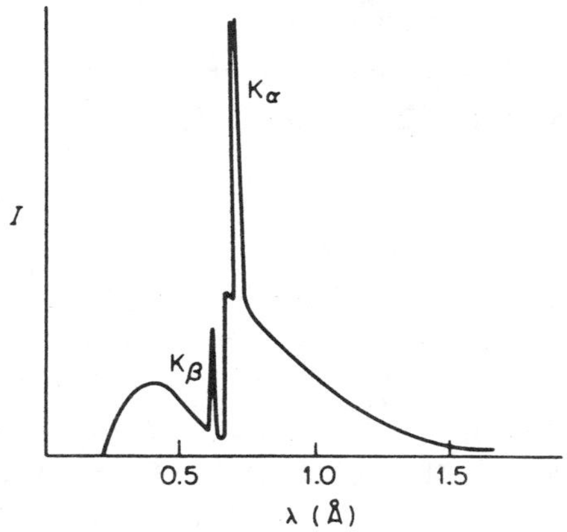

Figure 1.4. X-ray spectra showing effects of a β filter. Molybdenum radiation (50 kV) with 0.001-in. niobium β filter.

[5]This is actually true only for elements with $Z \leq 70$, but these include all the target materials whose characteristic radiations are commonly used.
[6]*International Tables*, Vol. III, pp. 78–79.
[7]*International Tables*, Vol. III, pp. 79–86.

2) only a very narrow band of wavelengths appears at a given crystal setting, and so the resulting beam is very nearly monochromatic. Although elegant in principle, this technique suffers from a number of disadvantages, among them the loss of intensity occurring during the process and certain other problems. Nevertheless crystal monochromators are now widely used in conjunction with diffractometers (see Section 5.10).

1.3. SELECTION OF RADIATION

The choice of radiation to be used for collecting diffraction data depends on a number of factors. Copper K_α was for many years the conventional choice for use with organic crystals and is still the best if the diffraction data are to be recorded photographically (see Chapters 5 and 6). It is sufficiently penetrating that it does not suffer too badly from absorption in the crystal or while passing through air, and at the same time it is recorded with reasonable efficiency on film. When used with a diffraction apparatus that can record all of the reflections theoretically accessible, it can provide enough data to more than adequately determine a structure.

The second common choice is Mo K_α. This is a more penetrating radiation and is less well adapted to use with film because of the low efficiency of recording. Nevertheless it is used to some extent in cases in which the apparatus is limited in its ability to record the available data (see the discussion of the precession camera, Section 5.9). It is generally the radiation of choice for use with diffractometers since these instruments (Section 5.10) use scintillation counters, which have nearly perfect counting efficiency for Mo K_α. Under these conditions, it is possible to use the harder radiation effectively and gain the advantage of its lesser absorption.

Wavelengths longer than that of Cu K_α do not usually offer any advantages except in the special case discussed below. If the crystal cell is very large, as in proteins, long-wavelength radiation will give better separation between the reflections but at the cost of losing some data. Absorption corrections are also increasingly a problem.

The elements present in the crystal may play a role in the choice of radiation. If one of them lies only a few atomic numbers below the target material, the X-rays will fall close to its K absorption edge. The consequences will be high specific absorption, causing a decrease in the accuracy of intensity measurements, and a large amount of diffusely scattered radiation (*X-ray fluorescence*) at the characteristic wavelength of the absorbing atom. This last is produced as the vacancy in the K shell of the absorber is filled by electrons from higher shells. It has the effect of increasing the background against which reflections must be measured. X-ray fluorescence will occur any time the incident radiation has a wavelength less than that of an absorption edge of the elements in the crystal, but it is less severe when the two are well separated. Elements

TABLE 1.1 Target Materials and Associated Constants

	Cr	Fe	Cu	Mo
Z	24	26	29	42
α_1 (Å)	2.2896	1.9360	1.5405	0.70926
α_2 (Å)	2.2935	1.9399	1.5443	0.71354
$\langle\alpha\rangle^a$ (Å)	2.2909	1.9373	1.5418	0.71069
β_1 (Å)	2.0848	1.7565	1.3922	0.63225
β filt	V, 0.4 mil[b]	Mn, 0.4 mil	Ni, 0.6 mil	Nb, 3 mils
α filt	Ti	Cr	Co	Y
Resolution (Å)	1.15	0.95	0.75	0.35
Critical potential (kV)	5.99	7.11	8.98	20.0

[a] $\langle\alpha\rangle$ is the intensity-weighted average of α_1 and α_2 and is the figure usually used for the wavelength when the two lines are not resolved.
[b] 1 mil = 0.001 in. = 0.025 mm.

below calcium cause little difficulty because the fluorescent radiation is so soft that it is absorbed by air.

Although specific absorption has the disadvantages described, it also produces some useful effects that may be lumped together as *dispersion* or *anomalous scattering*. These can sometimes provide helpful information as part of a structural analysis, and the radiation may then be chosen to maximize rather than minimize them.

Table 1.1 lists some of the commonly used target materials and gives various associated constants. The resolution value is an indication of the minimum resolvable separation of two carbon atoms, for example, when viewed with the radiation in question. It is only a rough approximation, however, as the actual value depends on the properties of the crystal studied.

1.4. X-RAY TUBES: CONSTRUCTION AND GEOMETRY[8]

The basic parts of an X-ray tube are a source of electrons and a metal anode that emits the X-rays. Tubes can be classified according to the nature of these parts.

The common *hot cathode tube* is very much like a television tube in construction. Electrons are liberated from a heated filament and accelerated by a high voltage toward the target anode (Fig. 1.5*a*). The tube is constructed as a permanently sealed unit, costs about $3500 (1988), and has a working life about 5000–10,000 hours. The drawbacks are its tendency to become "dirty" and emit spurious radiation as it ages, and the restriction to a single anode material. The first phenomenon is due to the slow deposition

[8] Guinier, *X-Ray Crystallographic Technology*, Chapter 2.

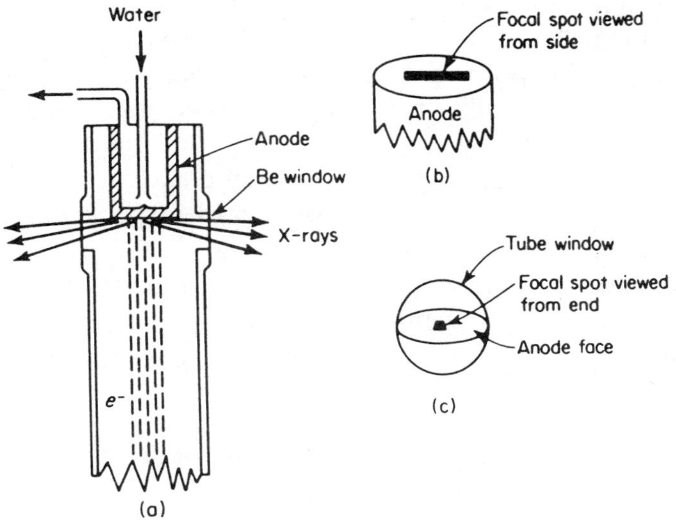

Figure 1.5. (*a*) Section along the axis of an X-ray tube. (*b*) Anode with focal spot viewed from side. (*c*) Focal spot viewed through tube window.

onto the anode and windows of tungsten and other elements (especially iron) evaporated from the filament assembly. In well-designed commercial tubes the problem is usually not a serious one. In attempts to escape both of these disadvantages, tubes have been built that could be demounted for cleaning or change of anode, but they are now rarely used.

Because of the high voltage through which the electrons are accelerated, the power dissipated at the anode is quite large (500–1500 W). In order to keep the anode from melting, it is made hollow and is cooled internally with circulating water. All commercial X-ray power supplies are provided with pressure- or flow-sensitive controls to shut down the electron beam if the cooling water flow falls below safe limits. Despite the cooling, however, the heat resistance of the anode still determines the maximum power of the tube. To increase the possible output and thus lessen the time required for obtaining data, *rotary anode tubes* are sometimes used.[9] Here the electron beam is directed onto the edge or face of a rotating wheel of the target material. With proper design, the origin of the X-rays remains in a fixed location but the anode moves under it and the heat generated is spread over a much larger area. Such tubes can handle at least ten times the power of those with stationary anodes. Unfortunately, they are expensive and complicated, requiring continuous evacuation and some extra maintenance, but they have now become relatively trouble-free and are widely used.

In a hot cathode tube, the beam of electrons arrives at the anode as an image of the filament, that is, a line ~10 mm × 1 mm (Fig. 1.5*b*). The

[9] See, for example, A. Taylor, *J. Sci. Instr.*, **26**, 225 (1949); *Rev. Sci. Instr.*, **27**, 757 (1956); D. A. Davies, A. McL. Mathieson, and G. M. Stiff, *Rev. Sci. Instr.*, **30**, 488 (1959).

X-rays are taken from the tube through *windows* of thin beryllium foil. Two of these are arranged so that they view the X-ray source from the end at an angle only a little away from the plane of the anode (usually 1–6°); thus the line image is foreshortened and appears as a rectangle, 1 mm × 0.2–1 mm depending on the takeoff angle. This is the so-called *point focus* (Fig. 1.5*c*). A third window affords a side view of the source and provides a *line focus*, which is used for X-ray diffraction from powder specimens but not for single-crystal studies.

Microfocus tubes have the apparent focal spot reduced to about 0.1 mm on a side. These require particular care in alignment but are now widely used. They have particular advantages for dealing with very small crystals where most of the usual beam is wasted.

The operating conditions for most X-ray tubes lie in the ranges 30–60 kV and 10–35 mA of tube current, depending on the anode material. The working voltage is several times the threshold potential because both the relative and absolute intensity of the characteristic radiation increase with voltage.

1.5. SYNCHROTRON RADIATION[10]

A recent addition to the list of X-ray sources are the giant particle accelerators known as storage rings. In these, electrons or positrons are injected into a very large evacuated loop and kept circulating at relativistic velocities by energy pumped in from powerful radio-frequency sources. To constrain the circulating particles to the chamber, external magnets, often superconducting, provide an inward acceleration. A consequence of this acceleration is the emission of *synchrotron radiation*. This radiation is a broad-spectrum (white) emission that resembles the white radiation of an X-ray tube but is immensely more intense (100 to 10^4 times the intensity of a conventional characteristic line). It is obtained from the storage ring through *beam lines* that are tangent to the circulating particle current. Because the particles are tightly bunched in the chamber, the emission is not continuous but occurs as a series of extremely short (~1 ns) pulses separated by longer (but only relatively, a few hundred nanoseconds) gaps. For most purposes, this pulsation is not a problem.

The radiation wavelength is a function of the size (radius) of the storage ring and the energy at which it is operated. It is described in terms of the *critical wavelength* λ_c given by

$$\lambda_c = 5.59R/E^3 \tag{1.3}$$

[10]R. Fourme and R. Kahn, in *Crystallography in Molecular Biology*, D. Moras, J. Drenth, B. Strandberg, D. Suck, and K. Wilson, Eds., Plenum, New York, 1987, pp. 27–44.

where R is the radius of curvature (in meters) in the magnetic field and E is the particle energy in gigaelectronvolts. This wavelength is approximately the most intense emission and is the midpoint of the distribution of radiated energy. The large rings have λ_c in the region of a few angstroms and contain in the mix of radiation a large amount in the 0.8–2.0 Å wavelengths of interest to crystallographers.

Rings particularly intended for radiation production contain additional devices (*wigglers* and *undulators*) to cause additional bending of the particle beam at locations that optimize the radiation generation. Wigglers cause sharper than usual bends in the particle current (and then a reverse bend so that there is no net deviation), leading to a shift of the radiation to shorter wavelengths and increasing the intensity in the range of interest to the crystallographer. Undulators create a series of small deviations such that the emissions produced at each turn are subject to interference with radiation from all the other turns. This results in an approximately monochromatic radiation source (or one in which the emission is concentrated in a few harmonically related lines) with vastly enhanced intensity (as much as 10^4) at the selected wavelengths.

The desired wavelength is usually selected by crystal monochromators (see above), often in connection with complicated focusing and reflecting arrangements to concentrate more of the available intensity on the sample. By suitable adjustments of the operating conditions almost any wavelength can be selected, and this ability to tune the radiation is potentially almost as important as the intensity gain.

The drawback to synchrotron sources is that they are extremely large and expensive installations, normally located at some distant place and much in demand, so the scheduling of data collection is complicated. Nonetheless there are cases for which synchrotrons are the only satisfactory tool, and their use is increasing, especially for the study of macromolecules.

1.6. SAFETY[11]

Like most scientific tools, X-ray equipment can be dangerous if mishandled. Although the radiation produced by the sources used is comparatively nonpenetrating, it presents a serious health hazard if proper precautions are not taken. The very fact of its "softness" is significant, since it means that the ionizing effect of the radiation is concentrated in a shallow region near

[11] *International Tables*, Vol. III, pp. 333–338; International Union of Crystallography, Commission on Crystallographic Apparatus, *Acta Cryst.*, **16**, 324, (1963); Radiation Safety for X-Ray Diffraction and Fluorescence Analysis Equipment, in *NBS Handbook*, Vol. 111, National Bureau of Standards, Boulder, CO, 1971; E. B. M. Martin, *A Guide to the Safe Use of X-Ray Diffraction and Spectrometry Equipment*, Science Reviews Ltd., Leeds, England, 1983; C. S. Barrett, J. V. Gilfrich, R. Jenkins, D. E. Leyden, J. C. Ross, and P. K. Predecki Eds., *Advances in X-Ray Analysis*, Vol. 30, Plenum, New York, 1987.

the surface of the body. The direct beam is particularly dangerous, since it represents a concentrated radiation source (several hundred roentgens per second) and brief exposure can cause serious injuries. Any diffraction equipment must have a beam stop to receive the direct beam that passes through the sample. Whenever it is necessary to work without a beam stop, for example, when aligning cameras, the beam intensity should be reduced to the lowest possible value and the experimenter should take particular care to keep his or her hands clear of it. Shutters should always be provided for covering the exit windows of the tube and should be kept closed whenever diffraction is not actually being recorded.

Scattered radiation is another problem, especially around the junction between the tube and the collimator. This junction should be designed with a labyrinth type of coupling so that no radiation can escape. The mere fact that the window cannot be seen is not enough, since double scattering can occur. An excellent study of this problem and of shutter designs has been made by the Apparatus and Standards Committee of the American Crystallographic Association,[12] and it should be consulted by anyone setting up a crystallographic laboratory. Scattering can also occur from the edges of the beam stop, from the crystal and its mounting, and from any other objects that intrude into the direct beam. In order to eliminate any slight risk from scattered radiation, modern diffractometers are generally furnished with surrounding shields. (Because of the softness of the radiation, Plexiglas is quite adequate, so it is possible to watch the operations easily.) Camera installations often do not have these, and although it should not be a problem it is advisable to check occasionally with a survey counter (be sure that it will detect soft radiation!) or by placing film badges near the cameras for several weeks.

The question of legal responsibility in X-ray diffraction laboratories is uncertain but increasingly serious. Licensing and inspection requirements vary greatly from state to state and from country to country. Liability in case of any mishaps is potentially a major problem despite the excellent safety record of such laboratories (X-ray analysis laboratories have not always been so fortunate).

If it is necessary to open the power supply, the operator should remember that it operates at very high voltages and great care must be taken. All power should be turned off, and any large condensers (which may be very large indeed) should be shorted out, allowed to stand 10–15 min, and shorted out again before any work is done.

[12]K. E. Beu, *American Crystallographic Association Apparatus and Standards Committee Report*, No. 1, 1962, Goodyear Atomic Corporation, P.O. Box 628, Piketon, OH 45661.

BIBLIOGRAPHY

Cullity, B. D., *Elements of X-Ray Diffraction*, Addison-Wesley, Reading, MA, 1956, Chapter 1.

Guinier, A., *X-Ray Crystallographic Technology*, Hilger and Watts, London, 1952, Chapters 1 and 2.

Henry, N. F. M., H. Lipson, and W. A. Wooster, *The Interpretation of X-Ray Diffraction Photographs*, Macmillan, London, 1960, pp. 25–33.

CHAPTER 2

DIFFRACTION OF X-RAYS

In this chapter, the groundwork is laid for an understanding of crystals and their interaction with X-rays. A development of the nature of lattices is followed by the derivation of Bragg's law. The concept of the reciprocal lattice is then introduced, and finally, the diffraction of X-rays is interpreted and discussed in terms of it.

2.1. LATTICES, PLANES, AND INDICES

The constancy of the external forms of well-developed crystals early led to the idea that they were built from blocks of a unit structure regularly repeated in space. Quantitative studies of the interfacial angles confirmed this idea and established a crystal as being constituted of these units stacked side to side in three dimensions.

As an introduction to crystal structures, it is convenient to consider as an analogy a two-dimensional array. The nature of such an array is illustrated in Fig. 2.1 by the regular repetition of a simple motif, a comma in this case, by translation along two directions in the plane. It is convenient to refer the array of commas to a lattice or grid system. Such a grid can be chosen in different ways. For an unlimited lattice there are, in fact, an infinite number of ways of drawing the grid lines, and in principle all are equally valid, although in practice matters of convenience and convention dictate the choice. Figure 2.2 shows three different ways of drawing the grid lines for the array in Fig. 2.1. It is important to note that the grid lines are drawn at equal intervals corresponding to the repeat distances of the array and that as a consequence *the surroundings of each grid line intersection, or lattice*

Figure 2.1. Regular two-dimensional array.

point, are identical. In finite lattices this is, of course, not true for points at the edges, but we will be dealing with lattices of such size that for practical purposes they can be considered infinite.

That area in Fig. 2.2 set off by successive grid lines in two grid-line directions is termed a *unit cell*. In a three-dimensional lattice, the unit cell is a volume element and can be defined as the *parallelepiped whose edges are successive grid lines* (Fig. 2.3). The unit cell is the "unit structure" referred to above that produces the macroscopic crystal when stacked side to side in three dimensions.

Note that a unit cell may contain a whole unit of the repeating motif as in Fig. 2.2b, or it may contain parts of several as in Figs. 2.2*a* and *c*. Although the unit cells can differ in both shape and position, nevertheless they have the same area (volume) as long as there is the equivalent of one unit motif per unit cell.

It must be emphasized that the lattice is a purely imaginary construct but a very necessary and useful one. It functions as a coordinate system to which the actual structure is referred. The three grid line directions or coordinate axes are termed x, y, and z and are ordinarily chosen to form a right-handed system, that is, a system in which the digits of the right hand point respectively along $+x$, $+y$, and $+z$ as indicated in Fig. 2.4. An equivalent view is that of a right-handed screw, which advances along $-z$ when rotated from $+x$ to $+y$, along $+x$ when rotated from $+y$ to $+z$, or along $+y$ when rotated from $+z$ to $+x$. The lengths of the unit cell edges along the x, y, and z axes, respectively, are labeled a, b, and c. These same symbols are often used for the axes as well. The angles between the axes are α, β, and γ, with α between b and c, β between a and c, and γ between a and b (see Fig. 2.3).

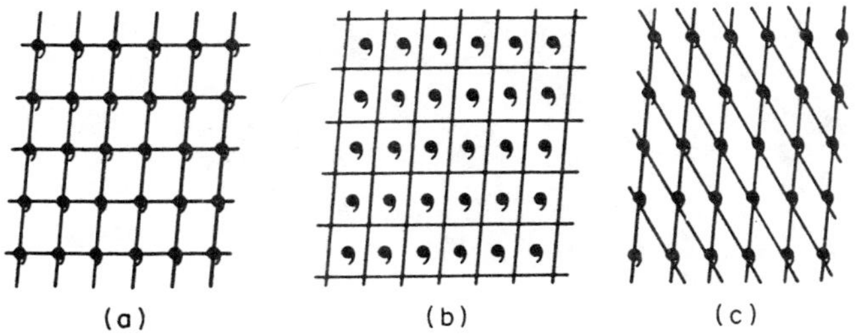

Figure 2.2. Three different grid systems referred to the array of Fig. 2.1.

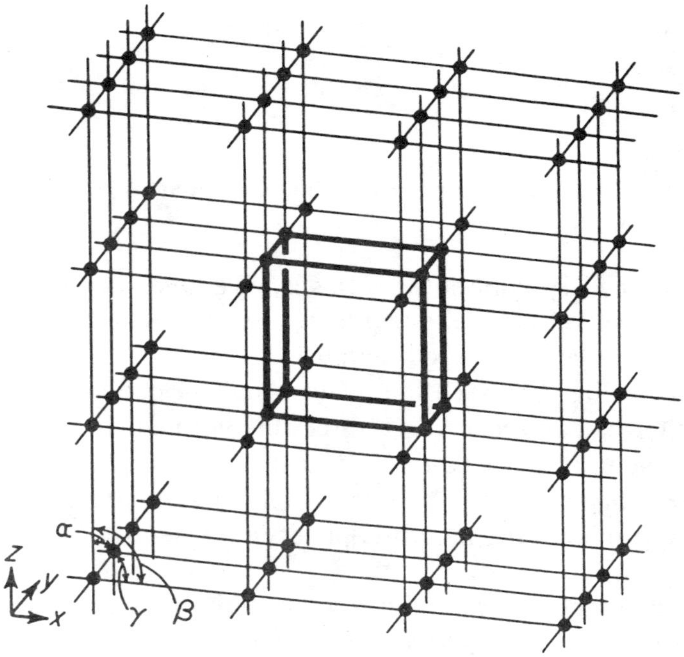

Figure 2.3. Three-dimensional lattice, showing unit cell (heavy lines).

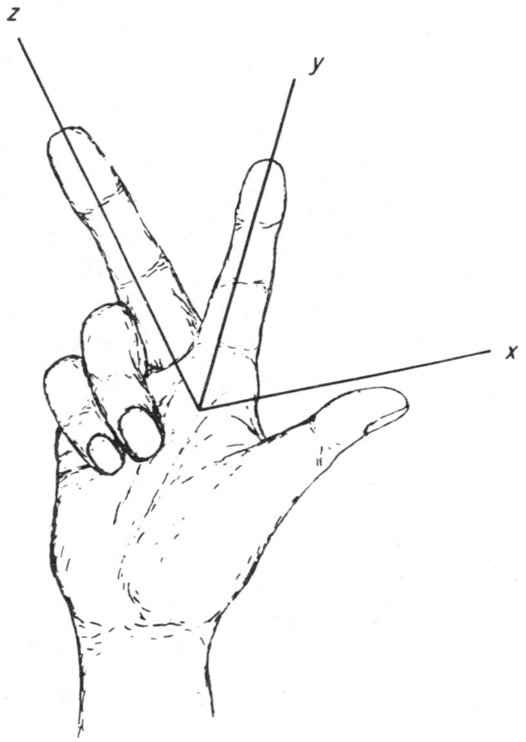

Figure 2.4. Right-hand rule.

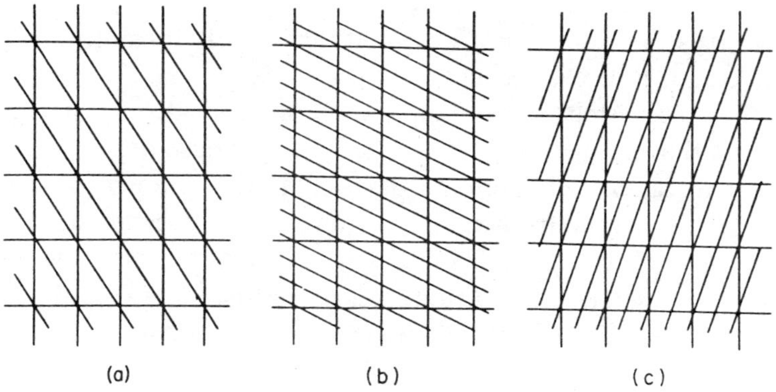

Figure 2.5 Three families of lattice "planes" in a two-dimensional lattice.

For use in the subsequent sections, it is necessary to consider sets of parallel lattice planes constructed so that for any given set every lattice point lies on some member of it. Figures 2.5*a*, *b*, and *c* show the same two-dimensional lattice with different sets of "planes" constructed in this way. These sets of planes are identified by three numbers in the three-dimensional case, one corresponding to each axis. It follows from the repetitive nature of the lattice that when such planes cut an edge of the unit cell the edge is always divided into an integral number of equal parts. These are, of course, common fractions of the unit translation; 1/1, 1/2, . . . , 1/*n*. The fractional intercepts on the three unit cell axes are used as a basis for a triple of numbers, the indices that characterize uniquely each possible set of planes. These indices are obtained by considering some lattice point as the origin and proceeding from it along the axes until the first member of a set of planes is reached. When the intercepts of the plane on the axes are expressed as fractions of the unit cell edge, their reciprocals are just the desired indices. Thus, in Fig. 2.6, plane 1 has intercepts $\frac{1}{2}, \frac{1}{2}, 1$ on the x, y, and z axes, respectively, and has indices (2, 2, 1).[1]

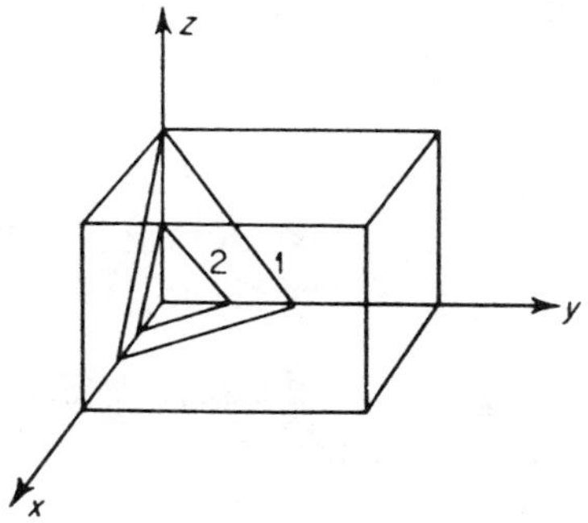

Figure 2.6. Example of a lattice plane and an interleaving plane.

[1]Alternatively, these indices can be regarded as showing the number of cuts made by the set of planes in one unit translation along each axial direction.

A special case arises when the planes in question are parallel to one or more of the axes. The intercept on a parallel axis is formally at infinity, so the corresponding index is its reciprocal, 0.

As we shall see, it is often convenient to consider additional sets of parallel planes that do not contain lattice points. These are interleaved so as to divide the distance between the original lattice planes into equal fractions. Thus, if the original lattice planes had the indices (h, k, l),[2] resulting from intercepts $1/h$, $1/k$, and $1/l$, a single interleaving plane would cut the axes at half these distances from the origin, that is, $\frac{1}{2}h$, $\frac{1}{2}k$, and $\frac{1}{2}l$, and have indices $(2h, 2k, 2l)$. For example, plane 2 in Fig. 2.6 has intercepts $\frac{1}{4}, \frac{1}{4}, \frac{1}{2}$ and indices (4, 4, 2).[3] In general, the addition of $n - 1$ interleaving planes between each pair of the set (h, k, l) will give the family of planes with indices (nh, nk, nl).

Classical crystallography was concerned with lattice planes primarily as they were exhibited in the exterior faces of the crystal. In this sense, the planes (2, 2, 1) and (4, 4, 2) are indistinguishable, and so the use of so-called Miller indices, that is, those having no common factor,[4] became customary. In dealing with X-ray diffraction, however, we shall find the general indices useful. Thus when indices are referred to subsequently without qualification, they will be general rather than Miller indices.

Miller indices can be used in any of three ways: to designate a set of lattice planes, a particular member of the set, or the face of a macroscopic crystal parallel to the set. Thus (010) is used to indicate the set of planes parallel to the xz plane and at $y = 0, b, 2b, 3b, \ldots$; the particular plane at $y = 0$; or the crystal face parallel to these. In contrast, $[x, y, z]$ indicates a direction in the lattice, that of a line segment from the origin to the point x, y, z. Frequently x, y, z are integers and may be confused with Miller indices. This occurs because locations in and around the unit cell are often specified by using the lengths of the cell edges as units. On this basis the lattice point at a distance a from the origin along the x axis has the coordinates 1, 0, 0, and the line segment connecting it to the origin is [100]. Thus the three cell axes are [100], [010], and [001], while (100), (010), and (001) are the yz, xz, and xy planes, respectively (Fig. 2.7).[5] Note that the plane (100) intersects the axis [100], although the two are not necessarily perpendicular, and similarly for the other planes and axes.

A third, related notation is {100}, and so on, which refers to a set of face planes that are equivalent by the symmetry of the crystal (see Chapter 3). Such a set is called a crystal *form*. The number of planes included will depend on the particular crystal and its symmetry; thus for a cubic crystal,

[2]These symbols are the ones that are universally used for the general representation of indices.

[3]Where there is no danger of misunderstanding, the commas separating the indices are customarily omitted. Thus, (4, 4, 2) is usually seen as (442), but (12, 4, 2) would remain as such.

[4]It can be shown that one of the characteristics of the indices of planes of lattice points is that they are relatively prime, that is, they have no common factor.

[5]These are more commonly referred to as the a, b, and c axes and the bc, ac, and ab planes.

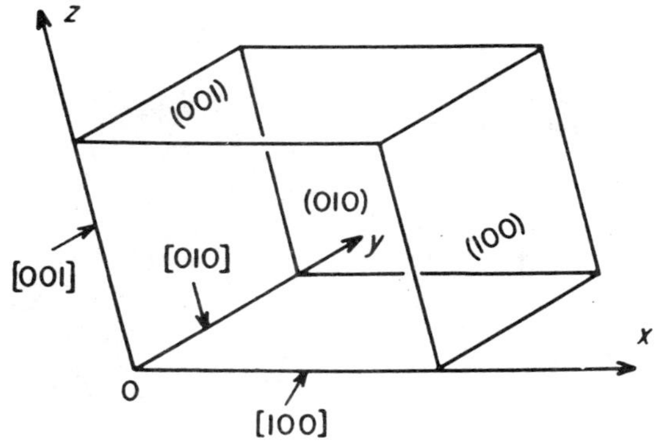

Figure 2.7. Unit cell showing bounding planes and edges.

{100} includes (100), (010), (001), ($\bar{1}$00), (0$\bar{1}$0), and (00$\bar{1}$),[6] while for a triclinic crystal it may include only (100).

The indices for the various planes in a lattice will depend on just how the unit cell is chosen. Transformation of the indices in changing from one unit cell to another follows certain well-established rules, which are treated in more detail in specialized texts.[7,8]

2.2. X-RAY DIFFRACTION

The diffraction of X-rays by crystals was discovered by Max von Laue in 1912, and the sequence of events that led to the discovery is one of the most fascinating chapters in the history of science.[9] Although X-rays had been discovered in 1895 by Roentgen, their nature was not known. During the years following their discovery, a number of determined efforts were made to prove them particles or waves. It was not, in fact, until diffraction by crystals was observed that their wave character was proved.

Following the experimental observation of X-ray diffraction early in 1912, von Laue showed that the phenomenon could be described in terms of diffraction from a three-dimensional grating.[10] In the same year, however, while engaged in experimental studies, W. L. Bragg[11] noticed the similarity of diffraction to ordinary reflection and deduced a simple equation treating diffraction as "reflection" from planes in the lattice. In order to

[6]It is standard crystallographic practice to place minus signs *over* indices. The plane ($\bar{1}$00) is one that cuts the $-x$ axis at $-a$ and lies parallel to the y and z axes.

[7]*International Tables*, Vol. I, pp. 15–21.

[8]Buerger, *X-Ray Crystallography*, pp. 10–28.

[9]See P. P. Ewald in *Fifty Years of X-Ray Diffraction*, P. P. Ewald, Ed., International Union of Crystallography, Utrecht, 1962, pp. 6–75.

[10]M. von Laue, *Sitz. math. phys. Klasse Bayer. Akad. Wiss.*, 303 (1912).

[11]W. L. Bragg, *Proc. Camb. Phil. Soc.*, **17**, 43 (1913).

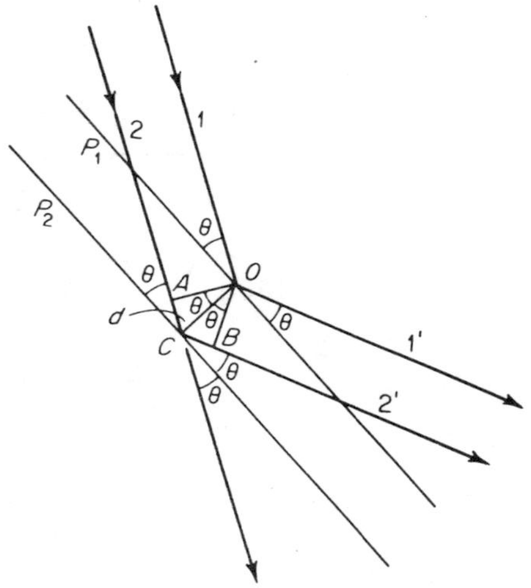

Figure 2.8. Construction showing conditions for diffraction.

derive the equation, we consider an X-ray beam incident on a pair of parallel planes P_1 and P_2 with interplanar spacing d (Fig. 2.8). The parallel incident rays 1 and 2 make an angle θ with these planes. Electrons assumed at O and C will be forced to vibrate by the oscillating field of the incident beam and, as vibrating charges, will radiate in all directions. For that particular direction[12] where the parallel secondary rays 1′ and 2′ emerge at angle θ as if reflected from the planes, a diffracted beam of maximum intensity will result if the waves represented by these rays are in phase. Dropping perpendiculars from O to A and B, respectively, it becomes evident that $\angle AOC = \angle BOC = \theta$. Hence $AC = BC$, and waves in ray 2′ will be in phase, that is, crest to crest, with those in 1′ if $AC + CB$ $(= 2AC)$ is an integral number of wavelengths λ. This is expressed by the equality

$$2AC = n\lambda \tag{2.1}$$

where n is an integer. By definition, $AC/d \equiv \sin\theta$, and by substitution in Eq. (2.1),

$$2d \sin\theta = n\lambda \tag{2.2}$$

This is *Bragg's law*.

The process of reflection is described above in terms of incident and reflected rays each making an angle θ with a fixed crystal plane. It can also be viewed as involving a fixed incident beam, in which case reflection occurs from planes set at the angle θ with respect to the beam and generates a reflected ray deviating through 2θ. This description resembles

[12]It can be shown (see Appendix A) that if one considers the simultaneous reflection of a large number of such rays, interference prevents the appearance of radiation in any other direction.

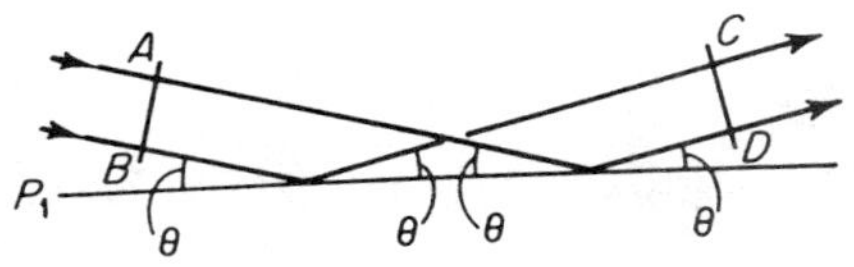

Figure 2.9. Reflection from two points in a plane.

more closely the actual experimental arrangements and is the more commonly used.

Though Fig. 2.8, on which the derivation is based, represents a special case, the result is, in fact, general. What holds for points O and C can be shown to hold for any pair of points in planes 1 and 2. This can be seen by recalling the elementary treatment of reflection. Figure 2.9 shows two parallel incident and reflected rays, where the angles θ between the rays and the plane are all equal. The path length by way of these rays (or any parallel rays) from the incident wave front AB to the emergent wave front CD is always the same provided the incident rays, the normals to the plane P at the points of incidence, and the reflected rays all lie in a plane. Thus the emergent rays shown, or any others similarly constructed, are in phase. It can now be seen by reference to Fig. 2.8 that any ray parallel to 1′ but from another point in plane P_1 will differ in phase by just $n\lambda$ not only from ray 2′ emergent from point C but also from any other parallel ray from any other point in plane P_2.

In the derivation of Bragg's law, electron density was assumed to be in the planes of Fig. 2.8. In actual structures, however, the electron density is distributed throughout the unit cell and does not lie in special planes. Nevertheless, the derivation is valid, since it can be shown that waves scattered from electron density not lying in the plane P (Fig. 2.10) can be added to give a resultant as if reflected from the plane. It is the variation in these resultants that accounts for the differing intensities of reflection observed for various planes (see Chapter 8).

In the derivation, reflections from only two planes were considered. In such a case the diffraction maxima would be broad and the various diffracted rays would virtually merge. In crystals, however, many hundreds or thousands of planes make up each of the mosaic blocks (see Chapter 4) that constitute the macroscopic crystal. Under these conditions, the diffraction maxima will be sharp and will occur only at clearly defined values of θ. Indeed, for real crystals the breadth of a reflection as measured in terms of the range of θ over which it can be observed is usually a small fraction of a degree and due mostly to the slight misalignment of the mosaic blocks

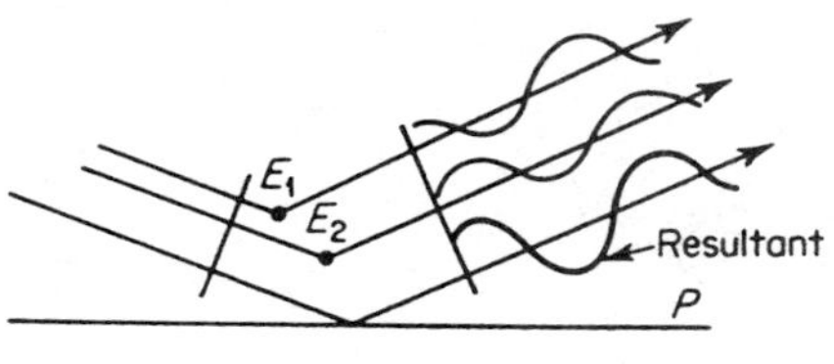

Figure 2.10. Diffraction from E_1 and E_2 as if reflected from plane P.

BIBLIOGRAPHY

Buerger, M. J., *X-Ray Crystallography*, Wiley, New York, 1942, pp. 4–47, 347–362.

Bunn, C. W., *Chemical Crystallography*, 2nd ed., Oxford University Press, London, 1961, pp. 120–125.

Gay, P., *The Crystalline State*, Oliver and Boyd, Edinburgh, 1972, pp. 15–33, 56–140.

Glusker, J. P., and K. N. Trueblood, *Crystal Structure Analysis*, 2nd ed., Oxford University Press, New York, 1985, pp. 11–41.

Guinier, A., *X-Ray Crystallographic Technology*, Hilger and Watts, London, 1952, Chapter III.

Henry, N. F. M., H. Lipson, and W. A. Wooster, *The Interpretation of X-Ray Diffraction Photographs*, Macmillan, London, 1960, pp. 34–41.

Jeffery, J. W., *Methods in X-Ray Crystallography*, Academic, London, 1971, pp. 18–31.

X-RAY DIFFRACTION METHODS

E. W. NUFFIELD

PROFESSOR OF GEOLOGY
UNIVERSITY OF TORONTO

JOHN WILEY & SONS, INC.,
NEW YORK · LONDON · SYDNEY

CHAPTER ONE

INTRODUCTION

HISTORICAL BACKGROUND

The Laue Experiments and the Bragg Equation

The investigation of the geometrical theory of crystal structure was completed by the end of the nineteenth century with the publication of the 230 space groups by Federov, Schoenflies, and Barlow. A number of English scientists then turned to problems connected with the determination of crystal structures. They devised three-dimensional models of possible structures, considered the packing of spheres, and even deduced the probable space groups of some minerals. However, the investigations were not systematic and attracted little attention, partly because the reality of the atom was still not universally accepted, but largely because there was no way to determine a space group and test the theory that the atoms of crystal structures were actually arranged in patterns predicted by space-group theory. Further progress toward the goal of a firm basis for the theory of crystal structure awaited advances in the studies of the x-rays discovered by Roentgen in 1895.

Wiechert and Stokes had concluded in 1896 that x-rays must be short waves consisting of electromagnetic pulses. Their wavelengths were thought to be of the order of 1 Å, based on estimates of 7×10^{-9} cm (Wien in 1907) and 4×10^{-9} cm (Sommerfeld in 1912). Nevertheless, a number of eminent physicists of the time, including W. H. Bragg, believed in the corpuscular theory of x-rays.

Perrin and Millikan had measured Avogadro's number [the number of molecules (or atoms) in a gram-molecular (or atomic) weight] and had obtained a value of 6.2×10^{23}. This provided the key for calculating the approximate volume occupied by a molecule or an atom:

$$\text{volume of one molecule} = \frac{\text{molecular weight}}{\text{Avogadro's number} \times \text{density}}$$

The compound NaCl, for example, with a molecular weight of 58.5 and a density of 2.2, gave a value of

$$\frac{58.5}{6.2 \times 10^{23} \times 2.2} = 42.9 \times 10^{-24}\,\text{cm}^3 = 42.9\,\text{Å}^3$$

for the volume of one molecule of NaCl. From this it followed that the atoms are spaced at intervals of about 2 Å in the NaCl structure.

The phenomenon of diffraction of visible light by ruled gratings was well known. Lord Rayleigh had frequently emphasized that the essential characteristic of a grating is the periodic repetition of its elements and not the nature of these elements. About 1910 M. von Laue elaborated on Lord Rayleigh's idea and arrived at an equation for the position of the diffraction maxima which could be extended without difficulty to the case of double periodicity as it exists in cross-gratings. Shortly thereafter it occurred to von Laue that crystals were supposed to be regular arrangements of matter on the same scale as the estimated order of wavelength of x-rays. He reasoned that if the assumptions concerning the internal structure of crystals were correct, and if x-rays were electromagnetic waves, crystals should act as three-dimensional diffraction gratings for the penetrating x-rays. At this time von Laue was an assistant lecturer in the physics department at Munich headed by Professor Summerfeld. It was arranged that Friedrich and Knipping, who had just completed their doctorates under Professor Roentgen, would undertake experiments to test the hypothesis.

A copper sulfate crystal, chosen for the first experiment, was placed in the path of a fine beam of x-rays; a photographic plate was used to record the effects. The first trials were unsuccessful because the plate was improperly positioned. However, when the plate was placed behind the crystal and normal to the beam, a pattern of spots in addition to the direct-beam spot was revealed when the plate was developed (Fig. 1-1). They obtained an identical but enlarged pattern when the crystal-to-plate distance was increased which indicated that the x-rays emanating from the crystal traveled in straight lines. They also found that the pattern was changed when the orientation of the crystal was altered. The choice of copper sulfate for the first experiment was unfortunate, because at this stage it was virtually impossible to interpret the diffraction effects from a triclinic crystal. When a crystal of cubic ZnS was substituted, it was found that the symmetry of the arrangement of spots on the plate was directly related to the orientation of the crystal in the beam. This finally appeared to prove the periodic arrangement of atoms in crystals, the wave nature of x-rays, and von Laue's diffraction theory. Admittedly, the ZnS crystal gave only a selection of the diffraction spots that von Laue had expected, but he explained this by ascribing to the atoms a strongly selective scattering power for x-rays and was thus led to believe in the existence of five characteristic wavelengths in the radiation.

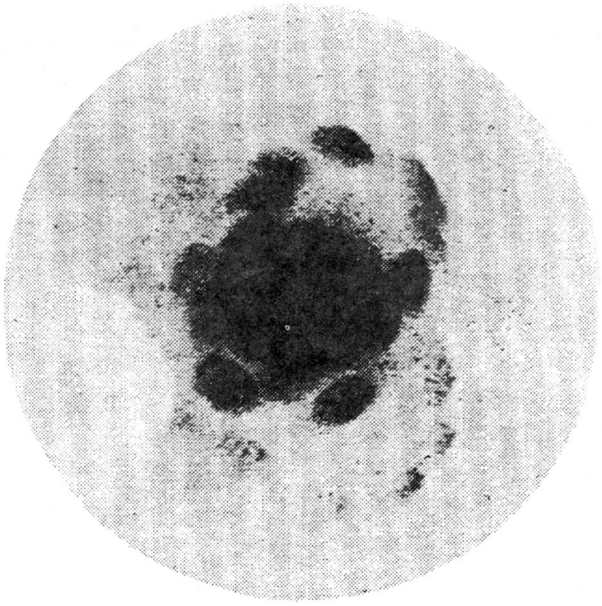

Fig. 1-1. The first x-ray diffraction photograph [P. P. Ewald, *Fifty Years of X-ray Diffraction*, N. V. A. Oosthoek, Utrecht, The Netherlands (1962)].

The experimental results and von Laue's interpretations were published in 1912 and aroused much interest. In England W. H. Bragg and his son W. L. Bragg immediately undertook experiments to test von Laue's conclusions. The younger Bragg, working at Cambridge, was soon satisfied that von Laue's photographs were due to diffraction, but concluded that von Laue's explanation for the spots had to be modified. He observed in his own experiments that the diffracted beam responsible for any spot was slightly converging—an observation that was easily explained, if the slightly diverging incident beam was being reflected by the crystal. This led him to picture the diffraction effect as a reflection of x-rays from the lattice planes of the crystal. He tested this by reflecting white x-rays from a mica plate set at a series of angles and obtained in every case a spot in the reflection position. This indicated that all wavelengths over a certain range were represented in the x-ray beam and that the reflection effect was equivalent to a selection from the continuous spectrum of a wavelength determined by the spacing of the lattice planes parallel to the plate surface of the mica crystal. From this Bragg derived a mathematical relation connecting the wavelength λ of the reflected x-radiation, the spacing d of the reflecting planes, and the angle of reflection θ. This relation

$$n\lambda = 2d \sin \theta$$

is now known as the Bragg law. Bragg was also able to explain why only a selection of diffraction spots appeared in von Laue's photographs of ZnS by ascribing to this compound an all-face-centered lattice instead of the primitive lattice von Laue had assumed. These results were communicated to the Cambridge Philosophical Society in November of 1912.

W. H. Bragg was much interested in the reflection concept and set up at Leeds the first x-ray spectrometer for accurately measuring the position and intensity of x-ray beams reflected from crystal planes. He was primarily interested in the nature of x-rays at this time. He satisfied himself that the reflected rays were really x-rays and confirmed that the spectrum of the incident beam was continuous. However, he found superimposed on this continuous range monochromatic components characteristic of the target. He constructed a number of x-ray tubes with different targets, with which he was able to show that the characteristic wavelengths were related to the atomic weights of the target metals. This was, in part, the groundwork for Moseley's discovery, published in 1914, of the mathematical relation between the characteristic wavelengths and the atomic number of the chemical element of which the target was composed.

W. L. Bragg had been able to deduce the atomic arrangements in NaCl and KCl from Laue photographs, but he had not been able to solve the structure of the diamond. W. H. Bragg found little difficulty with this structure when it was investigated with the x-ray spectrometer. Father and son then joined forces and collaborated in working out a number of structures, including ZnS, CaF_2, and FeS_2.

The Braggs used the NaCl structure to make still another important advance. X-ray diffraction photographs provided n and θ for the various reflections from a crystal, but could not evaluate λ without a knowledge of d. It was possible to establish the relative wavelength values of x-rays from different targets by reflection from a standard crystal (same value of d). Before absolute values of the wavelengths could be deduced, however, it was necessary to know the absolute values of the lattice constants of one compound. W. L. Bragg had shown that the Laue photographs of NaCl (and KCl) could be explained by two interpenetrating all-face-centered structures, one composed of Na atoms and the other of Cl atoms (Fig. 1-2)—in agreement with one of the structures postulated for this compound before the Laue experiments by Pope and

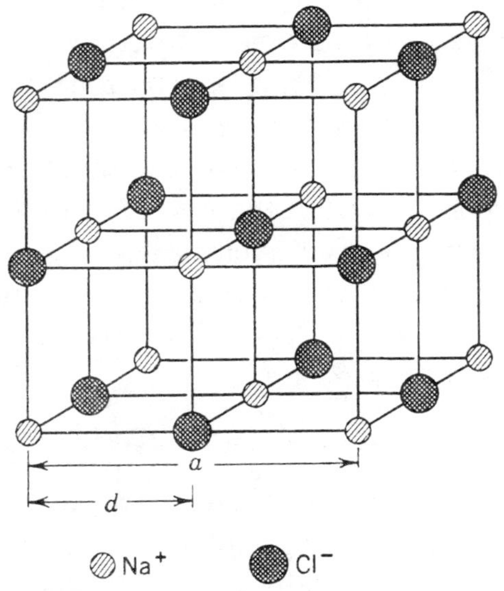

Fig. 1-2. The crystal structure of NaCl.

Barlow. The unit cell of this structure contained four molecules. By using an improved value for Avogadro's number (6.06×10^{23}), the volume of the cell was calculated to be

$$4 \times \frac{58.46}{6.06 \times 10^{23} \times 2.167} = 178.40 \times 10^{-24}\ \text{cm}^3 = 178.40\ \text{Å}^3$$

This corresponded to a cubic cell edge of 5.63 Å and, because of the all-face-centered nature of the structure, to a spacing of 2.815 Å for the $\{100\}$ planes. This first absolute spacing value provided an absolute value for the wavelengths of radiation reflected from the $\{100\}$ planes of NaCl. Alternatively, a known wavelength could be used to calculate the absolute lattice constants of an unknown crystal.

Wavelength Units

Soon after the first crystal structures had been determined, it became evident that x-ray measurements were more precise than measurements of constants, such as Avogadro's number, on which the absolute value of the $\{100\}$ spacing of NaCl was based. It seemed certain that the values of the constants would be progressively refined and would result in a changing series of values for the {100} spacing. To avoid the consequent confusion in the literature, Siegbahn, one of the foremost x-ray spectroscopists, proposed in 1925 to express x-ray wavelengths in terms of a new unit of measurement—the x unit, abbreviated xu. At this time the best value of the NaCl spacing was 2.814 Å. Siegbahn defined the x unit by assigning a value of 2814.00 xu to the fundamental NaCl spacing. This gave the unit a value as near to 10^{-11} cm, or 1/1000 Å, as the physical constants of the time allowed. A larger unit, equal to 1000 xu and abbreviated kxu or simply kx, became popular because its value was near 1 Å and therefore a more useful unit for expressing interatomic distances. Shortly thereafter it was found that the mineral calcite ($CaCO_3$) gave much sharper reflections than NaCl, and it came to be the standard crystal for measuring x-ray wavelengths.

Meanwhile, absolute x-ray wavelengths were being measured by means of diffraction by ruled gratings. With this technique, the wavelength is given by the relation

$$n\lambda = a[\cos\theta - \cos(\theta + \alpha)]$$

where n is of the order of the diffraction spectrum, a is the spacing of the grating, θ is the glancing angle of incidence, and $(\theta + \alpha)$ the glancing angle of diffraction. The values of a, θ, and α are capable of being measured with great accuracy, and today the ruled-grating method yields the best absolute wavelength values. As the technique developed to a high degree of precision, it became evident that absolute wavelengths determined by diffraction from crystals were lower by 0.2 per cent than the grating-determined values. This led to a thorough reevaluation of the constants involved in calculating the absolute value of the {100} spacing of NaCl—namely, the molecular weight, the density, and Avogadro's number. The investigation suggested that the only possible error of this magnitude lay in the determination of Avogadro's number. Eventually the error was traced to one of the constants—e, the charge on the electron—on which the number depended. A redetermination of e removed the discrepancy between crystal and ruled-grating values. However, the value of e, deduced by combining the two x-ray methods, was recognized as more accurate than the direct determination. Thus x-ray diffraction is responsible for finding errors in two fundamental physical constants, N and e, and for refining their values.

The new wavelength values came into general use in the early nineteen forties. Unfortunately, the literature for this period is somewhat confusing. Many crystallographers who used the Siegbahn kx values, wrongly stated their measurements in angstrom units. Consequently, the literature for the change-over period contains measurements both in angstrom units and in kx units but stated to be in angstrom units. Most of the data available before 1951 have been reviewed by Donnay and Nowacki.[1] It is advisable to consult the second edition[2] of this reference if any doubt exists. Values of wavelengths and lattice constants expressed in kx units are multiplied by the generally accepted factor 1.00202 to correct the 0.2 per cent discrepancy and to convert to angstrom units.

ELEMENTARY CRYSTALLOGRAPHY

The word *crystal* was used by the Greeks as early as 400 B.C. At first it referred specifically to transparent, crystallized quartz that was found in fine specimens in the high regions of the Alps. This mineral was believed to be ice—cooled and hardened to a permanent solid by the intense cold of the Alps. As a result of this belief, which persisted into the seventeenth century, the mineral became known as rock crystal from the Greek word *kyros*, meaning ice. There was much speculation about the origin of its hexagonal form, and by a natural association of ideas other minerals which showed faces, including those with metallic luster, were gradually spoken of as crystals. Eventually the word became a general term to describe any crystallized compound—that is, one bounded by faces—although "rock crystal" persists to this day as a varietal name for clear, crystallized quartz. Toward the end of the eighteenth century Rome de l'Isle used the term *crystallography* for the science concerned with the study of crystal forms of all substances, both transparent and opaque, that had formed by solidification in nature and in the laboratory.

The contemporary crystallographer is more concerned with the study of atomic arrangements, of which the crystal faces are one external expression. Because of this, the definition of the word crystal is changing and varies with the discipline. In physics and metallurgy, for example, "a region of matter within which the atoms are arranged in a three-dimensional translationally periodic pattern" (Buerger[3]) is a crystal, whether faces are present or not. The usage is not consistent in the earth sciences, even in the same field of concentration. Petrologists find the terms euhedral and anhedral useful in describing the fabric of rocks. Both words refer to grains that show optical continuity under the microscope. Euhedral implies a characteristic geometrical outline, anhedral the absence of crystal form. Some petrologists (Tyrrell[4]) speak

[1] J. D. H. Donnay and W. Nowacki, "Crystal Data," *Geol. Soc. Am. Mem.*, **60** (1954).
[2] *Crystal Data*, Second Edition, American Crystallographic Association, Monograph 5.
[3] M. J. Buerger, *Elementary Crystallography*, John Wiley and Sons, New York (1956).
[4] G. W. Tyrrel, *Principles of Petrology*, Methuen and Co. London (1929).

of both euhedral and anhedral grains as crystals, whereas others make the distinction of euhedral crystals and anhedral grains. The presence of faces is implicit in the definition of a crystal in descriptive mineralogy—"a crystal is a solid body bounded by plane natural surfaces which are the external expression of a regular internal arrangement of constituent atoms or ions" (Berry and Mason[5]). The word crystal is used in a curious way by many x-ray crystallographers. A specimen without faces but with continuous atomic arrangements qualifies as a crystal, if a crystallographic direction can be located and oriented in an x-ray beam—that is, if the specimen is amenable to the single crystal x-ray methods described in this book.

The orderly arrangement of atoms that constitute a crystal is known as the crystal structure. Some materials are obviously crystalline in composition but others, like the mineral limonite, are not. The ability to detect crystallinity improved enormously with the Laue experiments in 1912, which showed that x-rays are diffracted by crystals to give a characteristic x-ray pattern. Limonite was formerly classed as a mineral colloid, mainly because its earthy nature defied the usual microscopic tests for crystallinity. X-ray studies have shown that most specimens of this mineral produce a diffraction pattern characteristic of the mineral goethite ($HFeO_2$). These specimens of limonite might therefore be described as cryptocrystalline varieties of goethite. Some solids, such as glasses, appear to be obviously noncrystalline (amorphous), but they give weak and diffuse diffraction effects which indicate that their structures are at least partly ordered. Certain compounds give a range of patterns that vary from the diffraction effects of truly crystalline solids to the indistinct effects associated with amorphous materials. In these compounds, at least, there is no sharp distinction between the crystalline and amorphous states. It may be surmised that in the amorphous types there is a short-order range of crystallinity (individual crystals are only a few atoms in size), whereas in the highly ordered types the crystallinity is of a long-range order.

The Classification of Crystals

A crystal structure is like a three-dimensional wallpaper design in that it is an infinite repetition of some motif (a group of atoms). It is a periodic space pattern. Study has shown that there are 230 kinds of space pattern. Each crystal belongs to one of the 230 types, hence elementary crystallography is vitally concerned with the characteristics of

[5] L. G. Berry and B. Mason, *Mineralogy*, W. H. Freeman and Co., San Franscisco and London (1959).

the patterns. Because repetition is a fundamental property of the patterns, it is reasonable to base their classification on the repetition (symmetry) operations that yield them.

It is convenient, in developing the classification of crystals, to subdivide the elements of symmetry into three categories:

(1) translation (parallel periodic displacement);
(2) point group symmetry (rotation and rotation-inversion axes, reflection planes);
(3) space-group symmetry (screw axes, glide planes).

The Translation Lattices

The lattice is derived from the crystal structure by replacing each repeat motif with a point. The lattice is therefore a collection of equipoints that portrays the translational periodicity of the structure (hence the term translation lattice). This fundamental property of all crystalline structures limits the number of distinct two-dimensional lattices to the five shown in Fig. 1-3. These plane lattices can be systematically stacked

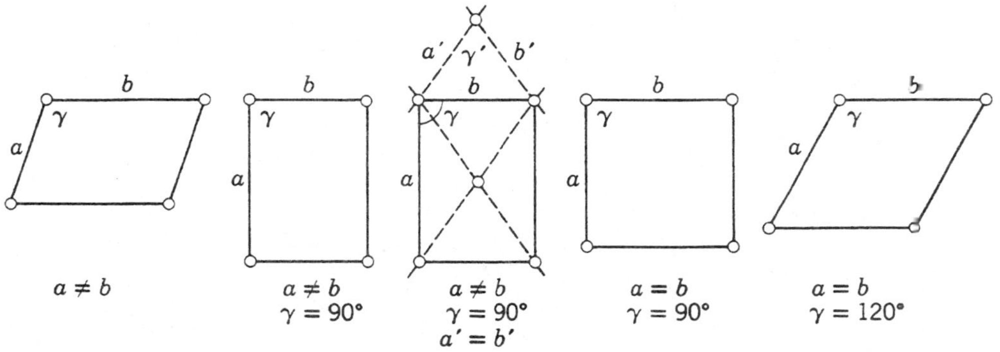

Fig. 1-3. The five plane lattices.

to realize only fourteen distinct space lattices (Fig. 1-4), referrable to six (or seven, if centered hexagonal lattices are referred to Miller rhombohedral axes) coordinate systems (Table 1-1). The names of some of the systems reflect the nature of the metrical properties: triclinic—three inclined axes; monoclinic—one inclined axis; orthorhombic—axes mutually perpendicular; isometric (cubic)—three mutually perpendicular equal axes. The remaining names, tetragonal and hexagonal, refer to the dominant symmetry of crystals belonging to these systems. A repeat unit of a lattice is known as the unit cell.

NOTATION OF LATTICE POINTS, ROWS, AND PLANES. Figure 1-5 illustrates the method of notating lattice points, rows, and planes on the

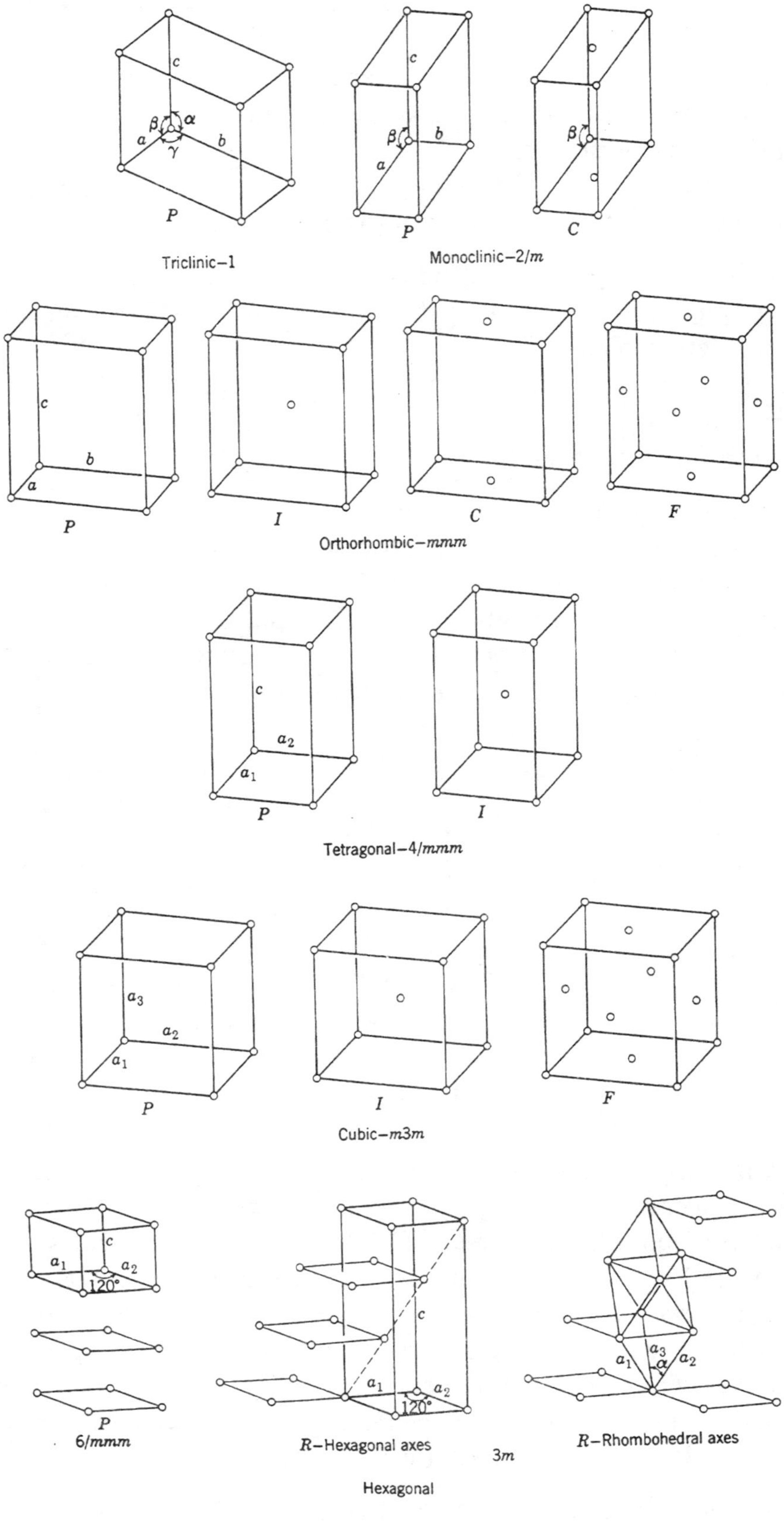

Fig. 1-4. The fourteen space lattices.

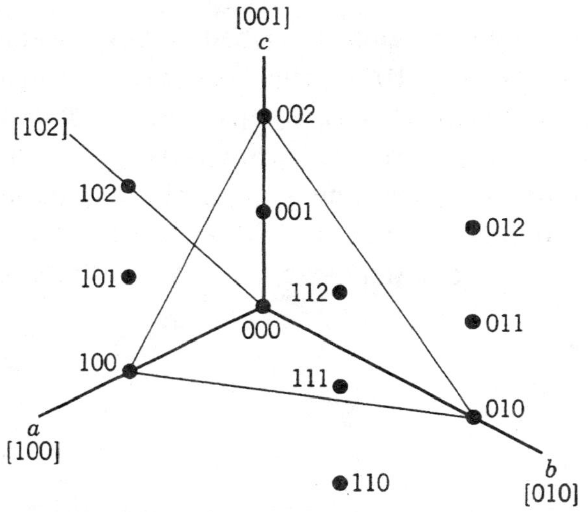

Fig. 1-5. Notation of lattice points, rows, and planes.

Table 1-1. The Fourteen Bravais Lattices

System	Type	Nature of Edges and Angles	Symmetry
Triclinic	P	$a \neq b \neq c$ $\alpha \neq \beta \neq \gamma$	$\bar{1}$
Monoclinic	P C (b = twofold axis)	$a \neq b \neq c$ $\alpha = \gamma = 90° \neq \beta$	$2/m$
	P B (c = twofold axis)	$a \neq b \neq c$ $\alpha = \beta = 90° \neq \gamma$	
Orthorhombic	P C (or A, B) I F	$a \neq b \neq c$ $\alpha = \beta = \gamma = 90°$	mmm
Tetragonal	P I	$a_1 = a_2 \neq c$ $\alpha = \beta = \gamma = 90°$	$4/mmm$
Hexagonal	R[a] P	$a_1 = a_2 \neq c$ $\alpha = \beta = 90°, \gamma = 120°$	$\bar{3}m$ $6/mmm$
Cubic	P I F	$a_1 = a_2 = a_3$ $\alpha = \beta = \gamma = 90°$	$m3m$

[a] Alternatively, a rhombohedral unit cell, characterized by edges and angles $a_1 = a_2 = a_3$; $\alpha < 120° \neq 90°$, can be chosen (see Fig. 1–3). This cell has one third the volume of the cell outlined by hexagonal axes.

basis of the coordinate systems described. Lattice points are specified without brackets—100, 101, 102; lattice rows are identified by brackets—[100] (the a axis), [010] (the b axis). Lattice planes are defined in terms of the Miller indices, which are the reciprocals of the intercepts of the planes on the coordinate axes. The general plane illustrated in Fig. 1-5c, for example, has intercepts 1a, 1b, and 2c. The Miller indices are therefore $\frac{1}{1}a, \frac{1}{1}b, \frac{1}{2}c = 2a\,2b\,1c$. The letters are usually omitted, and the indices

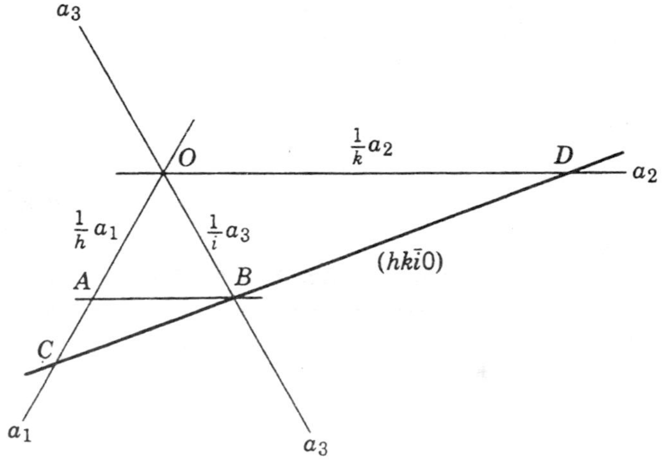

Fig. 1-6. Hexagonal indices.

are enclosed in parentheses; thus (221). If the calculations result in indices that have a common factor—for example, (422)—the factor is removed to give the simplest set of integers: (221). The symbol (221) therefore applies equally to all individuals of a stack of identical, parallel planes related by a simple translation operation. Braces { } are used to designate a family of planes related by the symmetry of the lattice. Thus, in the tetragonal system, {110} refers to the four planes (110), $(\bar{1}10)$, $(\bar{1}\bar{1}0)$, and $(1\bar{1}0)$; in the cubic system the same symbol stands for the twelve planes (110), $(\bar{1}10)$, $(\bar{1}\bar{1}0)$, $(1\bar{1}0)$, (101), $(10\bar{1})$, $(\bar{1}01)$, $(\bar{1}0\bar{1})$, (011), $(01\bar{1})$, $(0\bar{1}1)$, and $(0\bar{1}\bar{1})$.

The notation of hexagonal planes requires special attention. Hexagonal crystals are usually referred to the Bravais–Miller axes—a_1, a_2, a_3, and c. The three a axes are equivalent and, as a consequence, there should be a simple relation between the corresponding three indices. Figure 1-6 shows a plane with indices $(hk\bar{i}0)$ intersecting a set of hexagonal axes. The intercepts of the plane are the reciprocals of the indices, multiplied by the lattice period, a: $(1/h)a_1(1/k)a_2(1/i)a_3$. AB is drawn parallel to OD to construct two similar triangles OCD and ACB. OAB is an equilateral triangle. Then

$$\frac{OC}{OD} = \frac{AC}{AB} = \frac{OC - OA}{AB}$$

and

$$\frac{a_1/h}{a_2/k} = \frac{a_1/h - a_3/i}{a_3/i}$$

Because the axes are equivalent, this reduces to

$$\frac{1}{hi} = \frac{1}{hk} - \frac{1}{ki}$$

After multiplying by *hki*

$$k = i - h$$

The plane intersects the negative end of the a_3 axis and consequently, having regard for the sign of the *i* index,

$$h + k + i = 0$$

In other words, the sum of the indices is zero. For the sake of simplicity the *i* index is frequently replaced by a dot: $(hk \cdot l)$.

THE SPACING OF LATTICE PLANES. The perpendicular distance between the individuals of a stack of lattice planes is known as the *spacing* of the planes and is denoted by the letter *d* (Fig. 1-7). The value

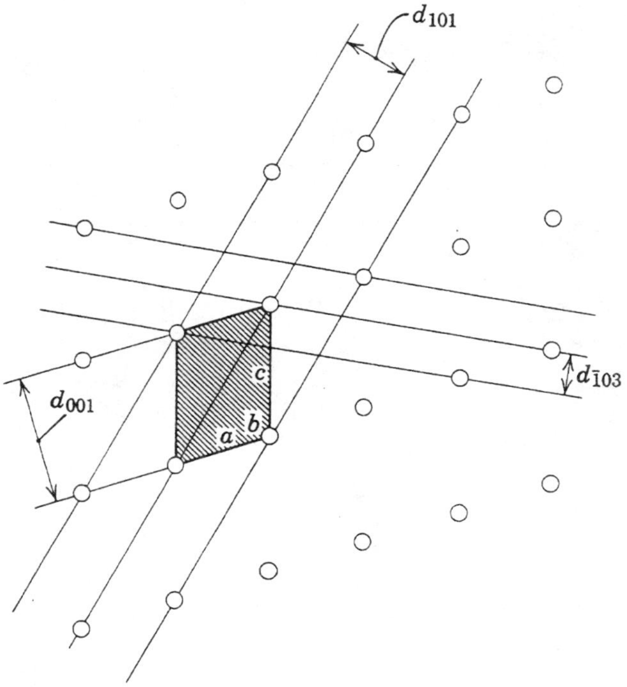

Fig. 1-7. Interplanar spacings.

Table 1-2. Values of the Interplanar Spacing (d_{hkl}) in the Six Crystal Systems

System	d_{hkl}
Cubic	$\left[\frac{1}{a^2}(h^2 + k^2 + l^2)\right]^{-1/2}$
Tetragonal	$\left[\frac{h^2 + k^2}{a^2} + \frac{l^2}{c^2}\right]^{-1/2}$
Orthorhombic	$\left[\frac{h^2}{a^2} + \frac{k^2}{b^2} + \frac{l^2}{c^2}\right]^{-1/2}$
Hexagonal	$\left[\frac{4}{3a^2}(h^2 + hk + k^2) + \frac{l^2}{c^2}\right]^{-1/2}$ hexagonal indexing
	$\left[\frac{1}{a^2}\frac{(h^2 + k^2 + l^2)\sin^2\alpha + 2(hk + kl + lh)(\cos^2\alpha - \cos\alpha)}{1 - 2\cos^3\alpha + 3\cos^2\alpha}\right]^{-1/2}$ rhombohedral indexing
Monoclinic	$\left[\frac{\frac{h^2}{a^2} + \frac{l^2}{c^2} - \frac{2hl\cos\beta}{ac}}{\sin^2\beta} + \frac{k^2}{b^2}\right]^{-1/2}$
Triclinic	$\left[\frac{\frac{h^2}{a^2}\sin^2\alpha + \frac{k^2}{b^2}\sin^2\beta + \frac{l^2}{c^2}\sin^2\gamma + \frac{2hk}{ab}(\cos\alpha\cos\beta - \cos\gamma) + \frac{2kl}{bc}(\cos\beta\cos\gamma - \cos\alpha) + \frac{2lh}{ca}(\cos\gamma\cos\alpha - \cos\beta)}{1 - \cos^2\alpha - \cos^2\beta - \cos^2\gamma + 2\cos\alpha\cos\beta\cos\gamma}\right]^{-1/2}$

of d depends on the dimensions of the unit cell in the manner shown in Table 1-2.

CHAPTER TWO

THE NATURE AND GENERATION OF X-RAYS

X-rays, along with visible light, form a part of the electromagnetic spectrum. The various types of radiation that are grouped under this heading are similar in nature and may be roughly distinguished or classified on the basis of wavelength (Table 2–1). The members of the spectrum have a dual nature. Under some conditions they act like waves—the study of the diffraction of x-rays is based on their wavelike nature. Under other conditions they behave like particles: their energy, for example, is radiated not continuously, as we would expect from a pure wave motion, but rather as bundles of waves, called quanta or photons. The energy of a quantum is proportional to the wavelength of the radiation in accordance with the Einstein equation

$$E = \frac{hc}{\lambda}$$

where E is the energy of each quantum, c is the speed of light, λ is the wavelength of the radiation, and h is a proportionality constant known as Planck's constant.

X-rays are generated when electrons, traveling at high speeds collide with the atoms of an obstacle. Broadly speaking, two types of interaction occur, and these result in two types of x-ray spectra—continuous and characteristic.

An x-ray tube is a device for promoting the interaction between high-speed electrons and matter. Its essential features are a source of electrons and two electrodes. A high voltage, applied across the tube, accelerates the electrons toward the anode, which is aptly called the target. X-rays are generated at the point of impact with this obstacle and radiate in all directions.

Table 2-1. Members of the Electromagnetic Spectrum

	Wavelength[a]
Gamma rays	0.0056–0.1 Å
X-rays	0.1–45 Å
Ultraviolet rays	45–3500 Å
Visible light	3500–7000 Å
Infrared rays	7000–2,000,000 Å
Etc.	

[a] After K. Krauskopf, *Fundamentals of Physical Science*, Third Edition, McGraw-Hill Co., New York (1953).

The Continuous Spectrum (White Radiation)

An electron is abruptly slowed and suffers a loss of energy as it enters the electric field surrounding the nucleus of an atom of the target. This results in the emission of a quantum of x-radiation whose wavelength is given by the expression

$$\Delta E = \frac{hc}{\lambda}$$

where ΔE is the loss in energy. An electron, accelerated by a difference in potential of V volts, has the energy eV (where e is the charge on the electron). If the electron is instantaneously stopped, the quantum energy is equal to the energy of the electron and the radiation has the wavelength

$$\lambda = \frac{hc}{eV} = \frac{(6.624 \times 10^{-27}\ \text{erg-sec}) \times (2.998 \times 10^{10}\ \text{cm/sec})}{(1.602 \times 10^{-20}\ \text{emu}) \times (V\ \text{volts})} = \frac{12{,}400}{V}\ \text{Å} \tag{1}$$

Normally an electron's energy is lost in a stepwise fashion by a series of encounters, giving rise to a number of quanta whose wavelengths are longer than if the energy were lost instantaneously. As a result, the spectrum from a stream of electrons exhibits a continuous range of wavelengths to a short wavelength limit, which represents the maximum electron energy transformed to x-radiation in a single encounter. The plot of intensity against wavelength (Fig. 2-1) is a smooth curve which begins abruptly at a short wavelength limit (maximum quantum energy), rises to a maximum (average quantum energy), and extends toward infinity (minimum quantum energy). An increase in the voltage across the x-ray tube increases the speed of the bombarding electrons; the electrons arrive at the target with greater energy, hence the average energy of the quanta is greater. As a consequence, the total intensity of the x-radiation is increased, and both the short wavelength limit and the intensity maximum of the spectrum shift to shorter wavelengths (higher energy). The wavelength distribution of the spectrum is independent

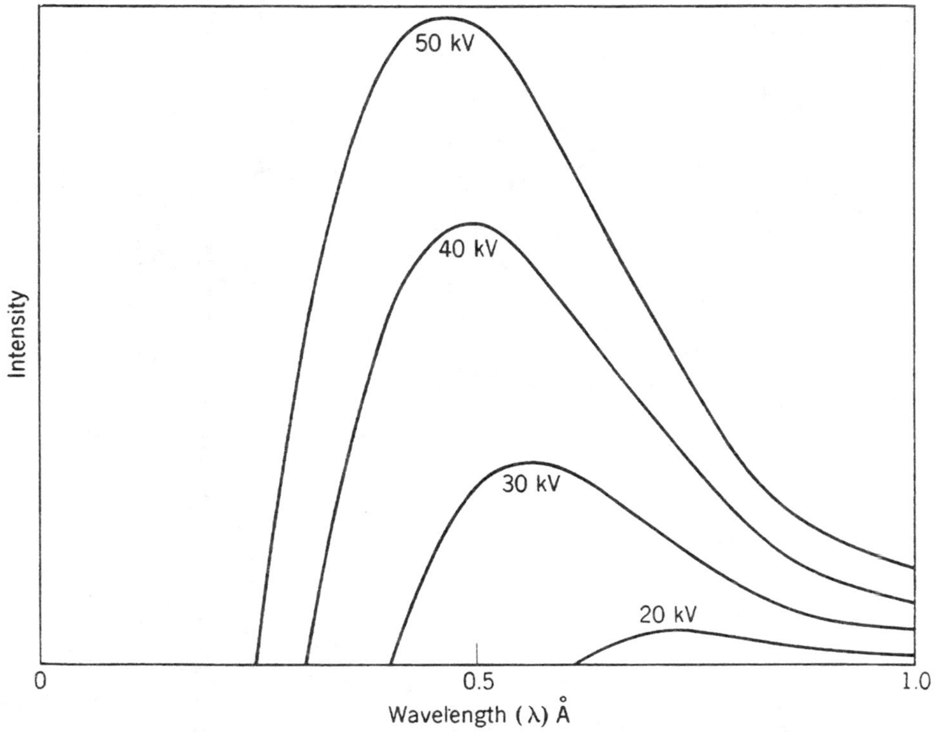

Fig. 2-1. Nature of the variation of the continuous spectrum with voltage (after C. T. Ulrey).

of the target material, but the total intensity of the radiation is proportional to the atomic number of the material. The target of an x-ray tube which is meant to function as an emitter of the continuous spectrum is, therefore, always manufactured from a heavy element.

Characteristic or Line Spectra

If the voltage across an x-ray tube is raised to a critical level, which depends on the element of the target, sharp peaks are superimposed on the smooth curve that represents the continuous spectrum (Fig. 2-2). The peaks occur in groups known as series and are designated *K*, *L*, *M* and *N* in order of increasing wavelength. In general, each series has the same appearance from one element to the next, but the given peak shifts to a shorter wavelength in passing from one element to the next heavier one. The peaks for a given target element always occur at the same wavelengths and are, therefore, *characteristic* spectra.

Characteristic spectra are produced when the bombarding electrons have sufficient energy to penetrate to the interior of the atoms of the

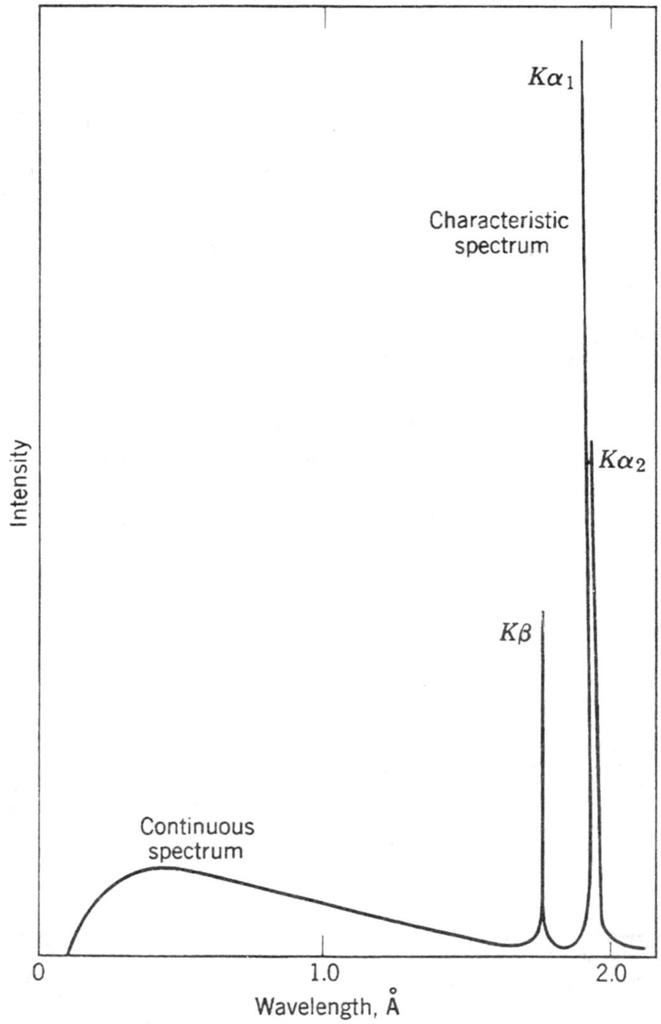

Fig. 2-2. The *K* characteristic peaks of iron superimposed on the continuous spectrum curve.

target and to dislodge electrons from their innermost shells. An atom may be pictured as a nucleus surrounded by shells of electrons. The inner or *K* shell can have two electrons, the *L* shell eight electrons, the *M* shell eighteen, and so on. The *K* shell electrons are the most difficult to dislodge. An expelled electron must be replaced, and the probability is that the vacancy will be filled from the next outer shell rather than from a more remote shell. This creates a new vacancy, which is filled from the next shell, or less probably from a more distant shell, and thus the atom returns to a normal state in a series of steps.

An electron moves to a lower energy level when it "falls in" to an inner shell. The transition is accompanied by the emission of energy in the form of x-radiation, the wavelength of which is precisely fixed by the difference in energy between the shells. Falling-in from the various levels

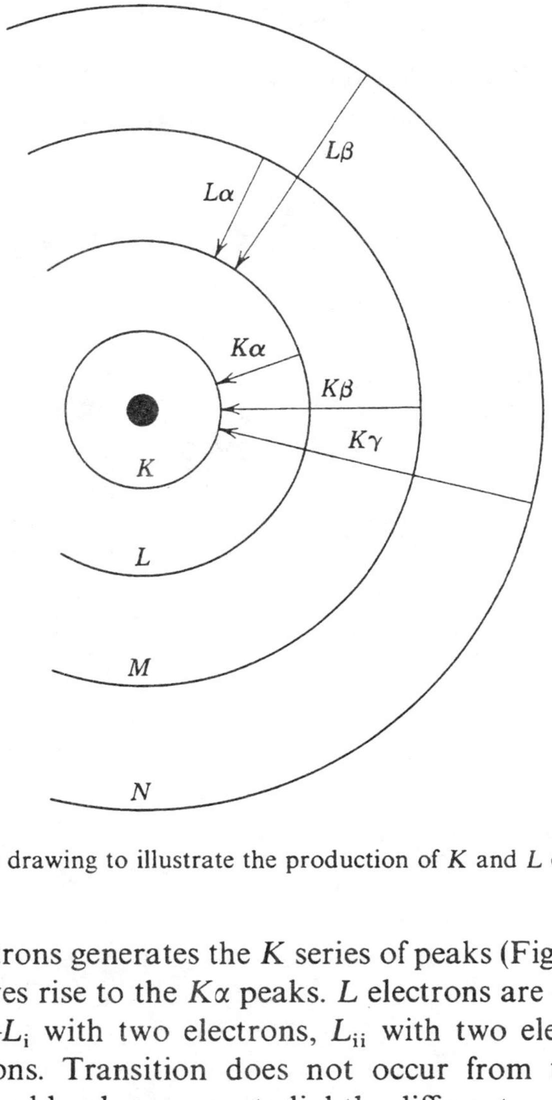

Fig. 2-3. Schematic drawing to illustrate the production of *K* and *L* characteristic peaks.

to replace *K* electrons generates the *K* series of peaks (Fig. 2-3). Falling-in of *L* electrons gives rise to the $K\alpha$ peaks. *L* electrons are distributed over three sublevels—L_i with two electrons, L_{ii} with two electrons, and L_{iii} with four electrons. Transition does not occur from the L_i sublevel. The L_{ii} and L_{iii} sublevels represent slightly different energy levels, and as a result the $K\alpha$ peak is actually a doublet whose individual peaks are designated, respectively, as α_2 and α_1. Similarly, the $K\beta$ peak is a closely spaced doublet, which arises from the transfer of electrons from two of the five *M* sublevels. A third doublet, the γ peak, is formed by electrons falling in from two of the five *N* sublevels. The total of such transfers gives rise to the K characteristic spectrum. The L spectrum is produced by electrons falling in from more distant shells to replace electrons expelled from the L shell. About 30 L peaks have been identified.

If the electron stream from the cathode of an x-ray tube has the energy to expel K electrons, obviously the more lightly held electrons in the other shells will also be expelled. Thus, if the K series of peaks is generated, as many additional series of peaks are generated as the electron configuration of the atoms in the target allows.

Table 2-2. Wavelengths, Absorption Edges, and Excitation Potentials

	$K\alpha_2$	$K\alpha_1$	$K\alpha^a$	$K\beta$	$K_{\text{abs edge}}$	Excitation Potential $\frac{12.4}{K_{\text{abs edge}}}$
Ag	0.56378 Å	0.55936 Å	0.5608 Å	0.49701 Å	0.4858 Å	25.5 kV
Mo	0.71354	0.70926	0·7107	0.63225	0.6197	20.0
Cu	1.54433	1.54051	1.5418	1.39217	1.380	8.98
Co	1.79278	1.78892	1.7902	1.62075	1.608	7.71
Fe	1.93991	1.93597	1.9373	1.75653	1.743	7.10
Cr	2.29351	2.28962	2.2909	2.08480	2.070	5.98

[a] Diffraction effects due to $K\alpha_1$ and $K\alpha_2$ are frequently not resolved on x-ray photographs. In this case an average wavelength, weighted in accordance with the ratio of the intensities of the peaks, is used:

$$\frac{2\alpha_1 + \alpha_2}{3}$$

The relative intensities of the peaks in a series are governed by the relative probabilities of falling in from the various shells. This depends partly on the number of electrons in each sublevel. Thus the chance of an electron falling in from the L_{iii} sublevel with four electrons should be twice that from the L_{ii} sublevel with two electrons. This is confirmed by an observed $K\alpha_1 : K\alpha_2$ intensity ratio of about 2:1 for all the elements. The intensity of the $K\beta$ component is not so readily predicted; the ratio, $\alpha_1 : \alpha_2 : \beta$, is observed to be about 10:5:2 for the radiation from a copper target. The $K\gamma$ component of the spectrum is much weaker and does not produce detectable diffraction effects.

Only the K spectrum, and in particular the intense $K\alpha$ and $K\beta$ peaks, is of significance in x-ray diffraction. The useful and practical wavelength range extends from about 0.7 to 2.3 Å. This radiation (Table 2-2) is provided by the K spectra of elements from atomic number 42 (molybdenum) down to 24 (chromium). Longer-wavelength radiation is too easily absorbed by the x-ray tube windows and by the air, and shorter-wavelength radiation—of wavelength values below 0.5 Å—is accompanied by a serious measure of white radiation. *L* peaks which fall into the useful range are, by comparison, much weaker.

The minimum voltage that must be applied to an x-ray tube to give the electron stream the energy to excite the *K* spectrum is given by the energy equation (1), in which λ corresponds to the wavelength of the *K* absorption edge of the target element

$$V_{\text{min}} = \frac{12{,}400}{\lambda_{K_{\text{abs edge}}}} \text{ (volts)}$$

This is known as the *excitation potential.* Table 2-2 lists the values of the *K* absorption edges and the excitation potentials for six useful *K* spectra. In contrast to the continuous spectrum, an adjustment of the voltage across the tube has no effect on the wavelengths of the characteristic peaks. The adjustment does affect the intensities, provided that the supply of bombarding electrons is not limited. An increase in the voltage causes an increase in the rate at which target electrons are expelled from their shells and therefore an increase in peak intensity. The continuous spectrum is simultaneously intensified. An operating voltage of several times the excitation potential provides a good ratio of characteristic-to-continuous radiation.

Fluorescence

The *K* characteristic spectrum of an element can also be excited by a beam of x-rays incident on the element, provided that the x-rays have the energy to eject *K* electrons from its atoms. The minimum energy (eV) depends on the element and corresponds to the wavelength of the absorption edge of the element

$$eV_{\text{min}} = \frac{hc}{\lambda_{K_{\text{abs edge}}}}$$

The absorption edge marks an abrupt change in the absorption coefficient of the element (Fig. 2-4). At the critical value, most of the energy of the incident radiation is utilized in ejecting *K* electrons, and consequently the x-rays are heavily absorbed. X-rays of shorter wavelengths (higher energy) have the energy to expel electrons from the *K* shell, but the probability of collision decreases rapidly with decreasing wavelength and the absorption effect falls off sharply. X-rays of longer wavelengths lack the energy to excite the *K* spectrum and are readily transmitted by the element. The absorption edge marks the boundary between transmission of incident radiation on the long-wavelength side and absorption of radiation with consequent generation of secondary radiation on the short-wavelength side. The secondary radiation is characteristic of the absorber, and therefore its wavelength is always longer than that of the exciter. When an element is generating x-radiation in this manner, it is said to be fluorescing; the secondary radiation is usually called fluorescent radiation.

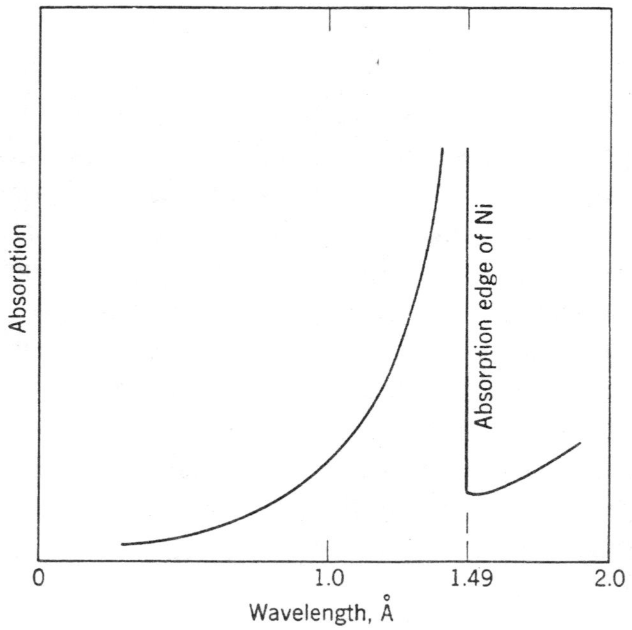

Fig. 2-4. Absorption edge of nickel.

The importance of fluorescence in x-ray diffraction studies can be illustrated by the effect of the $K\alpha$ component of an x-ray beam from a copper target on the element cobalt. Table 2-2 shows that the wavelength of the $K\alpha$ radiation (λ = 1.5418 Å) lies close to and on the short-wavelength side of the absorption edge of cobalt ($K_{\text{abs edge}}$ = 1.61 Å). As a result, the element fluoresces strongly in a Cu$K\alpha$ beam. If appreciable amounts of cobalt are present in a sample that is being photographed with this radiation, two undesirable effects will be observed. First, the diffraction pattern will be weakened because of the absorption of the incident radiation, and second, the fluorescent radiation generated in the sample will scatter in all directions in the camera, thereby increasing the background and obscuring the diffraction pattern. The elements iron and manganese (K absorption edges 1.74 and 1.90, respectively) behave in a similar manner with copper radiation.

Table 2-3. Fluorescent X-Rays

Element	Atomic Number	$K_{\text{abs edge}}$	Target	$\lambda_{K\alpha}$	Fluoresce Strongly
Ca	20	3.07 Å			
Sc	21	2.76			
Ti	22	2.50			
			Cr	2.2909 Å	Ti, Sc, Ca
V	23	2.27			
Cr	24	2.07			
			Fe	1.9373	Cr, V, Ti
Mn	25	1.90			
			Co	1.7902	Mn, Cr, V
Fe	26	1.74			
Co	27	1.61			
			Cu	1.5418	Co, Fe, Mn
Ni	28	1.49			
Cu	29	1.38			
Zn	30	1.28			
Ga	31	1.20			
Ge	32	1.12			
As	33	1.04			
Se	34	0.980			
Br	35	0.920			
Kr	36	0.865			
Rb	37	0.815			
Sr	38	0.770			
Y	39	0.728			
			Mo	0.7107	Y, Sr, Rb
Zr	40	0.689			
Nb	41	0.654			
Mo	42	0.621			
Tc	43	0.589			
			Ag	0.5608	Tc, Mo, Nb
Ru	44	0.560			

Table 2-3 lists the elements which, as experience has shown, fluoresce strongly in the $K\alpha$ radiation from common target materials. The table indicates that fluorescence occurs if the atomic number of the sample element is lower by at least two than that of a light target element (Cr to Cu) and lower by at least three when the target is made of molybdenum. Although the absorption effect falls off rapidly on the short-wavelength side of the absorption edge (Fig. 2-4), in general three elements fluoresce strongly with each target element. Thus titanium, vanadium, and chromium (atomic numbers 22 to 24) fluoresce strongly with iron radiation (atomic number 26). The radiation for a particular specimen must therefore be selected with some care. Table 2-3 shows that an element is transparent to x-rays that are excited by a target manufactured from this element or a lighter one. If it is necessary to use a heavier target element, fluorescence will not be serious if a large interval separates the *K* absorption edge of the element and the wavelength of the incident radiation. Titanium compounds, for example, give sharp patterns with little background when photographed with copper radiation.

The fluorescence phenomenon is turned to a useful purpose in x-ray spectroscopy. In this method of elemental analysis the sample is bathed in a beam of x-radiation. The *K* and/or *L* spectra of the elements are thereby excited, and the sample fluoresces. It remains only to determine the wavelengths of the characteristic peaks in the radiation emitted by

Table 2-4. β Filters

Element	Atomic Number	*K* Absorption Edge
Ti	22	2.50 Å
V	23	2.27
Cr	24	2.07
Mn	25	1.90
Fe	26	1.74
Co	27	1.61
Ni	28	1.49
Cu	29	1.38
Zn	30	1.28
Ga	31	1.20
Ge	32	1.12
As	33	1.04
Se	34	0.980
Br	35	0.920
Kr	36	0.865
Rb	37	0.815
Sr	38	0.770
Y	39	0.728
Zr	40	0.689
Nb	41	0.654
Mo	42	0.621
Tc	43	0.589
Ru	44	0.560
Rh	45	0.533
Pd	46	0.509
Ag	47	0.486

			Filter Data		
Target	$K\alpha$	$K\beta$	Filter	Thickness[a]	Loss of $K\alpha_1$
Cr	2.2909 Å	2.0848 Å	V (V_2O_5)	0.036 mm	48 %
Fe	1.9373	1.7565	Mn (MnO_2)	0.026	45
Co	1.7902	1.6208	Fe	0.012	39
Cu	1.5418	1.3922	Ni	0.015	45
Mo	0.7107	0.6323	Zr	0.081	57
Ag	0.5608	0.49701	Rh	0.062	59
			Pd	0.062	60

[a] To achieve a $K\alpha_1/K\beta$ ratio of 100/1. From *International Tables for X-ray Crystallography*, **3**, Kynoch Press, Birmingham (1962).

the sample and their intensities, to identify the elements, and to estimate their abundance.

β *Filters*

A monochromatic beam of x-rays is desirable for certain diffraction studies—especially when the sample is a powder. The reason for this is that the $K\beta$ component of the beam is sufficiently intense to produce its own diffraction pattern. When this is superimposed on the $K\alpha$ pattern, the difficulty of interpreting the diffraction effects is materially increased.

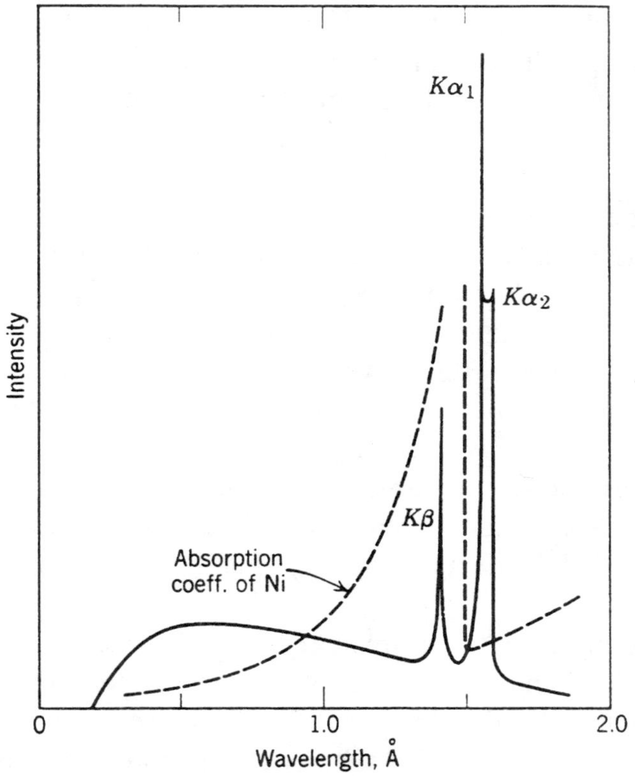

Fig. 2-5. Absorption curve for a nickel filter superimposed on the continuous and characteristic spectra from a copper target.

The absorption effect described in a preceding section and illustrated in Fig. 2-4 offers the means of removing the unwanted radiation to leave a beam that is essentially monochromatic. The element nickel, for example, has an absorption edge of 1.49 Å, intermediate between the wavelengths of $Cu_{K\alpha}$ (1.5418 Å) and $Cu_{K\beta}$ (1.3922 Å) radiation (Fig. 2-5). The element is therefore relatively transparent to the α radiation, but it strongly absorbs the β component of an x-ray beam from a copper target. Thus it can act as a β filter and, as indicated by Fig. 2-5, it can also reduce the intensity of the continuous spectrum. An examination of Table 2-4 shows that an element with the proper absorption edge is available for each of the commonly used target materials. The β filter naturally also reduces the intensity of the α component of the beam. X-radiation is always partly absorbed when it passes through matter—experiment shows that the intensity of the transmitted beam I_x, after passing through a thickness x, of an absorber is

$$I_x = I_0 e^{-\mu x}$$

in which I_0 is the intensity of the incident beam and μ is the linear absorption coefficient of the absorber. This coefficient is dependent on the density ρ of the absorber. The mass absorption coefficient μ/ρ, however, is independent of the physical state of the absorber, and therefore a more useful form of the absorption relation[1] is

$$I_x = I_0 e^{-(\mu/\rho)\rho x}$$

A filter thickness which increases the α/β intensity ratio to a value of about 600/1 is usually recommended in the literature. Unfortunately, the intensity of the α component is more than halved in the process. Parrish and Taylor have suggested a filter thickness sufficient only to increase the ratio to 100/1. The $K\beta$ diffraction effects are then not completely suppressed but appear only in association with the strongest $K\alpha$ effects and are easily recognized. The loss of $K\alpha$ intensity is still considerable, as shown in Table 2-4—a price in $K\alpha$ intensity must be paid to achieve a satisfactory reduction of the $K\beta$ component. If the loss is serious and the $K\beta$ effects are not confusing, the beam may be used in the unfiltered state.

The filter is inserted in the primary beam between the x-ray source and the sample in methods that use a film to record the diffraction effects. In other methods, the filter may be placed between the sample and the recording medium. This has the advantage of absorbing some of the incoherently scattered radiation from the sample, thereby reducing the background of the diffraction record.

X-Ray Diffraction Tubes

An x-ray tube was described as consisting essentially of a source of electrons and two electrodes. The electrons are produced in two ways, which gives rise to two kinds of tubes—cold-cathode or gas tubes and hot-cathode or filament tubes.

[1] The mass absorption coefficient of a compound M, with n elements is $(\mu/\rho)_M = \Sigma(\mu/\rho)_n W_n$, in which W_n is the weight fraction of the nth element.

GAS TUBES. The space between the electrodes in a gas tube is evacuated to a pressure of about 0.01 mm Hg and is maintained with the aid of a vacuum pump and a controlled air leak. When a voltage is applied to the tube, ions, which are present in the residual air, are attracted to the cathode, where they release electrons. The electrons, driven toward the anode or target, ionize the air in the process to provide more ions which in turn release more electrons from the cathode. X-rays are generated when the electrons collide with the atoms of the target. The generation of x-rays is inefficient in all diffraction tubes. About 99 per cent of the electron energy is converted to heat, and consequently the target must be constantly cooled by a flow of cold water to its underside.

A certain minimum voltage (the ionization potential) is required to give the electrons, released by the cathode, enough energy to ionize the residual air in their passage to the target. The ionization potential varies with the pressure of air in the tube. When the voltage is increased beyond the ionization potential, the speed of the electrons is increased. This results in a higher degree of ionization and consequently more electrons to carry the current. Hence the tube current (and therefore the intensity of the x-ray beam) depends on both the applied voltage and the gas pressure in the tube.

The cathode of a gas tube soon becomes pitted from the impact of ions and must be polished at frequent intervals. For this reason the tube is made demountable. The demountable feature has the advantage that targets of different metals may be easily interchanged to give a source of x-rays that has low initial and operating costs. The frequent service required by gas tubes, and their vacuum systems, weighs heavily against them today when the trend is toward facilities that offer push-button operation.

HOT CATHODE TUBES. In hot cathode tubes the electrons are supplied by a heated filament, which also acts as the cathode. The air pressure is much lower (of the order of 0.0001 mm Hg), which thus provides a near-vacuum in which no appreciable discharge can occur in the residual gas and ensures that all the current through the tube is carried by electrons emitted by the filament. The intensity of the beam generated by an x-ray tube depends on the availability of electrons. This is governed by the temperature of the filament in a hot cathode tube, and therefore the intensity of the beam developed by such a tube can be controlled with the current on the filament. For a given filament current, an increase in the voltage beyond the K excitation potential of the target element increases the intensity of the characteristic component of the beam only to the point at which all the electrons emitted by the filament are being directed at the target. A voltage increase beyond this level merely increases the speed of the available electrons and affects the quality of the continuous spectrum. At higher voltages the current in the tube is solely a function of the number of available electrons, which in turn is controlled by the filament current. Thus, in contrast to a gas tube, tube current and voltage are nearly independent variables in the operation of a hot cathode tube.

Most commercial tubes are of the hot cathode type and are permanently sealed off. The cost of such a tube is naturally higher than that of a gas tube manufactured in a university workshop, and a separate tube is required for each type of radiation. A commercial hot cathode tube has the advantage that it gives up to 2000 hours of trouble-free operation and provides the ultimate in convenience. One disadvantage must be mentioned. Vapor from the filament, which is usually made of tungsten wire, gradually plates on to the target and eventually contaminates the beam. Ignorance of this condition has on more than one occasion been responsible for the publication of incorrect data.

COMMERCIAL DIFFRACTION TUBES. The quality, versatility, and convenience of commercial diffraction tubes has been steadily improved in recent years. Beam intensity has been increased in a number of ways. One obvious method involves the use of lightweight window materials that offer better transmission (less absorption) of the beam. Most manufacturers now use thin-sheet beryllium (about 0.02 inch thick) or mica backed with beryllium. This is particularly important for the more easily absorbed long-wavelength radiations obtained from targets constructed of elements that are lighter than copper.

Beam intensity is also improved, in commercial tubes, by focusing the electron stream from the cathode to strike the perpendicularly situated target in a line focus, rather than a point focus. The focal spot is about 1 mm wide and 10 to 15 mm long in all-purpose diffraction tubes. The spot can be viewed either along its length or perpendicular to its length to give x-ray beams with distinctly different characteristics. When the spot is viewed end-on (Fig. 2-6*a*) at a small takeoff angle (angle between target surface and viewing direction), its long dimension is foreshortened to give a beam with small cross-sectional dimensions. Experience shows that the intensity of the beam decreases slightly as the takeoff angle is decreased to 10°, but falls off more rapidly below this point and drops sharply to zero below 3°. An angle of 6° proves to be a good compromise between the loss of intensity suffered at small takeoff angles and the gain of intensity obtained from a foreshortened view of a linear spot—at 6° the long dimension is foreshortened by a factor of 10.

The dimensions of the line focus are chosen to give a nearly square (roughly 1.0 by 1.0 mm) projected focal spot at this angle. This view of the target, often called the spot-focus view, and the symmetrical view from the opposite side of the target provide two highly concentrated x-ray beams of small, nearly equidimensional cross section. They are suitable for the majority of diffraction methods after they have been passed through pinhole systems to limit beam divergence and effective cross section in accordance with the particular needs of a project. More recently, so-called microfocus tubes with smaller focal spots (measuring

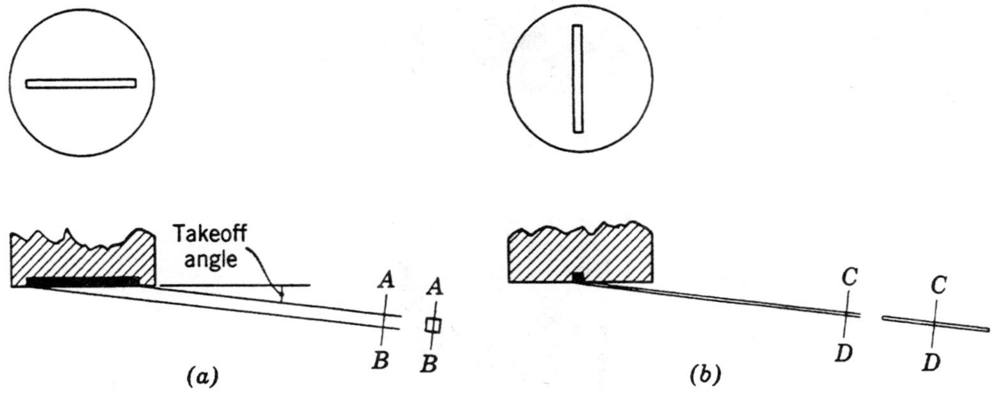

Fig. 2-6. Two low-angle views of a linear focal spot: (*a*) end-on view giving a beam of equal cross-sectional dimensions suitable for pinhole collimators, (*b*) side view giving a line-shaped beam suitable for collimator with rectangular slits and parallel plate assemblies.

in one case 0.4 by 8.0 mm) have been made available to provide even narrower beams. These tubes are more efficient for the study of tiny single crystals than the "standard" tubes described.

The short dimension of the focal spot is foreshortened when the view is perpendicular to the length of the spot. Consequently, at small takeoff angles the projection of the spot is very narrow and line-shaped. A 1.0 by 10.0 mm focal spot has a 0.1 by 10.0 mm projection when viewed at a takeoff angle of 6°. The side view is usually described as the line-focus view. Line-focus beams proved to be too weak for the small equant specimens (usually only a fraction of a millimeter in diameter) that are used in most types of diffraction studies and were largely ignored. At least two makes of commercial diffraction units did not provide access windows to these beams. The development of the North American Philips powder diffractometer, however, created an important use for the beams. The prime object of the diffractometer (described in detail in Chapter 5) is to attain the ultimate in resolution of the diffraction effects, aided by a long specimen-to-recorder distance. To this end, the instrument requires a powerful, highly collimated beam. It was found that the takeoff angle for the spot-focus beam had to be reduced to $1\frac{1}{2}$ or 2° to obtain a reasonable degree of resolving power, with a consequent considerable loss of intensity. This naturally led to the use of a large sample surface to strengthen the intensities to acceptable levels.

Fig. 2-7. Norelco x-ray diffraction tube. (Courtesy Philips Electronic Instruments).

It then became evident that the line-focus beam could be used to advantage with the diffractometer—the large sample surface (about 20 mm square) avoided the usual large loss of intensity with this beam, and an important gain in resolution was realized, even with the takeoff angle increased to 3° to improve the intensity. As a result of this discovery and of the increasing importance of the diffractometer, the market now offers several tubes, in place of one, with windows for viewing one or both of the line-focus beams.

X-Ray Generators

It is not difficult to construct a basic x-ray generator that will give years of satisfactory service; custom units, some equipped with demountable gas tubes, are not uncommon in university laboratories. Generally speaking, it is advisable to purchase a commercial unit if funds permit. Such a unit is the product of years of research and is normally equipped with many desirable features: convenient tube interchange without the necessity of realigning the recording instruments, automatic exposure timers, and safety devices to ensure that the tube is not operating without an adequate supply of cooling water. The unit is generally supplied with the manufacturer's offer to service the equipment. Finally, it is usually designed to take the refinements and accessories that will become a necessity as the scope of research in the laboratory broadens.